The Good Is One,
Its Manifestations Many

ROBERT CUMMINGS NEVILLE

The Good Is One, Its Manifestations Many

CONFUCIAN ESSAYS ON METAPHYSICS, MORALS, RITUALS, INSTITUTIONS, AND GENDERS

State University of New York Press

Published by
STATE UNIVERSITY OF NEW YORK PRESS, ALBANY

Printed in the United States of America

For information, contact
STATE UNIVERSITY OF NEW YORK PRESS, ALBANY, NY
www.sunypress.edu

Production, Laurie D. Searl
Marketing, Anne M. Valentine

Library of Congress Cataloging-in-Publication Data

Names: Neville, Robert C., author.
Title: The good is one, its manifestations many : Confucian essays on metaphysics, morals, rituals, institutions, and genders / Robert Cummings Neville.
Description: Albany : State University of New York Press, 2016. | Includes bibliographical references and index.
Identifiers: LCCN 2016007752 (print) | LCCN 2016035068 (ebook) | ISBN 9781438463414 (hardcover : alk. paper) | ISBN 9781438463421 (pbk. : alk. paper) | ISBN 9781438463438 (e-book)
Subjects: LCSH: Philosophy, Confucian—21st century.
Classification: LCC B5233.C6 N46 2016 (print) | LCC B5233.C6 (ebook) | DDC 181/.112—dc23
LC record available at https://lccn.loc.gov/2016007752

10 9 8 7 6 5 4 3 2 1

For Roger T. Ames, Cheng Chung-ying, and Tu Wei-ming

Friends, Mentors, Colleagues

The art of the cover of this volume is by Beth Neville, my wife, who has prepared art for many of my book covers. I thank her once again for doing this, with a line drawing this time. Her image is a humorous reference to me as a slightly quaint "Boston Confucian." On the left is a stereotypical drawing of Confucius, taken from a number of sources and modified by her style. On the right is a drawing of me in a suit in which I often teach, but wearing sneakers. I'm holding my brand-new mini-laptop and seem to be taking notes from Master Kung. Let no one think, however, that I intend to channel Confucius, any more than he intended in fact to channel the great sage emperors, however much he feigned doing so tongue in cheek. My intent in this book is to nudge contemporary Confucianism in new directions. Thanks to Beth for seeing the irony in this.

Contents

Preface

Just before our plane landed in Korea on our first visit to East Asia, my wife, Beth, told me, "Robert, I'm not going to walk eight paces behind you, and your Confucian friends will just have to cope." Such is the reputation of Confucianism for the demeaning of women even in its contemporary expressions. For several years, I have taught courses at Boston University on theological issues of gender identity. Many of our students from China and Korea cringe at what they take to be the bigotry of their home cultures, particularly their home church cultures, and they blame the bigotry on the legacy of Confucianism (even among East Asian Christians). The feminist women's movement and the LGBTQ revolution have been powerfully effective worldwide, particularly among intellectuals, although their practical success in combating the varieties of bigotry they oppose varies widely.

Contemporary Confucians have been slow to address this issue face-on, much to the chagrin of women studying Chinese philosophy from the perspective of feminism. Perhaps this is because of two themes that seem to be necessary default positions for Confucianism. One is the emphasis on fulfilling family responsibilities, modeling many other interpersonal relations on familial ways of showing humaneness. A second is the importance of exercising humaneness through the mature playing of rituals that define individuals in part through ritual roles. These two themes seem to set up Confucianism for devastating criticisms from those who emphasize the social construction of gender identities and roles, pointing out how unfair and hurtful many of those social constructions are.

In this collection of essays, I aim to show a way forward for contemporary Confucians, of whom I am one. Of course, I am not only a Confucian. Chapter 1 will show that I am a Platonist too. And nearly every chapter exhibits an appropriation and extension of American pragmatism. My identity as a philosopher works out of these three and many other intellectual and religion resources. Even as a Confucian, I am not every kind of Confucian, preferring an inspirational heritage from Xunzi to the ones from Mencius, preferring also Wang Yang-ming to Zhu Xi, although of course appreciating them all. Most obviously I am a Western Confucian, or more accurately a Boston Confucian, a movement I have helped to name and define as well as record.[1] Confucians working in Boston (and many other Western environments) live in cultures where some significant protections of women and sexual minorities are already written into law, even if far more still remains to be done.

To be fair historically, I doubt that Confucianism through the ages has been any worse on women and sexual minorities than most other religious or philosophical cultures. It seems that African Islam and some tribal religions today are about as hard on those groups as any culture has ever been. Most feminist and gender liberation movements in the last century or so have been directed against abusive bigotry in Christianity and Judaism. Although there have been saintly mothers in Buddhisms and Hinduisms, the lineages of authority often have been through males. I have never heard of a female Dalai Lama or Gyalwa Karmapa. Ancient Advaita Vedanta says that reincarnation is a comfort because you might have to wait many lives until you are born a male Brahmin, which is required in order to attain enlightenment and nirvana. The living heirs of all these cultures and religious traditions need to address the issues of bigotry related to gender identities. My concern here, however, is to build a Confucian response that addresses gender bigotry in all cultures, not only those in which Confucianism has been deeply formative for centuries.

Most of the time when these gender issues are raised, it is from the side of the liberationist critics who look at what Confucianism has to say about them. This inevitably brings up a reductionist vision of Confucianism, leaving out what does not pertain to gender and often expressing moral edginess regarding Confucian suppression of women. My approach here is the opposite: to attempt to develop a healthy and systematic contemporary version of Confucianism first and then to address the gender issues. Hence, the chapter devoted explicitly to the intellectual and practical issues of gender identity and respect is at the very end of the book. It is as if the first fourteen chapters are devoted to getting contemporary Confucianism ready to address feminist critiques, which is done only at the end and in a cursory way. This book is not a systematic feminist critique or a set of specific detailed instructions about how Confucianism ought to change its historical rituals so as to be more respectful of women (and sexual minorities). Many of the intervening chapters raise pertinent issues about gender, but the strands of argument are brought together only at the end. The reason for this order is that there are many themes in contemporary Confucianism that need to be addressed beforehand if a Confucian position is to be presented properly as a global philosophy with wisdom about the nature of gender identities and what to do to liberate them socially and politically.

By "Confucianism" here I mean the many streams of philosophy that relate back positively to Confucius and that have been called "Confucian" or "Ruist." I don't mean to suggest that these traditions are always fair to Confucius or are consistent with one another. Different periods of Confucian thought have existed and have interacted significantly with Buddhist and Daoist ideas and practices. Philosophies are significant, among other ways, by how they direct personal, social, and cultural life, and Confucianism has influenced these practical domains quite differently in different times and social contexts. A more elaborate discussion of the definition of Confucianism in is chapter 13.[2]

The focus in this book is not this history, not scholarly interpretations of important Confucians of the past nor of Confucianism in China and elsewhere. The focus rather is the construction of a contemporary version of Confucianism. Because I develop important themes that have been definitive of Confucianism in various times and places, I think my arguments here are in continuity with the kaleidoscopic traditions of historical Confucianism, and hence are Confucian in a living sense. Let me name here three of these themes that are elaborated from various angles in many of the essays in this book.

The first of the themes is metaphysics. Many Confucians and scholars of Confucianism suppose that Confucianism is primarily an ethical tradition oriented to guiding life and solving institutional and political problems. Metaphysics is too abstract and airy, they think, an elitist kind of play, and has not been developed in the Confucian tradition to anywhere near the extent it has been in South Asian, Islamic, or Western philosophies. There is a truth to this claim. Confucianism is probably the richest ethical tradition in global history. Some say that the Neo-Confucians got their interest in and vocabulary for metaphysics from Daoism and from Buddhism imported from South Asia. But Cheng Chung-ying develops a Chinese metaphysics out of the *Yijing* (see chapter 7). I find metaphysics in the Doctrine of the Mean, and I compare Zhu Xi and Plato on the same level of metaphysical generality (see chapter 1). Wu Kuang-ming denies the possibility of systematic metaphysics but practices it nevertheless with great verve even if in an anti-Confucian mode (see chapter 8). Moreover, recent Sinological scholars have begun to retrieve metaphysical themes. Stephen Angle's *Sagehood* is a remarkable analysis of the themes of harmony and principle (*li*). Two recent books by Brook Ziporyn, *Ironies of Oneness and Difference* and *Beyond Oneness and Difference: Li and the Coherence of Chinese Buddhist Thought and Its Antecedents*, are very serious metaphysical studies.

So Chinese, especially Confucian, metaphysics is back. But the metaphysics of the Confucian traditions needs to be brought up to date, and many Confucian thinkers in China and elsewhere are working on this. Except for perhaps the last three generations, Confucian metaphysics has not been developed during the last five hundred years in consonance with science, as happened to Western metaphysics from Hobbes, Descartes, and Locke up to Whitehead and Dewey, and so it is still too often uninformed and antiquarian. Confucian metaphysics needs to catch up not only on science but also on the development of a global economy and on the last half millennium of global politics. The classic themes of Confucianism need to be given articulation in relation to the other metaphysical systems in the global wrangles of philosophies. I regard my own metaphysical work as one way of being an up-to-date Confucian metaphysician. Because everyone's metaphysical assumptions, acknowledged or not, influence everything else they do, metaphysics is deeply practical. Chapters 1 through 8 here deal with dimensions of metaphysics in a Confucian mode. Chapter 1 begins an elaborate study of principle or *li*.

The second major theme of contemporary Confucianism I aim to address is the widespread suggestion that Confucianism can be understood fruitfully as a kind of "virtue ethics." Alasdair MacIntyre's 1984 *After Virtue* stimulated an exciting discussion, particularly among Western analytic philosophers, of the importance of becoming "traditioned" in virtues as the wellspring of moral action and character. This bears obvious superficial similarities to Confucian ethics. One of the finest full-scale defenses of this is Stephen Angle's *Sagehood*, mentioned earlier. The comparison is a common theme, however, in many journals devoted to Chinese and comparative philosophies and serves to connect Confucianism with Western analytic moral philosophy. Surely, the Confucians have attended to virtues. Antonio S. Cua's "Early Confucian Virtue Ethics: The Virtues of *Junzi*" makes a magnificent systematic study of this.

But I think that the virtue-ethics analogy gives a one-sided picture of Confucian ethics. The heart of Confucian, especially Neo-Confucian, ethics is the sage's practice of discerning possible harmonies or "coherences" (to use Angle's and Ziporyn's term) in the situation at hand. Although there are virtues of attention, and necessary skills of analysis to be learned, Confucian ethics is closer to Western "situation ethics," as found in Dewey, Whitehead, and many others.[3] It is a kind of "utilitarianism of principle" in principle's many manifestations. Confucian sages are and should be devoted to bringing about the best outcome, and if this compromises their personal virtue, so be it. This is what is argued here in chapter 1, which bears the title of this book. Angle's *Sagehood*, contrary to its intent, supports the same conclusion; I think his neglect of big-deal metaphysics causes him to fail to draw this conclusion, though he describes the process of discernment and effective action with suburb depth and clarity.

Roger Ames, in his wonderful *Confucian Role Ethics: A Vocabulary*, sees the limitations in the virtue-ethics analogy. He sees that Confucian personal virtue has no existence outside of the playing of ritual roles, and so the self is always a social self, not a private virtuous self. I agree with just about everything Ames affirms in that book but worry about what is left out. The limitation to the Confucian role-ethics theory is that it fails to stress enough the unique situations of discernment, choice, and action against-the-grain, things that fall outside the roles. Hence it sets itself up for criticism from feminists and other liberationists that it cannot take a sufficiently external position regarding ritual thinking to see that some rituals are disastrous and that Confucians need to be subversive (as Confucius himself tried to be). I suspect Ames's limitation here is his aversion to the metaphysical sides of Confucianism. Chapters 10 through 13 develop a non-virtue ethics approach to Confucian moral philosophy, though appreciative of the conception of virtue and the importance of ritual role-playing in Confucianism.

A third theme for the development of a rich Confucianism for our time is that of individualism versus social or group identification. Scholars commonly say that whereas Westerners are individualists, often to a fault, East Asians elevate the family or other group above individual satisfaction. Again there is much truth to this claim. Chinese athletes often put the victory of their team ahead of their own medals. Perhaps more than many Westerners, East Asians sacrifice themselves for the family. But I think this distinction is framed too much in Western categories of individuality and group identity. The Confucian tradition understands individuals as related to the Ten Thousand Things through the mediation of layers upon layers of institutions that are internal to the self, not alien. The self is constituted by learned semiosis in rituals, from learned postures to language itself all the way to ceremonial rituals. Rather than a Western self-other motif that defines individuality in contrast to group membership, Confucianism's basic motif is playing together in ritual roles. Self and other come to be distinguished within the roles. Individuality is achieved through individuation of role-framed actions with others, as well as through the spontaneity that is enabled from the perfection of those role-based habits, like a master pianist who can achieve transcendent creative freedom. This theme is developed explicitly in chapter 10 and is given depth through discussions of institutions and actions, individual and conjoint, from chapters 9 through 13. We need a Confucian way of understanding individuals and their social locations.

The key to a Confucian understanding of individuals and their social location is ritual. Confucius thought of himself as a teacher of ritual, and Xunzi elaborated a careful theory of ritual. The essays here approach ritual in two main ways. On the one hand, the Confucian tradition regarding ritual is very rich and not often understood in the West. Some of the chapters here, for instance 10, 11, and 14, work to give the Confucian conception of ritual a contemporary expression. On the other hand, the chief moral bent of Confucianism, I contend, is to analyze the personal and social situation in ritual terms, and to see many moral problems as failures of rituals. Moral correction frequently is to change bad rituals and invent new and better ones. The problems involved with the oppression of women and sexual minorities are mainly the function of oppressive rituals, and their remedy is to change the rituals, something more easily said than done (chapter 15). My emphasis on ritual stands in some contrast with the emphasis on the development of personal virtues more common among Confucian philosophers. I do not mean to deny the importance of personal virtues for the Confucian traditions, only to balance that emphasis with attention to ritual. Chapters 10, 11, and 14 elaborate how the inner virtues themselves are cultivated in the course of learning to play good rituals well.

This reconstruction of Confucianism is necessary, I believe, to give contemporary Confucianism the robust heft necessary to address the issues of gender identity that have been raised so effectively by the now-global sensitivities to abuse, oppression, and freedom. Surely, much more is needed as well, but these themes are enough for this volume and are summed up in chapter 14. Chapter 15 applies the themes to gender issues.

Although the multilayered argument preparing for the gender issues previously sketched sounds as if it needs a monograph, in fact the chapters here are developed from presentations made on special occasions. This book is a collection of essays somewhat rewritten to fit together. The plurality of angles of vision compensates, I hope, for the non-monographic organization. Although all the essays have been rewritten in great or small part for this volume, they still bear traces of their original contexts. I have not eliminated the first-person intimacy and flavors. Some are written for and with friends. Others are academically formal presentations.

Chapter 1, "The Good Is One, Its Manifestations Many," started as a keynote address by that name at the 2014 annual meeting of the Metaphysical Society of America that had as its theme East-West Comparative Philosophy, chosen by the president that year, Professor May Sim, and delivered at Holy Cross University. Few of the members of that society knew much about Chinese philosophy, and most thought that philosophy really did not get started until Aristotle took over from Plato. That situation affects the rhetoric of the chapter, which has not been published before. Chapter 2 had its origin in a paper, "Dimensions of Contemporary Confucian Cosmopolitanism," published in *Journal of Chinese Philosophy* 39/4 (December 2012), 594–613, and commissioned for that issue, portions of which are reprinted here with permission. Chapter 3 also began as a commission by *Journal of Chinese Philosophy*, though like the others from that journal, it was subject to peer review and revised with advice. It was in a thematic issue celebrating the fortieth anniversary of that journal and was published in *Journal of Chinese Philosophy* 40/S (2013), 59–75, under the title "Chinese Philosophy and Systematic Metaphysics." Much of that original publication is reused here by permission. Chapter 4 began as a talk at the 2009 meeting of the Eastern Division of the American Philosophical Association in New York and in revised form was published in *The Pluralist* 5/2 (Summer 2010), 45–56. Much of that published version is used here, with permission. These first four chapters together are about reorienting the metaphysics of contemporary Confucianism.

Chapter 5 began as a keynote address for the International Society for Chinese Philosophy at Buffalo, New York, in 2013, with the title it bears here. It has not been published before. Chapter 6 began as a lecture at Drew University in a series sponsored by the Hocking-Cabot Fund to honor William Ernest Hocking; it was published as "Metaphysics and World Philosophy: W. E. Hocking on Chinese Philosophy" in *A William Ernest Hocking Reader, with Commentary*, edited by John Lachs and D. Micah Hester (Nashville, TN: Vanderbilt University Press, 2004), 367–381, and is reprinted here with changes by permission. Chapter 7 began as "Cheng Chung-ying's Constructive Philosophy" in *The Imperative of Understanding: Chinese Philosophy, Comparative Philosophy, and Onto-Hermeneutics*, edited by On-cho Ng (New York, NY: Global Scholarly Publications, 2008), 107–121, used here by permission. Chapter 8 began as a talk on a panel about Kuang-ming Wu at the 2007 meeting of the American Philosophical Association, Eastern Division, and was published with a response from Wu as "Reflections on the Philosophy of Wu Kuang-ming" in *China-West Interculture: Toward the Philosophy of World Integration: Essays on Wu Kuang-ming's Thinking*, edited by Jay Goulding (New York, NY: Global Scholarly Publications, 2008), 174–82, and used here by permission. Chapter 9 began as a keynote address, "Spiritual Foundations and Chinese Culture," at a conference on that topic at Fu Jen Catholic University in Taipei, Taiwan, in December 2013. It retains its references to that conference and has not been published before. Chapters 5 through 9 orient my version of Confucianism to various positions in the contemporary academy.

Chapter 10 began as a brief panel presentation with Professors Cheng Chung-ying and Edward Casey called "Value and Selfhood: Pragmatism, Confucianism, and Phenomenology." A different version is in *Journal of Chinese Philosophy* 42/s (2015) and used with permission. Chapter 11 began as an essay in a Festschrift for Joel Kupperman, entitled *Moral Cultivation and Confucian Character: Engaging Joel J. Kupperman*, edited by Chenyang Li and Peimin Ni (Albany, NY: State University of New York Press, 2014), 151–168; the essay was called "Individual and Rituals," and parts are used here by permission. Chapter 12 began as a talk at the First Nishan Forum on World Religions, Nishan, China, 2010, that was published in both Chinese (under my Chinese name, Nan Lo-shan) and English in the informal *Proceedings of the First Nishan Forum on World Civilizations*, volume 2, 617–631. Chapter 13 appeared in an early draft entitled "Confucianism and Toleration" in *Journal of East-West Thought* 4/3 (September 2014), 25–38, and portions are used here by permission. Chapter 14 was first published as "Confucian Humanism (*Ren*) across Social Barriers" in *Confucian and Spiritual Traditions in Modern China and Beyond*, edited by Fenggang Yang and Joseph B. Tamney (Leiden/Boston: Brill, 2012), 295–307, and used here by permission. Chapter 15 was prepared, in a short version, for a keynote address at the 2015 meeting of the International Society for Chinese Philosophy at the Chinese University of Hong Kong and was written expressly for this volume.

Bibliographical information for references in the text and endnotes is given in the bibliography. This book obviously is written for people interested in Confucianism who read English, not only Sinologists but people in a broader public. Therefore, wherever practicable, I have cited Chinese texts as translated in Wing-tsit Chan's *Source Book in Chinese Philosophy*, a readily available volume. True, it is over fifty years old now, and many of the texts have been translated in ways reflective of more recent scholarship. Sinologists who care about these things know of the newer translations and can consult them instead. But the convenience of Chan's volume for amateurs in Chinese philosophy justifies its use. Besides, his middle-of-the-road approach to translation is a little like that of the translators of the New Revised Standard Version of the Bible who tried to avoid controversial translations. All quotations in this book from the Hebrew and Christian bibles, unless otherwise noted, are from that New Revised Standard Version, copyrighted in 1989 by the Division of Christian Education of the National Council of Churches of Christ in the United States of America.

This book is dedicated to three of the four people who have been my primary instructors in Chinese philosophy, Roger T. Ames, Cheng Chung-ying, and Tu Wei-ming. (The fourth, John H. Berthrong, was acknowledged with a dedication in my *Ritual and Deference*.) Because of these three, I feel comfortable in calling myself a Confucian, which requires in part a recognition by others of the legitimacy of that identity. They are very different people, however, each with his own distinctive approach to Confucianism. Ironically, I believe that I am closer to each of them than any of them is to the others. What great good fortune for me! I have commented on each of them in various writings, including in this volume. I hold them each in great affection and am humbled with gratitude that the affection seems to be reciprocated.

Chapter One

The Good Is One, Its Manifestations Many

Zhu Xi said,

> The Great Ultimate is nothing other than principle. . . . Fundamentally there is only one Great Ultimate, yet each of the myriad things has been endowed with it and each in itself possesses the Great Ultimate in its entirety. This is similar to the fact that there is only one moon in the sky but when its light is scattered upon rivers and lakes, it can be seen everywhere. It cannot be said that the moon has been split.[1]

Plato said,

> This, then, you must understand that I meant by the offspring of the good which the good begot to stand in a proportion with itself. As the good is in the intelligible region to reason and the objects of reason, so is this in the visible world to vision and the objects of vision. . . . In like manner, then, you are to say that the objects of knowledge not only receive from the presence of the good their being known, but their very existence and essence is derived to them from it, though the good itself is not essence but still transcends essence in dignity and surpassing power.[2]

At the beginning of the Western tradition, Plato pregnantly said that the ultimate *arche* of things is what he called the good, or the Form of the Good, that it is the source of all things that are good to the extent they partake of it, and that the good itself transcends all things that are structured so as to be good. The good is not itself a good thing. My quote is from the *Republic*; in a later work, the *Philebus*, Plato characterized the good as measure or proportion, that which makes all structured things measured or proportionate. Zhu Xi, a twelfth-century Neo-Confucian, was a great synthesizer of a millennium and a half of Chinese thought and said much the same, that "principle" (*li*) is the source of all coherence and goodness in things, manifest in every manifold, but itself transcending all structured things. I do not want to suggest that Plato was a paleo-Confucian or that Zhu Xi was a medieval Platonist. But I do want to say that I am a Platonist and a Confucian on the point that the metaphysical ultimate is the source of all things and is the source of goodness. The ethical implication of this Platonic-Confucian position is that moral discernment consists in finding the presence of goodness or coherence or harmony in things that are constantly changing. This chapter will reflect on this conjunction of metaphysics and ethics.

First, I want to present a hypothesis about the connection between the ultimate ground of things and the ground of value, a connection asserted vaguely in the quotes from Zhu Xi and Plato. My overall hypothesis will be that although the ultimate ground is the source of coherence or value in form, it is (1) also and on the same level the source of the multiplicity within which value is expressed in many manifestations, and (2) also the source of genuine otherness among things, and (3) also the source of the worth of the actual processive world for good or bad. Second, I want to focus on the ultimate as good and present the hypothesis that to have form is to have value, a point in which Zhu Xi and Plato also share in their different ways. I will not, however, develop equal attention to the ultimacy of plurality, otherness, and cumulative worth or meaning. Third, I will explore some of the implications for moral life of this understanding of value as coherence or harmony in form, developing contrasting emphases from Zhu Xi and Plato. For Zhu Xi, moral education and discernment have mainly to do with developing a purity of perception and action so that a fundamental human aesthetic faculty can operate with critical clarity and effectiveness. Plato shares the aesthetic sensibility but adds the complex dimension of dialectic to moral discernment. I will conclude with some hortatory remarks on character development, arguing that neither Zhu Xi nor Plato is to be regarded as a virtue-ethicist in any robust sense. The reason this frequent claim about them is false comes from their metaphysical conception of the nature of multiplicity.

ULTIMACY AND VALUE

Regarding ultimacy, I hold the uncommon view that there are five ultimates. Philosophers in most traditions have held that only one thing can be ultimate. Paul Weiss, founder of the Metaphysical Society of America, worked his way up to four ultimate modes of being.[3] Never wanting to miss a good idea, I agree with both views and synthesize them to get five. The root problematic of ultimacy has to do with the problem of the one and the many. The way I would frame that problem is to focus on the most abstract kind of multiplicity, the multiplicity of determinateness as such.[4] To be determinate is to be determinate with respect to something else, which implies something else with respect to which to be determinate. The world consists of determinate things that are determinate with respect to one another in at least some ways; they might also be partially indeterminate with respect to one another as allowed by the ways in which they are determinate. Notice how abstract this level of the discussion is. The world might be as described by Platonic processes and forms, Aristotelian substances, Plotinian emanations, Daoist flows, yin-yang vibrations, dharmas of consciousness, atoms and subatomic particles, fields of consciousness, Cahoonean orders of nature, or *f(x)*s. Whatever you might imagine! The notion of determinateness is vague, in the technical Peircean sense, with respect to what kinds of things can be determinate, and at this level of the argument all kinds of "worlds" are possible instantiations of determinateness.

One ultimate is whatever makes determinate things. Although the multiplicity of determinate things involves mutual conditioning so that they can be determinate with respect to one another, it still is the case that the determinate things are at least partly external to one another so as to be really different from one another. Without that, the multiplicity, and hence determinateness, would collapse. No determinate thing, no matter how great its own causal powers, can cause those elements of external things that are beyond the reach of its own causal powers, and the things would not be genuinely external if they did not have their own essential place beyond being conditioned. So I say the first ultimate is an ontological creative act that creates all the determinate things, whatever they turn out to be, including the temporal unfolding of processes that at any present time might be partly indeterminate regarding the future. There have been many concepts and metaphorical systems of this ontological creative act, and I will not discuss them here save to make one observation. Whatever accounts for the existence of the world of determinate things cannot itself be determinate, because it would then need a deeper ground to connect it with the things it allegedly creates. It is simply an act of making, like Plotinus's One as the source of the emanations, although emanation itself of course is determinate.

When we give a further analysis of determinateness, we find four more ultimate realities, which I call "cosmological" to contrast with the "ontological" because they are conditions of any determinate cosmos. Any determinate thing has both a multitude of components by virtue of which it is related to the other things with respect to which it is determinate, and at least some essential components by virtue of which it remains external to those others in some respects. Therefore, any determinate thing has a multiplicity of components and a form or pattern according to which they are together in that thing. Form and a multiplicity of components formed are ultimate conditions for any determinate things. I will argue shortly that having form means bearing value.

More than these two ultimates, however, any determinate thing has location in an existential field constituted by the ways it conditions and is conditioned by the other things. The easiest way to imagine this is with causal conditions in a space-time field, although from a properly abstract point of view the nature of the determinate things and their conditions determines what the existential field is like. That any determinate thing has existential location with reference to the things with respect to which it is determinate means that another ultimate condition is to be faced with things external to oneself. Those external things are conditionally related, but also significantly Other. From a human perspective, engaging genuine others is an ultimate condition over and above the ultimate conditions of having form that integrates one's components.

The fourth cosmological ultimate condition is that any determinate thing has the identity of getting its components together with its form in its place relative to other things. Identity here integrates the meaning of formal identity, identity of components, and identity of relations. Because form bears value, the ultimate condition of identity means a value-identity, which is very important on the human scale, however abstract it might seem on the level of the one and the many.

The five ultimates coimply one another. The four cosmological ultimates—form, components formed, existential location relative to others, and value-identity—are necessary together for there to be determinate things. But no determinate things would exist without the ontological creative act that makes them be rather than not be. Moreover, there would be no ontological creative act were there no determinate things created, because it cannot be determinate itself apart from what it creates. In what follows I am going to neglect the ultimates of existential location and value-identity except insofar as they show up in discussions of the ontological ultimate and of the ultimates of form and components formed.[5]

Before turning to the analysis of value, let me point out how Plato and Zhu Xi stand with regard to the ultimates. Plato says the Form of the Good is "beyond essence" and is the cause of all things that have essence. This is his way of saying that what I call the ontological creative act is not itself determinate but is the cause of everything that is. For him, the world is a maelstrom of processes that have form but are constantly moving beyond or out of the particular form they have. Because of the multiplicity of processes, there is a multiplicity of forms that unify them with proportion or value to some temporary extent. For Zhu Xi in the passage quoted, the Great Ultimate is identified with principle (*li*), or form, as the source of forms in the multiple things; in itself, principle is one and therefore not internally determinate. But for Zhu Xi, principle is not the only ultimate. He like other Neo-Confucians believed that *qi*, usually translated "material force," provides the multiplicity, the waves upon the lake, that principle informs with determinate shapes for each wave. Lying behind Zhu Xi's discussion is the argument of the earlier Neo-Confucian philosopher Zhou Dunyi, who said that the Great Ultimate is not itself the bottommost reality. Rather, the Great Ultimate arises from the Ultimate of Non-being, to use Wing-tsit Chan's translation of *wuji*. This dual-notion of Ultimate of Non-being and Great Ultimate is Zhou's way of saying that the ontological creative act is nothing without creating the world and, as creator, is the genesis of all determinate things, which he analyzes in terms of yin and yang that in tandem have pattern.[6] Zhu Xi drops emphasis on Zhou's Ultimate of Non-being and elides the Great Ultimate with principle, which is the source of pattern. He has great difficulty, then, saying what the source of material force or *qi* is, which is not to be reduced to principle. There is no material force that does not have principle as its form, and no determinate form that is not the form of some region of material force. At one point he says that principle creates material force, but he does not press the point. Scholars have disagreed over what to do with this conundrum in Zhu Xi's thought ever since.[7]

VALUE IN FORM

My hypothesis about form is this. Form is the schematization of pure unity to a structured multiplicity. If there were no multiplicity of determinate things for form to unify or make coherent, form would be pure indeterminate unity, like the Form of the Good or Zhu Xi's conception of principle as merely one. But if form were only pure indeterminate unity, this would not be determinate enough to make any sense; form requires determinate things to be formed. On the other hand, form is not merely a multiplicity of determinate things otherwise unrelated: form makes the multiplicity coherent in some way. Form is the pattern by which the multiple things cohere, their pattern or way of cohering. Some things cannot cohere because there is no form by virtue of which they might fit together.

This hypothesis about form will be expanded and defended in chapter 3. Here it can be made more concrete by reading it across the structure of temporality, which anyway is where it becomes interesting for ethics. Considering the three modes of time, future, present, and past, I propose to consider the future to be form relative to the actual world of things and decision points actualizing things.[8] Thus the future is possibilities whose essential components have to do with unity and whose conditional components are the things that have to be made coherent in the future. Future possibilities often contain alternative structures that might be actualized, such that selections or decisions in the mode of the present exclude some of the alternatives. The complexity of future possibilities consists in part in the fact that there are different possible structures for every date in the future, and a decision about the immediate future alters the alternatives in the medium run, which alters the possibilities in the long run. Therefore, the structure of possibilities in the future is a great kaleidoscope of shifting forms. When a possibility with its alternatives comes to the point of actualization, and a present decision process eliminates all the alternatives but one, that remaining form becomes the form of what is actualized. The past has the very complex form of all the forms actualized, and it bears the marks of all those possibilities that were excluded from actualization.

Now what does form have to do with value? Plato's name for the form beyond determinate essence is the Good. For Zhu Xi, too, anything that has principle has value. My hypothesis is this. Value is density of being, to use Leibniz's phrase.[9] It comes about in this way. Suppose there are five different things that need to be made coherent. One form for doing so might merely put them side by side in conjunction. But another form might combine certain of them so as to produce a sixth thing, and a seventh, eighth, and so forth. With every new kind of thing resulting from combination, new combinations are possible. So we can imagine a form as a hierarchy of levels of integration. The pattern of the hierarchy has both complexity and simplicity. Complexity refers to the diversity of things within it, whereas simplicity refers to their ways by which the things reinforce one another. I use the term "elegance" to indicate how complexity and simplicity are balanced in the hierarchy of a form, noting that for a given base multiplicity there might be many kinds and degrees of elegance. Whitehead in *Process and Reality* has a familiar analysis of great elegance in form in terms of what he calls contrasts, where elements of the pattern are made sharply determinate and reinforced to fit with and against one another. He parses contrast in terms of narrowness, width, triviality, and vagueness. This analysis of form shows how the same base multiplicity can be made coherent in a variety of ways that differ in richness or density of being. I propose that value is the identity a form has with respect to the density or richness of what it can make of its base multiplicity. Possibilities in the future are ways by which the base multiplicity can be made coherent, and they contain perhaps alternative kinds of richness as well as different degrees of it.

Why associate density of being in this sense with value? The long-run argument for this would require the analysis of many domains within which we make evaluations, showing that as we imaginatively alter the ways by which things might be made coherent, we see in some aesthetic sense how different patterns have different values. The real tests of imaginative evaluations come in instances where we realize that some previous valuation had been mistaken, perhaps because we misunderstood the base elements involved, or missed what happens when they are combined this way or that way. Although there is an immediacy in valuation, any valuation is always mediated by what we apprehend of the structure of the hierarchy of the forms involved. John Dewey's *Art as Experience* gives masterful accounts of how this aesthetic imagination works in matters of art and morals.

The notion of form plays many roles in Plato's thought. In the early and middle dialogues, it was often used in the sense of ideals, as when Socrates and his friends tried to define or find the forms of courage, friendship, justice, beauty, the immortal life, love, and so forth. These discussions usually had to do with varying the components and the patterns of integration so as to see what coheres or does not, and how certain combinations are of great value. The Neo-Confucian notion of principle also meant both form as structure and form as structure that harmonizes what should be harmonized. Grasping the principle in things is necessary for grasping their worth and responding appropriately.

As human beings regard the future, we know that what is possible is extraordinarily complex. On the one hand, the actual world for which the future is the structure of possibilities is itself complex and our understanding of it is limited. Especially, all the actual things in the world have value-identities because of the form that is in them, the possibilities that they have actualized. On the other hand, the possibilities relevant to any one of us are those that structure the environment in which we act, our actions are nearly always conjoint actions with others, and there are zillions of other decision points in our roughly contemporary world that are affecting what is possible. The possibilities relevant to our choices are implicated in a vastly wider field of possibilities that schematizes all the actual things and acting decision points to unity so that they are coherent. Add to this the complexities that come from contemporary physics of defining just what the present moment is relative to other things, and the nature of form as possibility for actualization, schematizing pure unity to the multiplicity of things to be unified, is mind-boggling. So I am going to change the topic.

ETHICS

The metaphysical construction of the world as value-laden because form has value is obviously important for ethics. I want to remark on four important implications of this. The first is that much of ethics is about how we come to know this value, about deliberation, discernment, taste, judgment, responsibility, guilt, and the like. Nevertheless, the Confucian-Platonic approach I am propounding provides a realistic foundation for ethics in the values that lie in the world. How we know these values-identities of things and respond to them is a different and related matter. But good and bad judgment ultimately comes down to being right or wrong about what is really valuable, including the value of doing something about something else that is valuable. Ethics is neither only a subjective projection of preferences nor a construction of what makes a good-willed subject, although surely much projection is involved in ethical life and the subjectivity of ethical agents needs many kinds of cultivation. I shall return to this shortly.

The second important thing about this theory of form and value is that, although it says that anything with form has a value, the values of things might be in serious conflict, the lesser values might ruin the greater, and from the perspective of human judgment many values are terrible, ugly, and bad. Perhaps we should always say, about this point, that every form bears values and/or disvalues, although this would suggest too simple a binary. Suffice it to say that the fact that everything has a value does not mean it is the right value in the right place at the right time relative to the other things that have value. Both Plato and Zhu Xi characterized value as "harmony," and harmony sometimes suggests too much sweetness and light: perfect storms are bad for genteel living.

The third important thing about this theory of form and value is that, while there are very many kinds of things with radically different kinds of value, in a general sense value is the same in each, namely, the coherence or harmony of the components of the form as previously described so as to have a certain patterned density of being with these components in this place. This is the meaning of the slogan "the good is one and its manifestations are many." So, on the one hand each kind of thing has a structure that must be learned, perhaps in esoteric detail, in order to apprehend its value. A person has to learn a lot of biochemistry to grasp the beauty and accomplishment of a self-regulating cell system; to understand what is at stake in the economy requires knowing a lot about how the economy works; to appreciate Bach deeply it helps to know music theory and to hear through that knowledge. But on the other hand, in all these different kinds of valuable things, the task of discernment is to grasp what makes them coherent, how their patterns have an inscape, as Gerard Manley Hopkins would say, and how things are conditioned in their own patterns by things surrounding in environing patterns.

The fourth important thing to say about this theory is that, regarding ethics, it entails that there is something in human beings that registers, mirrors, or responds to the values in things. This is an important epistemological claim. In the classic Confucian document, the Doctrine of the Mean, roughly contemporaneous with Plato, "Heaven" bequeaths to human nature an innate aesthetic sensitivity that picks up on the values in things and spontaneously responds in some appropriate way. The problem is that this value-responsive "heart/mind" is imagined to be at the inner core of a self that is constituted by many layers of physical, cultural, emotional, and cognitive conditions, including the conditioning of the self as a ritualized member of a society. The value of the things engaged has to be filtered through all these layers, many of which distort and others of which are underdeveloped. Therefore, the aesthetic perception is distorted. The same thing holds with the response, which has to work its way through all those layers into overt action, usually on distant things and people. Mencius likened the aesthetic response itself to the momentary flutter of the heart when a person sees a small child about to topple into a well. Although everyone would have that premature ventricular contraction, bad people will go on to blame the parents or complain that the water will taste bad for months; ill-trained people will rush to help and push the child over inadvertently. Most morally freighted situations are not as simple as this one: for instance, what all is at stake in setting an interest rate for the Federal Reserve Bank? Although the Confucians thought that all people, even small, mean-spirited ones, have this aesthetic responsiveness, that responsiveness needs to be cultivated through the many layers of self and society mediating any response to any thing in the world. Hence the Confucian obsession with education, in contrast to the philosophical Daoists who suggested that it all comes naturally.

Plato, too, believed that a kind of aesthetic sensibility lies at the heart of moral discernment, a matter of imagining and effecting balance, proportion, and due measure. In the *Statesman* he sharply contrasted the standard measure that consists in rules for mixing with the normative measure that consists in being able to judge just how much is enough.

Now let me pull together my claims about values resident in things with the aesthetic responses that need cultivation in order for moral judgment to be adept.

The cosmological theory of determinateness and the theory that values are resident in things as matters of their form add up to a basic general model for viewing possibilities. The many determinate things in the actual situation require that the possibilities for their future be plural. The plural possibilities are all harmonies, however, not substances that bear their characters as predicates of subjects. Each possibility has essential components that, if actualized, would make the thing definite. Each possibility also has conditional components that relate it to other possibilities. So no possibility would be a thing by itself for a thing by itself. Rather, each possibility would have intrinsic to its nature by virtue of its conditional components environments of other things that are also possibilities. There are environments within environments, environments containing environments, environments overlapping, and most importantly environments changing. Within a given possible harmony, all the components themselves are harmonies with their arrays of environing harmonies.

Consider, for instance, what to do about your younger brother, a grown man who is in physical, economic, and emotional decline and who both wants your help and resents it. Who is he? Obviously, he is the physical person located in and moving through neighborhoods. Dewey would counsel us to think of the person in his "situation," noting the organic functional definition of your brother as defined by interactions with things in the situation. I would press Dewey's point much further to say that the possibilities for your brother lie in nested arrays of harmonies that make up environments for all the determinate structures in your brother's life. Besides his body are his family relations, including his relation to you as a concerned and controversially responsible sibling. His family is determined in large measure not only by the DNA and the interactions of its particular members but also by its social situation constituted by class, professional affiliations, and so forth; by the educational system that has been available; by the health care system available for good or ill; by the local economy and its definition of possible jobs; by the physical characteristics of the neighborhood, its degree of sanitation, and its air quality. Farther in the background but still providing orientation for the things directly determining your brother's conditions are the environmental structures of province and nation, the historical situation regarding relations among nations, the technological and communications environment, and a host of other conditions such as global warming and solar radiation that few people think about, especially when concentrating on the problems of an individual.

An ethically wise person does not limit attention to the brother as such, because there is no such thing. There is only your brother in the array of environments, each of which has some kind of determinate, that is, harmonic structure. It is easy and common to think about your brother in terms of some of the proximate environments, including your family structure and his particular history growing up, working, and now coming to some grief. It may be important also to think about your brother directly in terms of the kind of family you have in a larger community, the kind of educational system available to him, what makes that educational system possible and has prevented it from being better, what the possibilities are for help improving physical and emotional help, what social conditions make those possible and prevent them from being better, or might improve them. Because people are determinate harmonies with somewhat determinate future possibilities, they are defined in part by what conditions them, and what conditions them is defined by further conditions, and so on. To be a thing at all is to be a harmony in an existential field with others, and that field is structured by the harmonies within it and their coherent connections. The Confucians have long recognized that loving your younger brother often means less face-to-face encounter than it does ministering to the institutions that constitute the relevant environment. There are institutions within institutions within institutions, all of which bear upon the possibilities for your brother. Western moralists have been somewhat surprised since the eighteenth century to learn that justice toward your brother does not mean only treating him a certain way, as in equal treatment before the law, but amending the environments within which he lives. The social structure of injustice was never out of mind for the Confucians. Plato's *Republic* makes the point as well.

Proper moral education therefore includes the acquisition of the knowledge, skills, and habits of thought to see people as having their identity, including their possibilities, defined by layers of harmonic environments. This is the way real possibilities are structured, according to my metaphysical analysis, and human moral vision needs to sort out the important structured variables. A significant part of this is to develop a culture that provides important signs for what to look for. Sometimes we understand these signs to be social values: think of family, or individual freedom, or equality of opportunity, or what makes for personal responsibility, or what makes for this or that form of social decision-making. If we do not have signs that discriminate the layers of harmonic structures in possibilities, we simply cannot discriminate them; cultures ought to be cultivated that do supply signs that show us what to look for.

On the other hand, the cultural availability of the signs is not enough. Individuals need to learn how to use them. If part of helping your brother is to improve the health care system, then you need to know how to vote on taxes and other legislation that is relevant, which means understanding the nature of the health care, the economic situation, and the political possibilities. Part of moral education then is gaining the most sophisticated education in the way these institutions work in their natural environment. What the culture delivers by way of commonsense ways of understanding is not enough if you care about the real possibilities for your brother. Innocent ignorance has a kind of attractive quality to it—the simple person has good instincts; nevertheless, well-intentioned simplicity can do great damage and simply misses the complexity of the environment defining your brother and cannot intervene in the relevant places.

Even with good relevant education, however, a moral actor needs the emotional purity to be able to accept, correctly assess, and act on what is known that might be helpful. The Confucians have thematized the problem here as selfishness. On the surface this means distorting what we allow ourselves to think about things because of a bias toward our own self-interest or the interest of the people and institutions with which we identify. But deeper down it means unjustified attachment to ways of thought and institutions that prevent coming to terms with what we can know. An ideology of stiff-upper-lip personal responsibility might prevent you from seeing that your brother needs help from a health professional; an ideology of looking to institutions to solve all problems might prevent you from directly helping your brother yourself. In the larger culture, political ideologies at their best are socially constructed values that allow us to discern the natural joints of the array of environing conditions for social life. But nearly always they are partial and obscure the values and disvalues of aspects of the environment that are morally relevant. Moral education involves concentrated and lifelong self-examination regarding the biases in our characters, and in our immediate social environment, that prevent discerning what we can otherwise know.

Moral knowledge is not only subjectively cognitive. It is also a matter of active inquiry and exploration, which requires cultivated abilities to act. In actual moral life we do not first study and decide what to do before doing anything. Our moral actions themselves are the arenas in which we discern the different layers of the morally relevant environments; we become wise through feedback. The acquisition of new elements of knowledge is part and parcel of acting better because of that. So moral education includes learning to become an adept agent, able to engage each relevant harmony in your brother and in the massive array of environments through which you share a world. The klutz who knocks the child into the well while trying to save her should have studied taiji and mastered his or her own body. It might be hard to learn how to talk to your brother. You have to learn how to be politically adept to improve the health system. The Confucian ideal regarding this point is to be a scholar-official. The scholarship is in coming to know, the officiating is virtuosity in acting. What is to be known and practiced is structured by the arrays of harmonies in the multilayered possibility structures of common life. In my remarks here I have concentrated on the development of knowledge or perception of the complex situation on things, especially people and institutions, in layers of environing contexts. A similar exploration needs to be undertaken about the complexities of acting where action requires engaging many of the relevant environing arrays, not only the matter at hand. This metaphysical position argues that real-life moral action requires intervening in many places—another meaning of the slogan the good is one and its manifestations are many.

Another aspect of this conception of addressing a multilayered array of possibilities is its dynamic character. I have spoken as if the paradigm is a decision maker in the present, operating in an actual environment formed by past decisions and faced with a complex array of possibilities defining the matters at hand. This is an oversimplification. Nearly every decision involves finding possibilities that would harmonize many ongoing processes at a sequence of moments in time, each of which has its own dynamic with myriad decisions or selective points. Moreover, nearly every decision itself takes time, sometimes a long time. Some decisions might seem to come at a specific moment, say a vote, after a period of deliberation. But most decisions are determinations of direction that then continue to be modified by feedback, perhaps significantly. A better way to think of moral action is to see it in a dynamic process of continually corrected perception of the complications of the possibilities and continually refocused action with regard to the changing arrays of possibilities. Deciding how to help your brother is likely to be a process of many parts, with some corrections of course, over the whole period of your interaction.

Implicit throughout these latter remarks on the ethics conditioned by this metaphysical vision is the assumption that the human mind, or heart/mind to use the Confucian phrase, has the capacity to grasp how things harmonize together, in various levels and shifting relationships. This is a kind of aesthetic capacity, to use the Western term. As I mentioned earlier, it is prominent in Plato and many others, including Leibniz, Whitehead, and Dewey, as well as being a standard motif from the very beginning of Confucianism, especially in those strands influenced by Mencius. The point of my metaphysical considerations, however, is to emphasize the complexity of harmonies within harmonies occasioned by the fact that any harmony has conditioning components from other harmonies that therefore constitute elements in its environment. The environment itself is a shifting nest of environments, many of which might be relevant for moral intervention. The aesthetic perception of a moral agent is not a single, one-time vision but a cultivated vision that grows with flexible inquiry and increased virtuosity in finding the potential harmonies within and behind the moral focus at hand.

In conclusion let me stress the fact that this metaphysical theory of the ultimate condition for determinateness, with its claim that anything determinate has form and therefore value, is a strong claim for moral realism. The fundamental moral metaphor is morally adept perception and response. We need to learn to perceive the world in the structures of its value-dimension and to respond by acting back through the complexities of those harmonic, or disharmonic, layers. Many people have thought it helpful to treat Confucian ethics as if it were an interesting analogue to virtue ethics. But virtue ethics is one of the attempts within Western philosophy to handle ethics primarily from the side of the subject, emphasizing the subject's character and how it is acquired through tradition and experience; this tradition suppresses analyses of what is good or bad objectively. I believe it is fundamentally misguided to see the Confucian traditions as building up virtues in the individual out of which actions flow. The Confucian traditions, at least insofar as they take seriously the metaphysical considerations of Zhu Xi, his ancestors, and descendants, rather treat virtues as learned capacities for discernment of the real. They are habits of perceiving this or that more acutely and responding adeptly. The habits themselves are not productive of actions but rather are elements in the complex perceptions that result in actions. It's always the real situation with its real multiple structuring of value-laden factors that is engaged. The strong emphasis on personal and social cultivation in the Confucian tradition is aimed to enhance engagement with the value-laden realities of nature, society, and human affairs. Where Aristotle indeed emphasized virtue ethics, Plato emphasized cultivation through his elaborate curriculum described in the *Republic*, including practical experience of governing the colonies so as to gain a sense of timing for how to intervene, all dominated by the ineluctable need for constant, imaginative dialectic. For Plato, ethical life is like statesmanship, dealing with realities that are difficult to comprehend and tease apart so that interventions can be effective. The failures of Confucianism have occurred when the emphasis on constant learning and sensitivity decays into acting on the basis of preformed ritualized habit.

That the good is one and its manifestations are many is a metaphysical characterization of reality that sponsors a seriously realistic approach to the moral life. The creation of the human moral subject is the evolution and cultivation of human beings to be elements within nature with the capacities to perceive something of the many manifestations, to grasp the kinds of value and disvalue displayed, and to act appropriately throughout the manifestations to enhance their value. Without a strong metaphysical hypothesis, our hypotheses about the moral life are likely to focus perversely on the moral subject and not on the value-laden realities subjects should be cultivated to address.

Chapter Two

Contemporary Confucian Cosmopolitanism

INTRODUCTION

The emphasis on metaphysics in the previous chapter situated the argument of this book in two important ways (among many others). First, it exploited the drive in metaphysics to find universality by weaving together Platonism and Confucianism, or at least Neo-Confucianism. This demonstrates that a contemporary Confucian can also be a Platonist and opens the matters of heritage to the subtle debates and qualifications that give precision and depth to developing philosophical identity. Second, it staked out the ground that Confucianism is not to be absorbed into virtue ethics too quickly but should balance itself toward a reading of the world with a realistic theory of value.

The present chapter aims to situate the argument of the book in yet another dimension, namely, the philosophy of community, a topic skirted in the previous chapter. From the outside perspective of some of its critics, the Confucian view of community might seem to be that of a ritualized inclusive social fabric where everyone, rich or poor, female or male, urban or rural, educated or not, has a role-determined place. There is considerable warrant for this view, although historically a ritualized inclusive social fabric has never worked and people have negotiated around broken boundaries. But from the inside I argue that contemporary Confucianism should identify communities with the ideals of cosmopolitanism. This reflects a genuine Confucian elitism. But the aim is that everyone should be elite, that is, cosmopolitan. This is a powerful echo of John Dewey's argument that proper participatory democracy would train all or most of the people to be articulate and competent to make good political judgments. Roger Ames and David Hall have made a detailed and subtle persuasive case for the resonances of Dewey and the Confucian tradition.[1]

Cosmopolitanism is an urgent need in today's world of conflicting cultures and political interests. Once upon a time, perhaps (but not likely), it was morally and politically satisfactory for large populations to be monocultural and for individuals to learn their culture from direct person-to-person contact with people they knew. We imagine this might have been the case for rural peasant societies. With the rise of cities, however, individuals interacted with people they did not know personally, and those interactions were culturally shaped. In modern societies the cities themselves are multicultural and individuals necessarily interact with people expressing different cultures. Cosmopolitanism in general is the trait of a culture whose members interact well with people of different cultures.

In our own late-modern societies, the venue is not only cities but social interactions across the globe involving different nations, ethnicities, religions, economies, political systems, and histories of war and peace, alliances and rebellions. Even this is not wholly unprecedented. But in the past the large-scale cross-cultural interactions were mostly in the hands of the elites. Today anyone with a computer can engage in such global interactions, sometimes with very serious, far-reaching consequences. Contemporary cosmopolitanism might not literally treat the entire cosmos as a city, but it does need to treat the interactive networks across global societies as a city.

In some respects, cosmopolitanism is itself a culture or trait of a culture, comprised of habits of interacting with others in ways that know about and appreciate serious cultural differences. In the United States, many people on the West and East Coasts fancy themselves to be far more cosmopolitan than people in the middle of the country, and many people in the middle regard "cosmopolitanism" as an effete putting on of airs. This situation registers that cosmopolitanism is rarely an actual culture if that means a culture truly alert to and appreciative of the relevant cultural differences. Rather, cosmopolitanism of this sort is at best an ideal. The volatility of the world situation, or even of the cultural-political situation in the United States, makes the actualization of a more nearly functional cosmopolitan culture an urgent need.

Lacking a robust, relevant, cosmopolitan culture in which people can be acculturated handily, the development of such a personal cosmopolitanism is a virtue for individuals who might pursue it. On the one hand, precisely because such a culture does not exist, it has to be invented, employing whatever means of cultural creativity and innovation are available. Much of this simply involves more education broadly deployed: ignorance turns the lack of cosmopolitanism into bigotry. But it also has to do with cultivating imaginative literature and the arts, religion and politics, so that they reveal new possibilities of healthy, appreciative, and respectful interactions. Cosmopolitanism is always particular, relating to the particular cultures to be engaged.

On the other hand, the attempt to develop robust, relevant cosmopolitanism is a virtue to be learned by individuals. Even if there were an actual cosmopolitan culture, it would be a difficult and elite culture that would have to be cultivated by individuals. Although we are not supposed to believe in "elites" in a democracy such as that of the United States, even less so in that of the People's Republic of China, in point of fact the virtues of citizenship are not automatically given. As John Dewey pointed out, creative citizenship in a democracy requires the acquisition of both knowledge and habits of communication and political maneuvering.[2] Jeffrey Stout, among many others, has pointed out the difficulties of attaining to effective public political *discourse*.[3] The discourse is just the beginning, however. The interactions that transform social habits and structures are far more difficult than problematic discourse. When the world of vast cultural differences manifests itself in many local neighborhoods, the virtues of cosmopolitanism need to be learned by just about everyone. Everyone needs to be elite in this regard, at least in many parts of the world.

The first contribution of contemporary Confucianism to the elite cultivation of cosmopolitanism is its millennia-long understanding of life to be principally an educational process whose goal is elite sagacity. Mencius said that the inborn "four beginnings" of virtue need to be cultivated into sophisticated habitual forms of perception and action.[4] Xunzi was less confident in the inborn powers of virtue and stressed even more the need to learn virtuous perceptions and behavior, especially through mastery of cultural semiotics in ritual.[5] Whereas in the past the Confucian educational ideal might have been intended only for the literate upper classes, now the need is to extend that ideal and the means of its achievement throughout most of the classes of society. Even in China and India, where masses of people are illiterate, the ideal is becoming relevant, especially as people take to computers before books. With regard to ideas and ideals, the boundaries separating social classes are becoming permeable as never before, although we should not overestimate the powers of education. Whereas many religious movements address the concerns of people in whatever class they are, Confucianism construes human concerns from the beginning to involve elite movement upward no matter what class one starts in. So Confucians are natural seekers after cosmopolitanism where that is the upward ideal.

In fact, the general Confucian emphasis on elite cultivation has two important strains that are relevant for the attainment of a cosmopolitan ideal. One is the emphasis on personal cultivation, thematized as sagehood. Tu Wei-ming has given that strain particular attention with regard to forms sagehood should take in the contemporary situation, and he has arrayed the classical texts and their historical development.[6] An emphasis to be added to Tu's, though he would not reject it, is that a sage in the Confucian tradition involves functioning as a scholar-official, that is, as engaged in public life. The other important Confucian strain is its emphasis on ritual as the cultivation of social habits, in this instance, of cosmopolitan behavior. For the Confucian tradition in general, habits are not the properties of individuals so much as they are of a ritual arena in which there are many players. The rituals have roles that are public and interactive, even when they are played by individuals. So the personal cultivation of ritual mastery is itself already the fostering of a cosmopolitan culture of interaction.[7]

In the remainder of this chapter I shall analyze five dimensions of cosmopolitanism as it is needed for the contemporary situation. With respect to each, a specific Confucian focus will be articulated, with the result being something of a plan for the advance of contemporary Confucianism, building on the past but addressing a somewhat new global situation.[8] The fostering of a wide variety of gender roles and freedom from oppressive ones is one sector of this global situation, as discussed in chapter 15.

DECISION-MAKING

The first dimension of cosmopolitanism to be addressed here is decision-making, a topic broached in chapter one. Simply to be human is to be faced with a future that contains alternative possibilities for actualization. Sometimes which alternatives are actualized depends on human choice, perhaps not as much as we like to think, but often in significant measure. Although the metaphysics of value is too abstruse a topic to engage here, it was introduced in chapter 1, and we know from experience that often the alternatives presented for choice have different kinds and degrees of value. Moreover, to actualize one alternative is to exclude the array of values (or disvalues) in the other alternatives. Choices rarely are made by individuals alone because most actions are conjoint actions. Any choice regarding the future must be compatible with other choices being made, as well as with the natural and social forces that are not to be understood in terms of choice.

Real possibilities, as argued in the previous chapter, are objective in the sense that it is in the nature of the future that it can be actualized in these diverse ways. This is a simple point. But the objective reality of real possibilities is always complicated in moral discussions by problems with the human discernment of what the alternatives are and what their kinds and degrees of value are. The real possibilities need to be interpreted in order to enter into human sensibilities and intentions. The interpretation needs to discern what the value-differences are in the alternatives. Sometimes the complexities of the discernment of what is at stake in choices lead thinkers to believe that all values are merely human projections onto a purely "factual" array of possibilities. But this is seriously counterintuitive to common moral experience. Philosophy provides the means to distinguish between accounts of the nature of real value-alternatives in future possibilities and the issues of signifying them in semiotic systems related to human culture, inquiry, and, of course, biased, interested, perspectives.

From Song Neo-Confucianism on, the Confucian tradition has developed an extraordinarily complex conversation about the nature of value in real possibilities and its discernment in human deliberative experience. Stephen Angle's *Sagehood: The Contemporary Significance of Neo-Confucian Philosophy* is an insightful explication of the metaphysics of *li* (principle, which he translates as "coherence").[9] On the one hand, *li* is the metaphysical principle that grounds the one-and-many and gives value to everything that exists. On the other hand, *li* structures the possibilities that present moral dilemmas for choice. And then, the Neo-Confucian argument is that *li* is the defining character of the human heart such that an intimate connection exists between value in possibilities and in their discernment. In this tradition are important differences in emphasis. Zhu Xi focused discernment on the study of the external objective situation. Wang Yang-ming stressed the presence of *li* in the heart/mind as the main avenue for discerning *li* in things. In a sense, neither would deny the point of the other, only its priority. Moreover, as Angle traces neatly, the real practices of the cultivation of sagehood involve so many stages that *li* is identified in many roles. Angle himself is interested in the ways by which the Confucians argue through particular moral situations, discerning harmonies that might be missed by ordinary reflection, acknowledging irreconcilable oppositions where they are obdurate, but then also being skilled in looking for larger background harmonies that are useful for contextualizing conflicts and working to minimize bad effects (or maximizing good effects where conflict is desirable).[10]

Jeffrey Stout, who is concerned about political discernment as well as personal moral issues, both genuinely Confucian themes, acknowledges that widespread agreement about political goals and ideals might be impossible and bases his argument for democracy on the possibility of political dialogue that is able to resolve piecemeal issues without a comprehensive cover of agreement.[11] His approach in practice is very much like Confucian deliberation in situations of great cultural divergences. But he regards metaphysical attempts to provide a background conception of value with potentials for articulating political harmony as themselves too contentious to risk political debate on.[12] He is scathing in his attack on Alasdair MacIntyre for advocating a return to some kind of cultural philosophy of ultimate values, because that ignores the genuine pluralism in late-modern societies.[13] The Confucian notion of *li*, however, is both metaphysical and epistemological, and in the latter guise it is perhaps abstract enough to rise above contentions about a pluralism of ultimate values. A contemporary Confucian could plug in to Stout's concerns, fortified with a robust metaphysics that would be helpful in mediating between issues of the real structures of possibilities containing alternatives with different values and the processes of representing them in moral discernment and interpretation.

Part of the metaphysics for contemporary Confucianism would be a constructive theory of coherence or harmony that shows all harmonies to have value, a theme to be developed further in chapter 3. A strong strain in Western philosophy also argues this and provides a comparative context for the development of a contemporary Confucian metaphysics, running from Leibniz and Jonathan Edwards through Charles Peirce, John Dewey, and Alfred North Whitehead.[14]

Confucian cosmopolitanism with regard to decision-making involves at least four elements. First is the Confucian recognition of the reality of value-laden possibilities with the attendant metaphysical theory to back this up. The metaphysical tradition of *li* can engage the alternative traditions in South Asia and the West in the matter of value-realism, a most important matter for contemporary cosmopolitanism. Second is the Confucian practice of discernment of the location of value-laden *li* among possibilities. The cosmopolitanism of this practice comes in the dialogue that cultivated Confucians would have with representatives of other cultures whose signs articulate possibilities and their values differently. Third is the cultivated Confucian resolve at making decisions and sticking to them through long processes of conjoint actions and reactions, shifting gears, tacking back and forth, wheeling and dealing so as to carry out a decision through the maelstrom of social and natural processes. Many choices involve acting through the interactions of different cultures. Fourth is the Confucian ideal of making one's decisions transparent. Despite all the levels of ritualized courtesy, the Confucian ideal is to minimize the distinction between the private and the public so that others might see the inner workings of one's heart/mind in the processes of discernment and decision-making. Cosmopolitanism requires transparency to others with different cultures and modes of discernment, a difficult task for self-presentation but one that is helpful for decision-making in conjoint actions.

ENGAGING OTHERS

The second dimension of cosmopolitanism that Confucianism addresses is the problematic of engaging others. By "others" is meant obviously other people, and in the context of cosmopolitanism this means people with other cultures. But Confucianism from the beginning has insisted that human beings are set within society, which in turn is set within a larger natural environment. Human beings are specialized parts of nature, and the respect due to other persons is continuous with the respect due to mountains and rivers. The great Neo-Confucian Zhou Dunyi was notorious for refusing to cut the grass outside his study because of such respect. For our purpose, however, the primary reference to "others" is to other people with perhaps different cultures from each other and from oneself.

Confucianism is famous for stressing the continuity between oneself and others, as in its slogan of "being one body with the world." Zhang Zai wrote, "Heaven is my father and Earth is my mother, and even such a small creature as I finds an intimate place in their midst. Therefore that which fills the universe I regard as my body and that which directs the universe I consider as my nature. All people are my brothers and sisters, and all things are my companions."[15] But the continuities are those of sympathy and identification, not those that obliterate real differences. When Wang Yang-ming wanted to defend the "one body with the world" thesis, he did so by reference to Mencius's example of empathy with a child about to fall into a well.[16] The importance of the stress on continuity in the "one body with the world" thesis is precisely because things, especially people, are quite different from oneself.

Engaging others, then, for the Confucian tradition entails recognizing that they might be very different indeed, a difference with which cosmopolitanism is required to cope. Confucian contributions to cosmopolitanism in the engagement of others who are very different, especially in culture and personal interests, consist in two principal themes, humaneness and ritual. Herbert Fingarette used these themes to read the whole of Confucianism in his little classic, *Confucius: The Secular as Sacred.*

Humaneness (*ren*) is a complicated theme in Confucian thought, with many different interpretations and stresses. For the purpose of the cosmopolitanism of engaging others, it can be interpreted in terms of two subthemes, appreciation and respect. Appreciation is the coming-to-know others as they are, not only or even primarily as they play roles relative to one's own interests. What the others are, of course, is primarily how they bear value, what their own value-structure is and what that means. Coming to know others is difficult enough when they are within a shared culture because it requires overcoming one's own impatience and selfishness. But when the others are from different cultures, and bear different cultural values, appreciation of them is difficult indeed. The Confucian stress on coming to know others in an appreciative way is especially important as a cosmopolitan virtue. Respect in this context is nothing more than treating others in ways that appreciate their own value-identities. Most affairs of life indeed involve utilitarian relations with others. Nevertheless, Confucian cosmopolitanism sets utilitarian relations in the larger context of appreciation and respect. A person who can do this is humane in the classical Confucian sense. In a world of cultural clashes, classical Confucian humaneness involves cosmopolitanism of appreciation and respect.

Ritual, as Fingarette noted, is an equally complicated Confucian emphasis. Xunzi's important analysis, connected with his concern for human nature being naturally untutored and hence "evil" unless it is ritualized, has been developed in many different ways.[17] For purposes of cosmopolitan engagement of others, ritual can be understood in some instances as a kind of dance with many different steps for different players. The dance itself accomplishes something, such as a greeting between strangers, or cooperation in an economic enterprise, or the negotiation of a military standoff. In the ritual dance, the dancers do not have to agree with one another, like one another, or share mutual goals save that of the dance. So long as they can perform the steps and interweave their various roles in the dance, they get along well enough to accomplish the purpose. Confucians emphasize the ritual character of just about all of society, which integrates the diverse and sometimes antagonistic interests of its many classes of participants and of individual wills. Cosmopolitanism in ritual performance means learning to dance with others who have different cultures and values so that social actions can be carried on. Cosmopolitan Confucianism calls attention to ritualized elements of social interactions and works creatively to perfect the rituals.

The ritual theme in Confucian cosmopolitanism plays back to enhance humaneness. In Western thought, the most common philosophical stance and popular attitude treats a self-world distinction as fundamental. In Levinas's focus on Otherness, for example, the supposition is that one is defined by one's own experience; the Other enters into that experience as an object; there is no way easily to leap from one's own subjectivity over the object-role of the Other to the Other's subjectivity. In Confucian ritual, however, one sees one's own identity in terms of the nexus of ritual roles played with others, just as, with appreciation and respect, one can see every other person as a player with a similar nexus. The ritual dance provides something of a neutral medium for self-and-other definition. Therefore, humaneness can be enhanced through relating to others not only as others to be appreciated and respected but also as fellow players in the rituals of interaction. Much of the cultivation of a

Confucian character, to be discussed in the next section, has to do with learning how to play ritual roles properly. Rituals working across cultures, especially antagonistic or competing cultures, provide the medium for enhanced cosmopolitanism.

Engaging others obviously relates to decision-making. Many decisions involve other people (or social institutions or elements in the natural environment) and every differential move with regard to engaging others involves decisions. Insofar as decisions are involved, engaging others requires the discernment of *li* and the carrying out of decisions. But engaging others cannot be reduced to mere good decision-making. Engaging others requires the deliberate cultivation of appropriate ways of appreciating the others, especially the differently cultured others, of responding to them appropriately, of finding means of ritual engagement with them that allows them their differences and of perfecting the playing of the appropriate ritual roles. There is no appreciation, respect, or ritual playing in general. Humaneness in this cosmopolitan sense is not about oneself. It is about the particular others in one's world. One's cosmopolitanism does not need to appreciate, respect, and dance with everyone, only with all the particular people in one's orbit.

ATTAINING WHOLENESS

The third important dimension of Confucian cosmopolitanism does have to do with cultivating oneself, namely, the integration of all the diverse elements of one's life into some kind of whole. The cosmopolitan dimension is that those elements reach out to others of very diverse cultures. The investments in appreciation and respect, and in ritual connections, lead to radically different orientations to those in the environment sometimes. How can these different orientations, the different educational projects, the different ways of showing respect, even the different rituals themselves, be integrated into a satisfyingly whole life? If one lived in a homogeneous culture, there would be patterns of integration that could function as models. But if one lives in a culturally pluralistic situation, there are competing models. Even if one positions oneself as a representative of a given culture (say, Boston Confucianism!), that culture would itself have to be cosmopolitan if it is to provide models of integration that allow for proper engagements of others and decisions about how to do that. As I argued earlier, such a cosmopolitan culture is still an ideal. The Confucian theme for wholeness is the project of becoming a sage, in this instance, a cosmopolitan sage.

Many current scholars associate Confucianism in general with virtue ethics of the sort made popular by Alasdair MacIntyre. Stephen Angle does this in his *Sagehood*, the main thesis of which is that Confucian virtue ethics can solve certain problems that are unresolved with various Western forms of virtue ethics. Virtue ethics distinguishes itself from moral positions that focus on decision-making, such as Kantian-style deontology, utilitarianism, or various forms of consequentialism. A gentle irony is to be found in my use of Angle's interpretation of the discernment of *li* as the principal Confucian tool for decision-making. Precisely because of its great worth in decision-making, Confucianism ought not be identified too closely with virtue ethics. With regard to decision-making, it is close to a kind of pragmatic, Deweyan, consequentialism. Virtue ethics also distinguishes itself from moral positions that focus on learning from engagement with others. Learning how to appreciate distant cultures involves far too much study of what is idiosyncratic in people in those cultures (from the perspective of one's own culture) to be mainly an element in the cultivation of one's own character. With respect to decision-making and engagement of others, Confucianism is not particularly well represented as a virtue ethics position.

Nevertheless, in respect of the project of attaining wholeness, Confucianism does indeed concentrate on the development of personal character and thus is akin to virtue ethics. To become a sage is to develop the kind of character that is good at decision-making and that is humane toward others with appropriate ritual mastery, although neither decision-making nor engaging others can be reduced to character. Relative to cosmopolitanism, the Confucian pursuit of sagehood has at least four main themes: commitment, purification of selfishness, transparent vulnerability, and poise.

A person needs to make a commitment to becoming a sage, and to renew that commitment whenever appropriate. It is always possible to rest in the character that develops naturally from one's social environment. Ordinarily, we think that one can be a decent person by achieving the ideals for a "good enough" life fostered by one's social group, no matter what the overall social group is. In these tough times of competing cultures, however, "good enough" is not good enough: by themselves, one's own culture's ideals are not sensitive to the issues of deciding about and engaging other, especially antagonistic, cultures. The times and situation today demand an elite cosmopolitanism. Therefore, it is not enough to go with the cultural flow: a commitment to the rigors of sagehood is morally and religiously important. Tu Wei-ming goes so far as to liken the commitment to sagehood to a Kierkegaardian existential decision.[18] Perhaps the Confucian commitment to sagehood is not as dramatic as Kierkegaard's existential decision, especially in its moments of renewal. But it does need constantly to push back against the pressure to let well enough alone in matters of one's own character.

Selfishness is the standard Confucian theme for accounting for moral turpitude. Selfishness has many forms, to be sure. The obvious ones can be pointed out by one's friends, and by one's own ordinary conscience. But the subtle forms of selfishness are the ones of which we are unaware and about which we deceive ourselves. Confucians long have emphasized self-examination, watching over our thoughts and emotions when we are alone and not subject to critical observation by others. The surface problem with selfishness is that it leads to putting one's own interests ahead of others when by all rights the others should go first. The deep structure of selfishness is that it distorts the way one perceives and responds to others. For instance, regarding perception it is important to learn about people different from oneself, and one's own organization of knowledge might be such as to prevent coming to appreciate others for what they are. So, one's very cultural modes of perception of other cultures might be selfish. Similarly, the Confucian conviction, for instance in the Doctrine of the Mean, that we all have an innate capacity to apprehend the values of the Ten Thousand Things in a kind of aesthetic way and then have an aesthetically appropriate response, as to a child about to topple into a well, can be blocked by selfishness. Although one intends to do well by others, one's actions can be sidetracked by selfishly structured modes of response. Therefore, a crucial element of Confucian sagehood is the practical uncovering and purgation of selfishness in all forms. Commitment to sagehood is a commitment to this self-examination and purgation. Purging selfishness takes on particular forms when the selfishness blocks appropriate responses to strikingly different people and cultures.

Transparent vulnerability is the positive side of purging selfishness. It means the character of being able to reach out to the relevant others and to be vulnerable to how they and their kinds of value impact one's own. This is not to say that one should always agree with or be pleased with the others. Sometimes opposition and conflict are appropriate, and this is a matter of making the right decisions. This is also not to be identified with the kind of learning involved in coming to understand and appreciate the others and their values. To appreciate others for what they are is one thing; to let that appreciation shape one's own character is another. Transparent vulnerability is having the character of letting what one learns about others register in oneself, a kind of cultivated sensitivity. Of course, each "other" is particular, and so this character is not general but directed to being able to relate vulnerably to particular cultures and types of people. The transparency so important to Confucians is a function of this cultured sensitivity. Westerners, especially Americans, like to be frank and say immediately what they think; they often take East Asians, especially Confucians, to be devious, the opposite of transparent. True transparency rarely comes with frankness, however, which is much too quick to work through the details of registering appreciation of the others. Transparency requires both the purging of selfishness and the achievement of genuine vulnerability to the others. Registering the value-identities of others requires working through many layers of interpretation, each made self-critical, and this is not done quickly, or communicated quickly.

Poise is the achieved ability to balance out the different domains of life. People organize themselves differently in response to different domains, for instance, family, the workplace, meetings with strangers, and various social and historical situations. Conceptually, these domains might be integrated by a worldview. Practically, the different orientations to the various domains need to be juggled according to the situation and doing so can be called poise. In this respect it is a little like a logger maintaining balance on a log that is spinning while moving downriver.[19] Looked at from the outside, poise is much like style, a personal way of integrating the movement from one domain to another where there is no formula. For people in a radically pluralistic society, deeply engaged with conflicting others and making decisions based on the true differences in values encountered, poise is a matter of keeping balanced. The Confucian emphases on balance without formula and the simultaneous playing of many ritual roles is an important contribution to cosmopolitanism.

Becoming a sage is a lifelong project of character cultivation. Very few sages-in-waiting live in communities that are so culturally homogeneous that they do not need to develop new characters adept at cosmopolitan skills of human interaction. As argued here, however, the precise kind of cosmopolitan character a sage needs depends on the particular diverse cultures and individual with which the sage might interact. There is no such thing as cosmopolitanism in general, nor a character vulnerable to diversity in general.

IDENTITY AND VALUE

The fourth dimension of a Confucian contribution to cosmopolitanism has to do with the basic question of the meaning of life. Or better put, what does one's life add up to? Or, what is one's true identity, all things considered? In many religious traditions these questions are asked in a context that supposes that one is under judgment by some anthropomorphically conceived God, and this supposition does not hold for Confucianism. Many people, Confucians and non-Confucians, believe that Confucianism is much too practical to be interested in what seems to be such a speculative question. Some believe that Confucianism is not a religion at all but only an ethical system. Nevertheless, three main Confucian themes do raise these questions in a profound way, and they bear upon cosmopolitanism: filial piety, the mandate of Heaven, and love with differences.

Let me make two brief philosophical points about value-identity.[20] First, a person's summed-up identity is not a purely factual matter, where the meaning of that is set in the context of a scientific distinction between fact and value. A person's true identity in absolute perspective is the many values embodied and achieved in the person's lifetime. Those values, of course, are borne by the facts of the person's life. The Confucian metaphysical way of putting this is that the person actualizes *li* in the particularities of life.

Second, a person's value-identity is not only the various accumulated elements of personal subjective identity, as it were, but also the effects the person has on others, on institutions, and on the environment. To some large extent, one controls the integration of the various parts of one's subjective value-identity, and this is what most people mean when they think about their own identity. But one also has important effects on others that by and large are under the control of those others; the others integrate those effects in their own subjective identity. But those effects are part of what can be called the objective value-identity of the one causing them. A simple illustration makes this dual subjective-objective identity clear. A college professor has a subjective identity growing from infancy and childhood through formal education, a career of teaching and writing, and perhaps retirement. But what the professor teaches has an objective identity within the students who can make of the teachings what they will. Despite the fact that the professor does not control much of what is done with the teaching by the students, the teacher's effects on students is part of the teacher's objective value-identity. In a philosophically individualistic culture there is a temptation to consider only the subjective value-identity of a person, relegating effects on others to the subjective value-identities of the others. But Confucianism insists that one's value-identity includes intimate connections with others: one is, among other things, one's influences on others, on institutions, and on the environment.

The bedrock Confucian theme for making this point is the emphasis on filiality, or filial piety. One's fundamental identity consists in individuating one's various roles with regard to parents, more remote ancestors, and siblings. Put in philosophic terms, this means taking into one's subjective value-identity the objective value-identities of the ancestors. In Confucian terms, this means learning virtue from them, fulfilling their responsibilities to oneself by attaining to the virtues they would teach. The importance of ceremonies of remembrance of ancestors is not only to keep their memory alive but to utilize them as means of incorporating their virtues in one's own life. Turned the other way, one's relations with the living, including one's siblings and one's children and grandchildren, involve acting in such ways as to foster their growing up with appropriate virtues. One's objective value-identity consists in significant measure in influencing others in the family for the better, often in ritually prescribed ways, and one's subjective value-identity consists in significant measure in receiving the objective value-identity of others into one's subjective value-identity in ways that honor those others.

All this is to say that one's value-identity, the meaning of one's life, what one's life adds up to, is never only a property of oneself but always also a property of people in relation to oneself. The paradigm of family relations is generalized in Confucianism to ever broader structures of social relations. The Great Learning defined value-identity, which it called "manifesting the clear character," in terms of the metaphor of roots and branches. At the root are the apparently inward matters of will and knowledge (the tradition debated the priority of those two) which in turn affect the mind in the sense of the acting heart/mind, the habits of personal life, the cultivation of family relations, the regulation of the state, and the achievement of peace in the world. The branches of "manifesting the clear character" extend throughout the world and the person is analogized to the emperor. The point to notice is that even the most apparently inward elements of subjective value-identity are causally connected in the roots and branches metaphor to the more external expressions. Even one's own "interior" will has its identity in how it manifests itself in external things. The Confucian tradition has always emphasized the continuity of inner and outer, never the distinction of subjective from objective. The theme of direct unity of thought and action was developed especially by Wang Yang-ming.[21]

Apparently orthogonal to the theme of filiality is that of finding the mandate of Heaven. Of course, everyone wants to develop one's own talents and interests. One's family tries the best it can to educate and foster those talents and interests. Our educational systems are bent on making the most of those talents and interests. Yet very often the affairs of one's life call upon one to do and become things quite different from what one would expect, given those talents and interests. Wang Yang-ming wanted nothing more than to be a philosopher and teacher, and yet the affairs of his watch made him into a general, a military leader. Confucians have thematized this dissonance between personal preference and responding to the needs of the day as "finding the mandate of Heaven" for oneself. Subjective preference is one thing and objective need for one to act in important ways, establishing one's objective value-identity, is another. The theme of the mandate of Heaven is another way of saying that one's value-identity is an objective function of one's need to affect others as much as it is a subjective function of developing one's personal identity.

An extremely important element of the mandate of Heaven in the present circumstance for many people is the need to develop cosmopolitan identities, skilled to relate well to others. Part of the meaning of contemporary life is to be an effective cosmopolitan person, in ways such as those discussed here. So, the value-identity by which one is to be identified and judged, placed in the family history, includes one's accomplishments objectively and subjectively with cosmopolitan life.

Another Confucian way of making this point comes from the ancient theme of "love with differences." Whereas the Mohists said that love should be universal, Confucians said that love should have different characters according to different objects. They had in mind that one should love one's intimate family members with a closeness and attention to the particularities of family roles that is different from the ways one should love one's neighbors, which again is different from the ways one should love the citizens of one's nation and the citizens of other nations. In the present circumstance the Confucian point can be developed so as to love people in other cultures in ways appropriate to those other cultures as has been discussed here. These skills at differential appreciation and respect are functions of "engaging others," in the language of this chapter. One's value-identity, with respect to this sense of cosmopolitanism, includes how one functions in engaging the plurality of cultures and individuals within them that come within the bounds of one's objective effects on others. One's poise expresses how one subjectively integrates these different ways of being humanly related.

The Confucian contribution to cosmopolitanism in respect of the dimension of value-identity begins with the recognition of the extension of one's identity through family relations to others, marks that need to include a plurality of cultures among the diversity of social relations analogized to the family as dictated by the mandate of Heaven in our time, and then sets limits on the family analogy by noting the radical differences that appear when being conscious of loving with differences.

RELIGION AND ONTOLOGICAL PIETY

The fifth and final dimension of the Confucian contribution to cosmopolitanism addresses the issue of the foundation of religions. Nearly all religious traditions have some way of saying that the world is radically contingent and attempt to answer the question of why there is something rather than nothing. The answers to this question are astonishingly diverse. There have been three main metaphors, however, that have been elaborated in countless ways to answer the ultimate why question. One is the metaphor of the person, shaped to transcendent dimensions and superhuman powers, who is said to create the world; theisms are common in West and South Asia, not so much in East Asia. Another is the metaphor of consciousness, purified and identified as the substratum for all definite and changing things, as in the South Asian notions of Atman-Brahman and Buddha-mind. The third metaphor is spontaneous emergence, as in the Dao that cannot be named or the Non-being that gives rise to the Great Ultimate, which in turn gives rise to yang, then yin, and so forth, in the thought of Zhou Dunyi. These metaphorical developments are not exclusive to different religions. All religions personify creative forces, all have meditative traditions that focus on consciousness as the locus of the ground of being, and all have non-personal themes of spontaneous emergence. Nevertheless, the religions organize and deploy these deep metaphors differently.

In certain respects, these differences in ways of addressing the question of the ground of the world's existence are esoteric matters for comparativists. In other respects, however, religious people take their own existential identity to be tied up with the authority of their own religious traditions. Often they see other religions or religiously based civilizations to be threatening, as detailed by Samuel Huntington in his *The Clash of Civilizations and the Remaking of World Order.* All too often religious people go to war to defend the authority of their tradition's way of relating the world to its ultimate ground. Some secular thinkers try to ascribe these wars to economic or tribal/ethnic conflicts. But beneath these conflicts, the impetus to violence at the risk of one's own welfare comes from defensiveness about the authority of one's tradition's articulation of ultimate reality in the sense of the ontological question, why there is something rather than nothing, and this religious base for violence is usually overt. Of course, the diverse ontological commitments blend into all sorts of other cultural commitments so that economic and tribal/ethnic conflicts take on ultimate seriousness.

The urgency for cosmopolitanism in our time comes from the threat of violence in many parts of the world. Therefore, a significant element of the engagement of others with appreciation and respect, and making good decisions about them, consists in engaging their religious elements. On a superficial level, this might seem to be a matter of engaging different cultural systems with regard to their religious elements. But engaging the systems as the social sciences study them does not get at the deep commitment those systems evoke. It does not recognize the deep piety, the apprehension of contingency and the surprise of existence, the ways by which people define their own value-identity in terms of the authoritative grounding of existence as such. Cosmopolitan engagement of diverse cultures and their members requires an empathic appreciation of their ultimate religious sensibilities.

To appreciate and respect the ontological commitments of other cultures is difficult if not impossible if one does not have such ontological commitments oneself. There is no context for empathy or for registering the religious commitments of others within one's own vulnerability. Strange as it sounds, I think cosmopolitanism in any serious sense requires a certain kind of religious virtuosity. For those who believe themselves to be secular and cosmopolitan, this is not good news. For those who think Confucianism is only an ethical culture and not a religious one, it seems a stumbling block. For those who think the ontological commitments of religion are all bogus, the task of engaging other cultures in their religious depths seems beside the point. But for those who appreciate the ultimacy in religious commitments and see that ultimacy as connected with ways of coping with the contingency of existence, cosmopolitan religiosity is a crucial virtue. Dismissing other people's religions is not likely to engage them well so as to bring about peace in the world. Every religion today needs to be cosmopolitan and hence appreciate and respect the religions of others.

The special contribution of Confucianism to religious cosmopolitanism lies in the conjunction of two themes: non-being and Heaven. Pervasive throughout Daoism as well as Confucianism is the conviction that anything specific or determinate comes from that which has no characters (*wuji*). Only the determinate needs to be explained; the indeterminate does not. What explains is not some higher order principle but the spontaneous emergence of the determinate from non-being. Wangbi and Zhou Dunyi are important figures in the development of this idea. The advantage of the theme of non-being as an ontological principle for the religious engagement of other religious cultures is that it does not presuppose any particular character in the ground of being. In fact, it presupposes that there is no such character. Therefore, there is no competition with other religions that ascribe personality or a particular pulse of consciousness to their representations of the ultimate ground. It can tolerate any metaphor for the spontaneous emergence.

The importance of the theme of Heaven is that all things, including all religious cultures, are embraced under Heaven.[22] This theme was developed by the Neo-Confucians into the detailed category of *li*, or principle, or coherence. But I mean it here in the older sense that all things in reality are embraced together. This means, in the current situation, that all religious sensibilities need to be embraced together. Confucians can use the notion of *li* to find some coherence or harmony behind the conflicts; or they might use the notion to articulate the incommensurability of certain conflicts—Angle has shown that Confucians are not committed to the assumption that harmony is possible, only to the search for possible background ways to bring harmony about. The practical implication is that the theme of Heaven means that no religious commitment can be left out of the cosmopolitan project of appreciation and respect.

Together, the themes of non-being and Heaven provide a rich religious culture for Confucians to reach out to other religious cultures and register them in the cosmopolitan heart/mind. In the philosophical scene, the master at this is Cheng Chung-ying, whose many writings about what he calls "ontological hermeneutics" lay the groundwork for comparative approaches to the ontological questions from a Confucian standpoint; chapter 7 examines his work in more detail.

CONCLUSION

In this chapter I have identified five dimensions of cosmopolitanism, though doubtless there are many more. These are cosmopolitanism in: decision-making, engaging others, attaining personal wholeness, the ultimate value-identity of life, and religious sensibility. The distinctions between these five dimensions are not particularly Confucian in origin, although I have cited Confucian themes to elaborate each one. In the course of this chapter the following Confucian themes have been discussed: Mencius's "Four Beginnings," ritual, life as cultivated education, sagehood, public versus private life, *li* (principle or coherence) in metaphysics and epistemology, heart/mind, harmony, value, resolve in decision-making, transparency, persons and society in nature, Heaven (and Earth), "one body with the world," Mencius's child on the lip of the well, humaneness, Confucianism and virtue ethics, commitment, character development, selfishness, self-examination, the Mean, vulnerability, poise and balance, filiality, the Mandate of Heaven, "love with differences," "roots and branches," "manifesting of the clear character," rectification of the will and the investigation of things, the unity of thought and action, non-being (*wuji*), "all under Heaven," and Confucianism as an ethical system rather than a religious philosophy. The result of this is a non-systematic but fairly capacious interpretation of how Confucianism can address the issues of cosmopolitanism. In all, I address Confucianism as a living tradition that is facing up to how it might extend itself in light of the need for cosmopolitanism.

Chapter Three

Systematic Metaphysics and the Problem of Value

The first two chapters of this book have staked out a terrain for the development of contemporary Confucianism. This and the following two deepen the themes, beginning with metaphysics.

SYSTEMATIC METAPHYSICS AND SCIENTIFIC REDUCTIONISM

"Systematic metaphysics" is a designation that deserves both a readily comprehensible colloquial meaning and a more precise meaning as a term of art in global philosophy. In the former sense, "systematic metaphysics" means a set of connected ideas about the kinds of processes and things that are real in the universe, ideas that provide intellectual orientation at the most general level and also sometimes orientation for the guidance of life. Most of the great philosophers East and West have explicit or implicit systematic metaphysical theories in this sense and this is one of the things that make them "great philosophers." Many ways exist by which these metaphysical ideas can be connected, and so there are many different forms of "system."

As a term of art in global philosophy, "systematic metaphysics" can usefully be defined as a conceptual language with associated implications for behavior that allows for the recognition and acknowledgment of all processes and things in the world along with their general connections. Whitehead put it this way: Philosophy is the endeavor to frame a coherent, logical, necessary system of general ideas in terms of which every element of our experience can be interpreted. By this notion of "interpretation" I mean that everything of which we are conscious, as enjoyed, perceived, willed, or thought, shall have the character of a particular instance of the general scheme.[1] Acknowledging again that there are many forms of such systems, the point to stress here is the anti-reductionist force of systematic metaphysics. Systematic metaphysics is thus to be understood in contrast to scientific reductionism, about which an important word needs to be said as a prelude to discussing Chinese systematic metaphysics.

Reductionism is the very heart of modern science. To "explain" something, according to most spokespeople for modern science, is to translate the phenomenon to be explained into an ideal language that itself is so perspicuous that it does not need to be explained further, at least within the science at hand. From the time of Plato in the West, the "ideal" ideal language has been mathematical. Or, where the mathematics is inadequate or too far from the phenomenon for a translation to be made, the ideal language has been "theoretical" in some sense. An explanatory theory might be a classification system, as in Aristotle, or a model, as in a social scientific theory. In our time, it often is assumed or hoped that the ideal language for a given science is satisfactory for that science but can itself be translated or "reduced" to some more basic language. For instance, some scientists hope that the language of psychology can be reduced to the language of neurology, which in turn can be reduced to that of biochemistry, then to chemistry, and then to physics of more and more basic sorts.

Philosophers and scientists have puzzled deeply in the last three centuries about the exact nature of explanation by means of translation or reduction to an ideal language, and many controversies remain. Immanuel Kant made a decisive contribution to this discussion when he argued that any knowing that is true about objects is itself a reconstruction of the objects by the mind taking off from sensation. The real objects, the "things in themselves," are not known at all. Whatever is known is only the disciplined construction of "objects" of scientific investigation according to the transcendental structures of the subjective mind. In fact, what we call "objects" are subjective representations in mind insofar as the subjective representations are objectively ordered by logic and empirical sensation. The "objective world" for science is not the "real world out there of things in themselves" but rather the constructed world of scientific knowing. The objectivity of science consists precisely in not making any claims about the real world transcending knowledge but rather limiting its claims to what the world "appears" to be when reconstructed according to the twin sources of sensation and transcendentally disciplined scientific logic.

Not many contemporary scientists are conscious of being Kantians. They think rather that their work is objective because it expresses only those claims about the subject matter that can be represented in the terms of their core theories or ideal languages. These ideal languages are supplemented by theoretical interpretations of their instruments of analysis such as machines and statistical procedures. They are supplemented further by specialized communities of scientists who have developed good taste in experimental design and evaluating results, specialized journals with peer review processes, specialized working groups, specialized professional associations, and specialized university educational departments and procedures. The sciences are far less formalized than Kant imagined. But they do take his point that the validity of their results depends *both* on the logical, personal, and social discipline with which they translate their subject matter into the ideal explanatory language of their specialty *and* on the careful refusal to suggest anything about the subject matter that cannot be so translated in explanation. This is scientific reductionism at its purist and best, the kind of reductionism that has allowed astonishing progress in the last several centuries, progress increasing in its rapidity within our own time.

Reductionism is a bad thing, of course, when a science says that what its specialty explains is all there is to the subject matter. Consider religion, for instance. A sociologist such as Émile Durkheim might explain a lot about religion when it is translated into the ways a religious culture stabilizes or destabilizes a social structure; that is good reductionism. But if the sociologist says that religion is to be understood *as* a function of social structure, that religion is nothing more except that, then this is bad reductionism. A psychologist such as Sigmund Freud or Jonathan Haidt might explain a lot about religion when it is translated into the language of psychological theories, good reductionism. But if the psychologist says that this explains the whole of religion or even its most important elements, this is bad reductionism. If a theologian explains religion as the response of a group of people to a divine revelation, this might explain a lot about that religious group; this is a good reductionism if the claims to revelation can be justified. But if the theologian forgets about the social functions and psychological workings of religion, that theology is bad reductionism. All reductionism leaves out everything in the subject matter that cannot be translated into the explanatory ideal language. When reductionism remembers that it is leaving out things that might be important, and that it is making claims only about that part of the subject matter that can be reconstructed within its specialized theories and procedures, it is good. When reductionism forgets about what it is leaving out and claims to be speaking about the subject matter as such, it is bad.

Systematic metaphysics is the opposite of scientific reductionism. Its system of general ideas in principle ought not leave out anything whatsoever. If the metaphysical system allows for articulating the social structures of things but leaves out the psychological, the system is flawed and needs to be amended. As Whitehead said, anything whatsoever that can be experienced in any way needs to be explicable as an instance of the general ideas. A metaphysical theory is refuted, or at least flawed and in need of amendment, if anything can be found of which it cannot give an adequate account.

We need to recognize, of course, that every metaphysical system, like every scientific theory, is historically located. It is responsive to the problems that dominate its time, enriched by its particular cultural history, and subject to the vagaries of the original creative geniuses in its place. These historical contingencies shape the form, content, and orientation of any metaphysical system. Nevertheless, systematic metaphysics in any period is needed as a civilized balance to the reductive intellectual approaches of the time. It is needed to show just what any reductive explanation leaves out, and how. If a science becomes abused as a bad reductionism, claiming that the world simply is the way it says and no way else, then systematic metaphysics needs to hold up a mirror to reality and show what does not register in the reductionisms at hand.

Systematic metaphysics cannot do this by being a super science, a totalization of all reductionisms plausible at the moment. Rather its general ideas need to be "vague" in the logical sense of being able to interpret subject matters that are contradictorily interpreted on lower levels of generality. For instance, systematic metaphysics needs to be able to interpret religion in such a way as to be able to register positively the sociologist's claim that religion is a social function and also to register positively the psychologist's claim that religion is a psychological phenomenon. Metaphysics needs to be able to interpret cosmology so as to register the truth in the Big Bang theory, while allowing that there might be many Big Bangs, or maybe even a Steady State theory that has plausibility. The vagueness in metaphysical ideas means that metaphysics cannot decide between disputes on lower levels of generality, but must allow those to be fought out on their own terms.[2] Sometimes scientists think of this vagueness as a flaw. But what metaphysics provides as a corrective to scientific reductionisms is space to register what the reductive ideal language ignores, marginalizes, distorts, or denies. To use the language of interpretation more forcefully, any subject matter can be interpreted in an infinite number of respects, and civilized societies have focused on finding the most important respects. Any scientific reduction interprets its subject matter in the respects in which the subject can be represented in its ideal language. The job of systematic metaphysics is to insure that no one respect of interpretation is allowed to define the whole so as to obscure other respects in which it might be important to interpret the subject matter.

METAPHYSICS AND OUR CIVILIZATION

The civilizing role of systematic metaphysics is not merely an academic matter. Crucial to the health of a civilization is a set of vague ideas about what is really real so that all the realities of life, both daily life and its peak and problematic moments, can be registered and understood in relation to one another. Those ideas provide orientation so that a civilization does not haplessly exclude something important. While professional systematic metaphysicians need to be as precise as possible about their vague ideas, those ideas need also to pervade cultural sensibilities. When philosophers and scientists are critical of the vagueness of metaphysics, this often means that they are more preoccupied with professional precision than with the function of metaphysics in civilization.

Consider the great systematic metaphysics built around the notion of *li* (principle) and its associated ideas that was developed in various critical ways by the Neo-Confucians. To be sure, this metaphysics was based on ancient sources and most often its Neo-Confucian expressions took the form of commentaries on those sources. There were other sources in Buddhism, Daoism, and creative genius that also contributed. Reflect, however, on the range of significance the metaphysics of *li* has. Sometimes it is used as a fundamental ontological category for understanding how there is anything at all; the debates about its relation to *qi* or material force concern this. Sometimes it is the focal point for understanding the issues of order and disorder in the cosmos. This is continuous with the consideration of the nature of order and disorder in society. Sometimes *li* is understood as the source of value in the cosmos, and sometimes as the source of justice relative to injustice in the state. In nearly all of the great Neo-Confucian thinkers *li* is at the heart of what it means to be human. It is also the crucial point of discernment in issues of how to be moral.[3] A great thinker such as Wang Yang-ming stressed how *li* defines the heart of human psychology and is the source of identification with other things so that "the whole world is one body."[4]

Because of the integrating cultural significance of *li* or principle, and its intellectual ancestor "Heaven," Chinese civilization rarely if ever has been tempted to make a serious split between nature and the human social sphere, as has been so prevalent in Western cultures from the Bible onward (see chapter 15). The sudden "discovery" of ecological thinking in the West would never have been an experience of "discovery" for the traditional Chinese, even if at times nature has been treated as exploitatively as people have in China. Because of the integrative nature of the notion of *li*, Chinese civilization has seen no divisive opposition between the individual and society, or between body and mind, or between subject and object. All the matters that Western cultures have signified by these troubled dichotomies have been registered in the systematic metaphysics of *li*, but not as dichotomies.

Consider the topic of the civilizationally disastrous dichotomy between fact and value that has plagued the culture of Western science but that the metaphysics of principle never would allow. In ways that will be discussed in more detail shortly, Western modern science has taught that what can be known are only facts. Knowledge is knowledge of facts. Both human beings and environing nature can be known in terms of fact, but not as having value. Valuation therefore cannot be based in knowing about value in things but rather as a function of human subjectivity. Western interpretations of this subjectivity of valuation have veered from sheer subjective emotion to the will to power; but in both cases and all those in between the valuation is arbitrarily placed on things, arbitrary as a subjective projection onto the things. The flip side of this is that things themselves have no value in this reduction. Therefore, anything can be done to them. The environment can be treated as nothing but resources for human projects. People can be treated according to the will of people who have the power. Even the human process of scientific pursuit of curiosity can be treated as nothing but a power game, as so many post-modern thinkers assert. Western nihilism has often been traced to the conviction that "anything is permitted" regarding things because they have no intrinsic worth. Although it would be a wild exaggeration to say that the atrocities of war and environmental degradation that have dominated the last century are the result of the fact/value dichotomy, surely that cultural assumption has contributed significantly to those disasters.

What exactly is the source of the fact/value dichotomy in Western scientific civilization? Of course, any phenomenon as pervasive as this must be reinforced from ten thousand directions. But three factors can be singled out: the language of science, the asymmetry of the usual scientific explanation, and the exclusion of the paideia of the discernment of value.

The first is the language of science when its ideal is mathematics. Mathematics represents things in certain kinds of relationships that preclude the registering of the values things might have. True, the mathematical relations are often astonishingly beautiful in an aesthetic sense, but they do not express the values in the things they interpret. For the ancients in the West, the celestial spheres had their "music," yet the moderns do not hear that. Of course, the mathematical relations among things that science explains are true of the things in the proper reductive sense. Science has "proved" this in so many ways it would be foolish to deny the point, even if "vitalists" and some others have tried to do so. But the scientific language just leaves out what it cannot register, and it cannot register value.

The social sciences, for which the hope of a mathematical language seems still distant, develop theories of functions that things perform that might have value in the sense of fulfilling the function. But the function is thought to be understandable only in terms of what Aristotle called "efficient" causes, causes that work from behind. Modern science was careful to exclude "behaving for the sake of some value" from its explanatory repertoire. Terrence Deacon has argued persuasively that the fault in this instance has been to think that only what is "complete," that is, wholly actual, can explain some possibility being actualized.[5] At any rate, the general point is that modern scientific language cannot register the value in things. When reductive modesty is forgotten, then it is assumed that the nature understood by science has no value. When the whole civilization grants dominating authority to the language of science, the language for registering value gets subjectivized. In fact (pun intended), we forget to speak any languages of value save those of human projection. The Neo-Confucian language of *li*, by contrast, never allows valuation to be separated from discerning the facts of the matter.

The second source of the fact/value dichotomy is the scientific intellectual strategy of explaining the more complex by the less. Descartes put it in an extreme form. He said in his *Rules for the Regulating of the Mind* that to understand something we should break it down into simples and then see how the simples fit together to make up the complex subject matter. A simple he defined as something that could be understood perfectly clearly and thoroughly in itself, and his ideal was a mathematic relation or equation. This of course assumes that reality is made up of simples and their compositions of complex realities, instead of things intrinsically related to one another whose contours are a function of perspective. But even without this assumption, the sense of explanation employed in science takes the base language, that which is perspicuous and not in need of further explanation, to be the "simple" from which complex relations in the subject matter are to be built up. As Descartes said, once we have broken the phenomenon into simples, how we put them back together to get the original complex is a matter of our own will in building, and we can understand our constructive will. This is the idea behind the use of "models" in explanation—we understand the model because we built it, and then we understand the phenomenon when we show how it fits the model. The pervasive assumption in the sciences is that understanding builds from below, from the simpler things that are supposed to explain how the complex things work.

But value most likely is a function of things in relations with others, and in relations with their own internal parts. This idea will be defended at length later. Now the point to note is that when things are reduced to their simpler elements, their value just disappears. Things have value only in their relations, often in their changing relations. When things are decomposed into their simpler elements, the value is lost. The Romantics have made much of this point, claiming that science "murders to dissect." You can't get to the parts without destroying the harmony of the whole, and when the parts are put back together, the best you get is Frankenstein's monster.

Some might think that this explanation of the complex by the less complex is also a prominent theme in Chinese philosophy. For instance, in various ways the *Daodejing*, *Wangbi*, and *Zhou Dunyi*, among many others, indicate that the source of all things is non-being. The philosophical rationale for this is that non-being is the only "thing" that does not need explanation. Even the mostly indeterminate Great Ultimate that is pregnant with the yang-yin movements of *qi* is to be understood as resting in that which has no qualities whatsoever. This point, which is to say that any "order" whatsoever needs explanation, is different from the point that complex things are composites of simpler things. For the Chinese traditions, in various ways, things are not merely the sum of their parts but have their identities in relation to environing factors. Nothing can be isolated entirely from its environing harmonies so as to have an identity or value merely in itself, according to the Chinese sensibility. But the Western Cartesian, and then modern scientific, strategies for analysis assume, indeed assert, that things are to be understood as composites of their parts, which in turn are to be understood as composites, each level of composition having its appropriate language of reductive explanation.

The third element of modern scientific culture that fosters the fact/value dichotomy is that the privileging of scientific inquiry displaces and eventually delegitimizes the educative cultural practices that make for the disciplined discernment of values in things. Ancient cultures East and West knew that, however value-laden common experience is, often common valuations are mistaken. Education is required to improve discernment, to know what to look for in mistaken value judgments, to acquire aesthetic habits of appreciation that penetrate to the depths of what makes things valuable. One thinks of Plato's elaborate epistemology for the discernment of justice in the *Republic* and Aristotle's practical reason based on learned habits of balanced judgment in the *Nichomachean Ethics*. Similarly, in ancient China the education to become a "superior person" was the subject of much debate concerning the proper mix of ritual practice, deliberation, learning not to be selfish, and opening oneself to the more or less spontaneous growth of the four virtues from their "sprouts," as Mencius famously argued. Confucius counted on a seventy-year education for him to be able to trust his intuitive impulses. The Neo-Confucians refined this cultivated sense of discerning what to do and be relative to the values of the things in the world into an elite sense of sagehood, as Stephen Angle has so luminously shown.[6]

The culture of modern science, however, with its commitment to the subjectivity of all values as projected onto a world of fact-alone, finds little use for the disciplines of discerning the values of things in the world. Calculating self-interest is fine, but not learning how to be sensitive to the worth things have on their own in relation to other things beyond oneself. Immanuel Kant, in his *Critique of Judgment*, developed an exquisitely subtle theory of taste, but it was a theory of the subjective structure of the mind transcendentally considered as the condition for the possibility of making value-judgments, not a theory about how the mind relates to values in things.[7] So for much of late-modern Western scientific culture, the disciplined arts of discernment of value have languished and to a large measure disappeared. Apart from calculating self-interest, what is there to know about value if it is not resident in things engaged in knowing ways? The study of morals drifts toward the study of preference, or of self-consistency of will. Alasdair MacIntyre has inspired a countermeasure against the languishing of the disciplines of discernment with his emphasis on tradition. Indeed, appropriating a tradition with some thoroughness is a crucial part of learning the depths of value. But his philosophy has been accused of relativism because it does not give an account of what makes things really valuable such that subtle traditions can discern them.

Needless to say to those acquainted with Chinese philosophy, the education of the would-be sage in the discernment of values in things has always been front and center. Philosophy, even moral and political philosophy, has never been a purely theoretical venture in Chinese traditions. Even to do theoretical philosophy requires a kind of value-sensitive personal and communal cultivation, focusing on sincerity and ritual as well as many other things. Indeed, sometimes the Confucian tradition is read as moral philosophy alone, downplaying both theoretical metaphysics and the religious dimensions of the tradition. This is not the place to explore this point in detail, but it illustrates the ease with which it is seen that the Chinese tradition has not let the arts of value-discernment slip.

The argument of this section has built toward the conclusion that, whereas the culture of modern science in the West has elaborated a deep and very bad dichotomy between fact and value, the Chinese tradition has been careful not to do so. With respect to the scientific reduction to languages that exclude the registration of value, the cultural systematic metaphysics of *li* has been a counterweight. It remains to be seen whether Chinese culture can accommodate Western science without losing that counterweight, a point to which the next section will return obliquely. With respect to the scientific strategy of explaining things by their components, treating things merely as composites, the Chinese tradition has insisted that things have their identity and value only with internal relations to things in their environment. With respect to cultivating the deep arts of the discernment of value as forms of cognition and orientations for action, the Chinese tradition has insisted on them and rejected any suggestion that valuation is mere subjective projection.

A CONTEMPORARY CONFUCIAN THEORY OF VALUE

Suppose it is the case, as argued earlier, that scientific reduction interprets the subject matter only in the respect relevant to the theories, languages, and procedures of the specific sciences, leaving out the rest and often forgetting what is left out. Suppose it is the case, also as argued earlier, that the most egregious case of this is the scientific representation of the world as being factual but not as having value, reducing away the value dimensions and then leading to the now deeply engrained cultural sensibility that values are all subjective. And suppose the Chinese philosophical tradition offers an alternative to the conception of the world as exhibiting the fact/value dichotomy. Is the Chinese tradition right to do this? Or has traditional Chinese philosophy simply not learned the lesson of modern science, namely, that the world is an array of facts with no intrinsic value and that valuations are indeed merely subjective projections, preferences, emotional inclinations, arbitrary tastes?

The answer to that last question depends on the development of a viable, contemporary theory of value that is an authentic extension of the Confucian tradition, based on the systematic metaphysics of *li*, and that is able to register and legitimate proper modern scientific reductionisms as valid in their place. The Neo-Confucians did not have modern science with which to conjure. Contemporary Confucians do. This section will sketch such a theory, elaborating what has been said in the previous two chapters. It will have three parts. First is a set of comments on the Neo-Confucian theory of principle so as to establish the traditional root. Second is a formal theory of value, abstractly stated in terms of harmony. Third is a reflection on how the systematic metaphysics built around their theory of value can appreciate and register our scientific knowledge as well as valuational appreciation and knowledge.

The concept of *li*, usually translated "principle," for instance by Wing-tsit Chan in his massively influential *A Source Book in Chinese Philosophy*, is perhaps the most central notion in Neo-Confucianism from Zhou Dunyi to Wang Yang-ming.[8] It is the pivot around which most of the other important concepts were debated. "Principle," however, has not been a satisfying or even perspicuous translation. Its strength is that it connotes that *li* is the arche or source of order and value. But the modern connotation of "principle" is that it is something like a rule or equation or explanatory axiom that is determinate and that explains something else. This does not quite fit because *li* in itself, apart from its manifestations, is not something determinate as such. Moreover, *li* is the source of value in things, which is not suggested by "principle." Rather, it is that which makes other things determinate when it is manifest in them. With great subtlety, contemporary Sinologists such as Stephen C. Angle and Brook Ziporyn have argued that something like "coherence" is a better translation because what *li* does in its manifestations is make things cohere, both internally and with one another.[9] At least two strengths lie in this line of interpretation. One is that it makes great sense of *li* in its manifestations. A second is that it sets up the discussion of how such coherence can be discerned at many levels of reality so that *li* can be explored in every context from the immediately moral to the more generally political to the environing elements of nature and the cosmos. But the translation as "coherence" does not get at the sense in which *li* is one and in some way stands behind, or underneath, or deeply within, its multiple manifestations. The metaphysical or ontological sense of origin is obscured.

The point of this essay, however, is not to engage the niceties of translation but rather to present a contemporary theory of value that "just happens" to make sense of *li* as one as well as many in its manifestations. The theory of value begins with a metaphysical theory of reality consisting of "harmonies." This theory of harmony bears significant relation to the Chinese concept of *he*, usually translated "harmony."[10] But it is a more basic notion than *he* is usually taken to be. Here is the theory.[11]

The most abstract characterization of things in the world is that they are determinate. To be determinate is to be something rather than something else, this rather than that, and to be something rather than nothing at all. The theory of that to be determinate is to be a harmony of two kinds of components, conditional and essential. The "conditional" components are the ways by which other harmonies condition the thing so that it is determinate with respect to them; causal factors are obvious but by no means the only examples. As each harmony has conditional features from the things with respect to which it is determinate, it also contributes conditional features to the other things that are determinate with respect to it. The "essential" components are those that give the harmony its own-being, integrating the conditional components. Without essential components, a harmony would have no reality to be conditioned by other things and thus would not have conditional components either. A harmony is just the fitting together of its conditional and essential components. This idea of determinateness is an extraordinarily abstract notion, in fact the most abstract notion possible, applying to anything that is what it is rather than being something else. Harmonies can be large or small, statically together at once or played out in time like a piece of music or a person's life. Some harmonies interweave through each other as components and then as external conditioning things. The components of a harmony of course are determinate and so themselves are harmonies (whose components are harmonies all the way down).

As harmonies, all determinate things have four transcendental features. All have the form or pattern of the harmony, the multiplicity of components formed, existential relations to other harmonies by virtue of the field of conditional components, and the value achieved by getting these components together with this form in this existential location relative to other harmonies. There must be a plurality of harmonies because a determinate thing by itself would have to be determinate with respect to some other things to be determinate at all. Furthermore, the plurality of determinate things would not be possible if there were not a context deeper than their mutual conditioning that allows them to be external to one another by virtue of essential components and related by virtue of conditional ones.[12] These theoretical claims are all extraordinarily complex, but the focus here is on form and value.

Form, as a harmony, has pure unity as its essential component and the multiplicity of things to unify as its conditional components, according to this metaphysical hypothesis. If there were no multiplicity, pure unity would be indeterminate and not the unity of anything. If there were a multiplicity of things with no unity, they could not be related to one another enough to be determinate and hence could not even be multiple. Form therefore is a harmony that requires essential unity as well as a conditioning multiplicity to give it determinate shape, or pattern. In any case of multiplicity there must be a pattern in terms of which they are unified at least enough to be relevantly different.

Perhaps this is best understood in the case of future possibilities. The form of those possibilities has to have a structure relevant to the already actual things that need a future locus. Future possibilities often have forms that contain alternative possible actualization, like Aristotle's famous "sea-battle or no-sea-battle tomorrow." What happens in a present moment when the alternatives become selectively actualized affects the structures of possibilities for later dates. In a temporally advancing field of harmonies actualizing possibilities, arrays of selections or decisions among proximate possibilities determine constantly shifting forms for more remote ones. As the actual multiplicities change, the forms that would unify them change. When possibilities bearing alternative forms for actualization are decided upon, only one alternative is actualized and the others are excluded. Form in the world, then, has three distinguishable modalities: as future possibilities that might contain alternatives, as present structures of selection or choice, and as actualized in concrete things that are then in the past and that are constantly added to as present time passes.

We now have a rudimentary expression of *li*. As "one" it is the essential component of pure unity and as "many" it is structured patterns by which multiplicities are unified. The dependence of *li* on an external multiplicity is the locus of the Neo-Confucian debates about the relation of *li* and *qi*. There is no *li* in the sense of form unless there is also *qi* providing a multiplicity of things to be formed and the energy of present selective temporality. On the other hand, there is no multiplicity in *qi* that is not already formed by the *li* possibilities that have been actualized within the things and their ongoing processes. *Li* as form has no determinateness without the conditioning components that come from the multiplicity in *qi* and whatever else makes up the actual world bearing form.

Where does value fit in? Attention now must be paid, however briefly, to the nature of form as pattern. Suppose, as an unrealistically simplistic model, that there are five harmonies that need to be unified with a form. The lowest level of form would be mere conjunction, although how things can be merely conjoined is not a simple matter to understand. Suppose further, however, that each of the five things is combined with another of the five so as to produce new harmonies out of the combination; that form now contains at least ten things. Suppose that the combinations increase so that many more different harmonies are now contained within the form. Imagine this form as a hierarchy in which the original multiplicity is supplemented on higher levels by new things arising in combination. Value is the "density of being" achieved by the formal integration of the multiplicity. The value has two dimensions, complexity and simplicity. Complexity marks the differences that remain or are achieved by the hierarchy of form. Simplicity marks the ways by which the hierarchy maintains sharp contrast in the vertical lines in the hierarchy so that the "top" has sharp definiteness.[13] Degrees of value consist in optimizing the complexity and simplicity. But that can be done in many different ways, so there are many kinds of value that can be borne by the form that unites the original five harmonies into a new one. It is not always possible to say what the comparison of those kinds of values might be.

Whatever has form has the value of getting the components together in the ways the form exhibits. As possibilities, forms bear the values of different alternatives for actualization, although all the alternatives bear some value. Some alternatives, of course as we know from human life, bear terrible, disastrous value for other things. In the present processes of selection among alternatives, the form choosing determines the value of the selection process. In the human case where there is some free choice among alternatives, the value-identity of the alternatives chosen relative to those excluded by the choice determines a kind of moral identity for the chooser. Insofar as humans have some choice and control over what gets actualized, they lie under obligation, a profound Confucian point. Once possibilities are actualized, their form is what bears the value of the actual states of affairs. The world is filled with things of differential value because of the forms actualized in them (and the other forms excluded—what "might have been otherwise").

The case for this theory of value cannot be made persuasive without discussing how value is discerned in human valuations. Making that case will not be attempted here, though it comes up in nearly every chapter of this book. Reflection on moral deliberation, the creative process of artists, the role of conscience in human self-definition in decision-making, and the many ways in which we appraise social states of affairs and the natural environment: in all of these things we notice the complexity and simplicity of the things under consideration, imaginatively varying them and aesthetically appreciating them. There is an immediacy in valuations of many kinds that lends itself to aesthetic metaphors. But that immediacy is internally mediated by the ways in which the valuation is aware of the components in their combinations and their alternatives. Valuations are seen to be wrong when we come to appreciate something we had not discerned before.

The disciplines of discernment so important to all ancient cultures and especially to the Confucian tradition down to the present day are ways of cultivating a learned ability to apprehend how the forms in things bear the values they do, either as possibilities, as matters of determining a person's own character, or in appreciating and knowing what to do with the world as actualized and in process of change. Regarding the future, there are layers of proximity and distance, each with their formal patterns perhaps containing alternatives. With regard to the proximate world within which a person participates, there are harmonies within harmonies close and far, interweaving in unexpected ways. A sage learns to discern these, looking for the distant conditions for possible harmony as well as the actualities at hand. As Wang Yang-ming emphasized as much as anyone, it is because the innermost moves of heart/mind are themselves harmonizations of multiplicities that it is possible through learned discernment to see and act with reference to the most distant harmonic forms in the Ten Thousand Things. To discern a form in any mode at any level is to appreciate it as having a value-identity. How well the form is discerned constitutes how well its value is appreciated.

Despite the complexities of discerning value in things, note that the value itself is a function of the things' forms, not of the discerning subject. Why we value as we do is often largely a function of human learning and habits of discernment. But what we value, by means of which we correct our mis-valuations, is the density of being in the forms in possibilities, choices, and actual things. Whereas valuation is subjective in some sense, value is in the things and valuation is the knowledge of them, however fallible.

This account has selected certain themes concerning value to discuss as being extensions of Confucian systematic metaphysics. So much has been left out or alluded to obliquely that the argument is slightly embarrassing. But if the abstract theory of harmony and value is read back through the great Neo-Confucian discussions, the other themes with which the abstract theory is connected will become apparent.

The final reflection here is to note that this very rich theory of value stretching through all things in the cosmos, including the projects of civilized life, in no way obviates what the sciences can learn about the structures or behaviors of things. The harmonies and collections of harmonies that can be analyzed for their value-identities can also be analyzed for other aspects of their form and powers. All things with mass and energy can be understood in part by the laws of motion. Evolutionary lines of causation can be discerned. Social and psychological structures are aspects of some harmonies, and themselves constitute a kind of harmony that can function as a component in other harmonies. With a systematic metaphysics that includes a contemporary elaboration of the classical Neo-Confucian theory of *li*, we can appreciate the truth in scientific reductions without letting that blind us to the multifarious dimensions of value that reality bears and that should be able to orient human life.

Chapter Four

New Projects for Chinese Philosophy

The general thesis of this chapter is that contemporary Chinese philosophy needs to be more creative than it is. It proposes eight new projects for Chinese philosophy to undertake that require creativity. But first it asks what the term "Chinese philosophy" means in the current philosophical context.

To some people, it means the tradition of philosophy in China from the ancient world of the Zhou texts, the Confucians, Daoists, and other schools, through its development up to the point where Western intellectual influences became prominent in the nineteenth century.[1] An appendix to this conception is the attempt to recover the vitality of the historical Chinese schools after the onslaught of Western thought (and modernization), a project associated with many of the New Confucians.[2] The limitation of this conception by itself is that Chinese philosophy was never sealed off and confined to the Chinese "until serious Western influence." Buddhism was only the most prominent of the many "foreign" philosophical influences on China. The Silk Road centers such as Turfan hosted important Muslim, Christian, and Zoroastrian institutions of learning and practice, and surely those influenced intellectual life in China. Xian was a multicultural city from ancient times. As we give up predefining philosophy, as we should, by paradigmatic names such as "Confucianism" and "Daoism," or "Platonism" and "Aristotelianism" for that matter, we shall become more aware of the eclectic nature of the "traditions" of philosophy.

To others, the first, quasi-ethnic, meaning of "Chinese philosophy" is augmented with the scholarly and philosophical study of that historical tradition, not necessarily by philosophers who are Chinese.[3] These, including me, are philosophers who study Chinese philosophy, as well as other kinds of philosophy. Today most philosophers educated in China are also well versed in Western philosophical traditions and contemporary movements. Insofar as this work is not limited to intellectual history but also takes the form of critical commentary, we are extending the tradition of Chinese philosophy into a wider public as a kind of philosophy worth noticing by everyone.

Yet there is something incomplete about this second conception of Chinese philosophy. Philosophy of any sort deals with first-order philosophical issues. One philosopher can learn from another as a resource for contextualizing, formulating, and addressing those issues. In this sense "Chinese philosophy" is the use of the traditions of philosophy that once were or now are associated with China as resources for addressing contemporary first-order problems. Some traditions of philosophy use the genre of commentary on other philosophers to address first-order issues, and this has happened in China, especially in the Neo-Confucian period, as it has in the Western Medieval period. Commentators are not repeaters of those on whom they comment. They raise new questions and bring forward hermeneutical stances that reflect their own time, not the time of their subjects. For a commentator to attempt to limn out what is true and false in the subject of commentary is to assume the plausibility conditions of the commentator, not the subject, and those plausibility conditions reflect the philosophical problems of the commentator. When we read the *Daodejing* or *Zhu Xi*, as historians we try to say what issues they addressed in their own terms, but what we say about that reflects our own first-order problems. To be aware of this and address our own first-order questions in the hermeneutical circle with the Chinese traditions is extremely important. This leads to the eight new projects for Chinese philosophy.

CREATIVE FIRST-ORDER ISSUES

The first project I want to urge for Chinese philosophy is that it take up the task of being creative about the first-order philosophical issues of our own time explicitly. In the mid-1980s my wife and I visited the city of Chongqing and toured a school for the training of visual artists, mainly painters. The school was perched on a high bluff overlooking the deep gorges where three rivers joined to constitute the Yangtze, a wild and spectacular scene of natural heights and depths, forests, mists, and swirling waters. Inside the school the students were learning only to paint Song dynasty landscapes in the style with which we all are familiar, modeled on the tame karst mountains of the Li River valley, some thousand miles away. No one looked out the window.

Chinese philosophy today is a little like that art school: it is slow to look at the first-order issues in front of it. Of course contemporary Chinese philosophers have looked out the window at Western philosophical traditions, as their predecessors did at South Asian traditions a millennium and a half earlier. In fact, one of the most important twentieth-century dynamics was the rejection of the Chinese traditions in China in favor of the Western philosophy of Marxism. As a result, however, many contemporary Chinese philosophers have turned back to the classical Chinese traditions in order to show them to be better than the Western, or to repristinate them so that they can compete in contemporary global philosophical discussions. To a significant degree, this historical retrieval is necessary in order to make those classical traditions accessible after a generation of neglect, or worse. Nevertheless, it is time for Chinese philosophers to address first-order questions directly and demonstrate the resourcefulness of Chinese traditions in dealing with them. The question should not be, What would Confucius say about the human orientation to the natural environment? (Ecology has posed new, urgent, philosophical issues.) Rather, it should be, What should we say about the human orientation to the natural environment, we who have been steeped in Confucian philosophy?

In order to ask this second kind of question, Chinese philosophers need explicitly to be creative, recognizing that we are undertaking something new, not just repeating or applying Chinese traditions. Traditions themselves, of course, are creative when they live into new circumstances. Confucius said he was merely handing down the traditions of the ancients, but most scholars now think he was lying when he said that: he was inventing those ancient traditions as authoritative for his own time. So my first new project for Chinese philosophy is that it orients itself explicitly to making creative contributions to contemporary first-order philosophical issues.

RE-SORTING THE CANON

The second new project for Chinese philosophy is that it consciously re-sort its canon. This project was already begun in the mid-twentieth century by some of the New Confucians such as Mou Zongsan, who debated whether Zhu Xi or Wang Yang-ming was the true conduit of the Mencian line of Confucianism. In the last two decades there has been an extraordinary retrieval of Xunzi, who had been read out of the primary canon of the Four Books by Zhu Xi. These two movements are interestingly different. The first was really about how to interpret Mencius in light of twentieth-century interests, especially interests in German idealism.

The second was about how Xunzi elaborated many Confucian ideas that had been suppressed in the subsequent Confucian tradition but that are particularly good for understanding our own issues, particularly his naturalism, realism, ritual theory, and understanding of convention.[4] The retrieval of Xunzi is far more important than the debate about whether Zhu Xi or Wang Yang-ming was better on Mencius because it lets the unfolding of contemporary issues direct the interest in the past. Xunzi offers a way for contemporary Chinese philosophers to be creative.

This point can be generalized with the observation that the attempt to establish an "authoritative past" obscures and marginalizes much philosophy whereas the search through the past for resources for creative advance is far more likely to be creative. We have learned the lesson from postmodernism that the various figures of the past should be studied in their own terms and contexts, as free as possible from some larger authoritative narrative that assigns them roles. Once we have this array of historical figures understood on their own terms, we can take responsibility for employing those whose thought can contribute to a creative advance. So, we should lighten up on the reins of policing traditions of Confucianism, Daoism, Buddhism, and the rest, and look at thinkers in their own contexts as relating to these and perhaps many other influences. Where is the influence of Muslim philosophy in China, or Western philosophy in Dang dynasty Christianity? Where is the Jewish philosophy that must have existed in the large Jewish communities in China? A new way of historical reading can create a new set of traditions. Then those thinkers might be quite different when we look to them for contributions to a contemporary canon of Chinese philosophy. Thus the second new project for Chinese philosophy is to learn to read its history with a new eye, not filtered through the lenses of attempts to find an authoritative past. The past has its own integrity and all positions should be respected. The authority of the past consists in what worth it has for our own questions, and that authority changes as the questions change.

GLOBAL PORTABILITY

The third new project for Chinese philosophy builds on but corrects the second and is to inquire into what is portable from the Chinese past into the present philosophical discussions. Philosophy now is global, with participants from all philosophical cultures. For the purpose of the contemporary philosophical conversation it is not possible, however, simply to pluck a figure from here and a figure from there. Each philosopher has a social, cultural, and historical context. How much of that context needs to be carried into the present conversation in order for that philosopher's thought to flourish helpfully? Not all parts of the context, of course, because our own context cannot tolerate everything. But to determine the portability of philosophers, particularly, in this instance, Chinese philosophers, is itself an interesting philosophical question.[5] I believe this is a third new project for Chinese philosophy.

The first three projects I am proposing for Chinese philosophy—becoming explicitly creative in this new conversation, re-sorting its canon for contemporary needs, and rethinking the portability of classical Chinese philosophy into the global context—all are about Chinese philosophy itself. A conscious irony lies in this, because my main message is that Chinese philosophy needs to look outside itself to see what it can do with regard to contemporary philosophical issues that arise from a much larger and more pluralistic context than obtained in earlier stages of Chinese philosophy. So the next several projects I will mention look outward.

COSMOGONY

The fourth new project is to enter into the discussion of cosmogony, the arising of the cosmos.[6] The *terminus ad quem* for this discussion today is set by physicists' renderings of the cosmos as expanding from an initial big bang, or several big bangs, an idea that had little or no play in the Chinese traditions although considerable play in the South Asian traditions.[7] The cosmogonic question, which is not addressed by the physicists, is how there could be a cosmos described by their equations. In the global conversation three main strategies exist for answering this question, nearly all of which find representative expressions in most of the major philosophical and religious cultures.[8] One is that the cosmos, under whatever description science gives it, is created by a God who is not part of that cosmos in any ordinary sense. This strategy has had little play in Chinese philosophical discussions since the worship of Shangdi gave way to awe at Heaven and its partner Earth back in the time of the Zhou. Many Chinese philosophers today, however, are friendly to Western process philosophy, whose God is very much a determinate being who is conceived to account for the order of things, as the Confucian idea of Heaven was supposed to do. That friendliness should be cultivated with the great care required for cooking a fish if the Chinese tradition is to avoid having to accept a transcendent determinate God.[9]

The second cosmogonic strategy is to say that the cosmos arises from some primordial fullness of being that contains within itself all the actuality, perhaps in infinite form, that the cosmos has in finite form, to use Thomas Aquinas's formulation. A similar point is made by Neo-Platonism that informs other Christian traditions as well as Muslim ones. Some of the main traditions of Shaivism make the same point, about the world arising from the fullness of Shiva and then dissolving back into that infinite fullness. Chinese philosophy has acknowledged fullness of being in its various conceptions of *taiji*, but not given it primacy in cosmogonic discussions.

The third cosmogonic strategy is to say that the cosmos arises from nothing by a kind of creativity that makes something new. This strategy is represented by traditions of creation *ex nihilo* in Christianity and Islam and various Hindu philosophies. In China it is the dominant tradition, illustrated by the opening lines of the *Daodejing*, by Wangbi, and by the classic statement of Neo-Confucian cosmogony in Zhou Dunyi, among other sources. In the last, the fullness of being, *taiji*, is secondary to *wuji*, which Wing-tsit Chan translates as the "Ultimate of Non-being"; literally, it means "having no characters or determinateness."[10] Whereas cosmogony by a determinate God or by the fullness of being involves no creativity, since everything in the cosmic effect is already in God or the plenitude principle, cosmogony out of Non-being is wholly creative in the sense of the making of new reality. I commend the development of Non-being or *ex nihilo* cosmogony in the contemporary cosmogonic discussion, not only for its expression of creativity at an ontological level but also for its approach to cosmogonic explanation. As Charles Peirce pointed out, order is itself what most needs explanation; chaos or Non-being does not need explanation. All those philosophical strategies that insist that the ontological cause of the cosmos must contain within itself all the actuality and complexity of the cosmos, the understanding of which is derived from an understanding of the cosmogonic source, fail to be basic enough for cosmogony. For, it is always necessary to ask for an account of the origin of the plenitude or complexity of the source. Only the Non-being strategy is fundamental enough for cosmogony. Its causal principle is creativity of novelty, a powerful theme in Chinese philosophy and elsewhere, that needs to be elaborated in contemporary cosmogonic discussions.

COSMOLOGY

The fifth new project for Chinese philosophy lies in philosophical cosmology. How should we understand nature philosophically, given what science is showing us in the fruitful reductionist ways of science? Here the Chinese traditions, nearly all of them, bring two important themes to the discussion. Most Western philosophical cosmologies since the modern era accept the philosophical reduction of value out of nature, as is typical in modern science according to the discussion in the previous chapter.[11] Whitehead reacted against this by developing a scientifically sophisticated cosmology that does express value as a transcendental trait of any natural thing.[12] The Chinese traditions never did entertain seriously conceptions of nature that reduced it to facts without value. They therefore can throw their weight into the cosmological discussions behind conceptions like Whitehead's and the pragmatists', and develop conceptions of nature and value of their own.

The second important cosmological theme in Chinese philosophy is to consider human society as part of nature, and nature as continuous with human society. Some people have stressed the ethical orientation of Confucianism, and there is truth in this stress. But unlike ethical traditions in many other traditions, Confucianism always set ethical concerns within a wider natural cosmology. It was able to do this, of course, because of the continuity of value from human to natural affairs, and vice versa. In our time, as Thomas Berry has reminded us, in reference to Chinese philosophy, it is imperative to understand human affairs as modulations within natural affairs, and to behave accordingly.[13]

Philosophical cosmology is among the most important philosophical tasks of our time. Without it we cannot understand the sciences of nature that, by themselves, tend to tell us that nature is without intrinsic value. Without it we cannot understand nature as constitutive of human life and society and are likely to continue to overvalue human history and its conflicts relative to the depths of nature within us. Without philosophical cosmology we cannot understand the roles of human habitation within the evolution of cosmic nature, thinking at most of the Earth as it is subject to human influence. Without philosophical cosmology, we cannot understand the meaning of human life in any larger perspective than the projections of human ambitions and we cannot understand the true implications of human ambitions outside the ken of human interests.

Kant mistakenly and disastrously taught that philosophical cosmology is impossible and that the only viable alternative is philosophy of science, an epistemological-only enterprise. The resulting scientific cosmologies are reductive to extreme degrees, particularly with reference to value. The older traditional cosmologies associated with religious and cultural traditions are innocent of science and blatantly inapplicable to the cosmos as we know it to be through science so far as it goes. This is true of the traditional Chinese cosmologies as well: it simply is not helpful to cite Heavenly Principle and material force today without translating them into what can represent scientific knowledge in nonreductive ways. Pragmatism and process philosophy seem to be the only vital enterprises of philosophical cosmology today that understand science and aim to represent its findings without scientific reductionism. They would be enormously deepened by participation from Chinese philosophers who would bring the deep interests of conceiving human life and society, replete with moral analyses, in natural, value-laden, cosmic terms.

RITUAL STUDIES

The sixth new project I urge upon Chinese philosophers is to bring into the study of human origins the rich Chinese understanding of ritual, especially that stemming from Xunzi but also as developed through millennia of engagements with the problems of human life. Confucian ritual theory can be translated into the language of pragmatic semiotic theory without much difficulty: any habit with a vague meaningful character as defined within a semiotic code is a learned ritual. Evolutionary biologists are now coming to understand the origin of human culture and language in terms of the development of semiotic forms of reference that employ symbolic patterns of signs rather than merely indexical causal references.[14] Current evolutionary theory, however, looks only to evolutionary adaptiveness to understand the growth of human meaningful behavior, ignoring or downplaying the senses in which ritual behavior becomes self-corrective and expansive on its own terms. If beliefs are held only because those who hold them pass on their genes with greater success, then there is no reason to believe that beliefs are true or false.

Without the contributions of Chinese understandings of the subtlety of ritual, and like considerations, it will remain possible for the understanding of human origins to remain wholly materialistic, an absurd position that cannot account for the evolution of minds to produce accounts of true and critically tested theories. Most discussions within the circles of those who think of themselves as Chinese philosophers, however, do not connect with the scientific discussions of human origins. The language of the sciences needs to be brought into the Chinese philosophical discussions.

RITUAL AND CULTURE

A seventh new project for Chinese philosophy is related to the point about ritual. Among the most important topics for any philosophy in our time is the understanding of the different world cultures with their own philosophies, philosophies explicit in textual traditions and implicit in the ways by which cultures conceive the world and what is important in it. The day is past when it is plausible to think of only Western philosophy as real philosophy, just as the day passed earlier when the Chinese could think of Chinese philosophy as the only real philosophy. Representatives of the diverse cultural traditions need to learn to engage one another. This means that the paideia for philosophy for anyone now needs to include a strong dose of comparative philosophy. All philosophers need to know the core texts and motifs of the world's cultures, just as it used to be thought in the West that all philosophers need to know Plato and Aristotle. Despite enormous strides in recent years to translate those core texts into global languages such as English and Chinese, making global comparative philosophy possible on a large scale, most philosophers still find themselves in situations defined by the familiar versus the strange. How should we behave in situations defined by this distinction of familiar versus strange?

One of the most important points to understand about the Chinese conception of ritual is that large-scale social rituals are designed so that people who are very different from one another in culture, class, and real interests can still interact together in productive ways. The ancient Chinese rejected the response to social chaos that says that a strongman is required to impose order, obliterating all cultural, class, and personal interests save his own, although sometimes the imposition of order might be helpful temporarily. Rather, the only response that respects genuine differences of culture, class, and interests is the development of rituals that allow the competing groups and individuals to dance together.

In the present philosophical situation, we cannot have any one tradition lay down the ground rules for what counts as philosophy or cultural criticism. Each position needs to have the space to make its case. Hence we need to develop rituals of intercultural philosophical engagement. This is already happening in the proliferation in America of societies devoted to Chinese-Western philosophical comparison. Much more, however, needs to be done to reshape the rituals of academic philosophy in America and across the world to create the contexts within which different philosophical cultures can engage one another. Among the important engagements are those dealing with cosmogony, cosmology, and human origins.

RITUAL AND POLITICS

An eighth and final new project for Chinese philosophy is to bring ritual theory to the analysis of global moral and political issues. Here the context is not academic philosophy but the intellectual life of the real players in morals and politics. The analysis I just gave of the function of ritual to allow people with different and competing cultures, classes, and interest to work together productively applies in spades to the domain of global politics and moral conflict. There are three parts to this new project. One is to promote ritual analyses of the social habits that surround the engagements of different cultures with one another, particularly those that involve conflict. Western moral analyses have tended to focus on actions themselves, whereas much more is to be learned by understanding the ritual contexts within which actions take place, because those ritual contexts supply the semiotic meanings and values that lie behind actions. Meaningful actions are not possible without the ritual structures that give them meaning, and Chinese philosophers can point this out, case by case.

The second part of the new project is to criticize the rituals that are operative, showing just how they are good or bad and inventing new ones where appropriate. Despite his claim to be traditional, Confucius was one of the most creative, innovative philosophers ever! The third part of the new project is to call attention to the need for global rituals of political and moral interactions, rituals that give space for cooperation and disagreement and that make the efforts at resolution, even when they are at cross-purposes, be meaningful in terms of one another.

Long ago I argued, following Hsu Sung-peng, that creativity within the processes of time, according to Daoism, introduces genuine novelty as a matter of "yang-extension" that is to be applauded so long as the novelty can be reconciled with what had gone before, a matter of "yin-consolidation."[15] That might have been a good, though partial, point about Daoism. But now I have my doubts about circumscribing the legitimacy of creativity to what can be reconciled with what has been before. I have been recommending eight new projects for Chinese philosophy that require Chinese philosophers to venture far enough beyond the several traditions of Chinese philosophy that they might well not be able to get back. When Chinese philosophy engages contemporary natural sciences, for instance, does it have to extend too far from its classical conceptions to carry over what is important in those conceptions to the new conversations? This is a problem in the portability of the traditions of Chinese philosophy the answer to which is not yet clear. To my knowledge, though I would hope to be mistaken, the practices of contemporary science in China are not much connected with the older Chinese philosophical traditions. So I leave that as an open question.

The main point of my remarks concerning the last five projects for Chinese philosophy is that the global philosophical situation needs the contributions of Chinese philosophers. Contemporary cosmogony needs the Chinese emphasis on creativity as novelty and on understanding as moving from the simple or indeterminate to the complex or determinate. Contemporary cosmology needs the Chinese emphasis on value in nature and on the understanding of human society as part of nature. The contemporary understanding of the origins of human nature needs the Chinese emphasis on ritual in semiotics such that we can understand the evolution of the human as a matter of learning as well as success at passing on genes. The contemporary practices of global philosophy need the Chinese understanding of ritual for bringing together incommensurate cultures. The contemporary political and moral situation needs a

Chinese analysis of its conflicts as functions of adequate and inadequate rituals, with the invention of more civilized rituals that make living with conflict possible. These are all urgent philosophical needs, in somewhat different senses of urgency.

In order for Chinese philosophy to rise to these and other needs, it will have to look to itself to become aware of the difficulties and risks of the portability of its traditions into these contemporary conversations, the third project I advocated. To do this, it will have to re-sort its canon, determining which elements show promise for contemporary contributions, the second project. Both of these projects themselves have a long history within Chinese philosophy. In the contemporary situation, however, when many kinds of Chinese philosophers are most concerned to recover their "own" traditions in the face of recent hostility to them, these projects require an about-face, a turning outward. In this sense, Chinese philosophy is called upon to be creative explicitly, venturing into novelty, which is the new project with which I began.

CHAPTER FIVE

Philosophy's Fight between Engagement and Distance

A Confucian Resolution

PHILOSOPHY AND THE AXIAL AGE

Philosophy invented itself during the Axial Age in the civilizations of East Asia, South Asia, and West Asia through a series of radical cognitive transformations, of which I shall mention four.[1] First was that at least some individuals in all those civilizations came to identify themselves most importantly as being human. The alternative had been to identify most importantly with one's tribe or kinship group. In some Pre–Axial Age societies, the very word for "people" was the name of their tribe, such that those people outside that in-group were regarded as somehow subhuman. The Axial Age civilizations defined humanity in interestingly different ways, although all fairly close together when seen from the distance of our standpoint. The philosophic point was that all people were to be regarded as human, however humanity was defined. Humanity is universal. For practical purposes, of course, an individual's location in a kinship group has specific duties within that in-group that do not apply to people in the out-groups, and often these duties are more important to self-identity than merely being human. Nevertheless, the early philosophers found ways to say that the *most* important matters of life have to do with fulfilling one's humanity, not merely with in-group success.

The second radical cognitive transformation, a corollary of the first, was to conceive of both compassion and justice to be owed to all human beings, not only to those in one's in-group. Before the Axial Age, the received wisdom was to be kind and just to one's friends and to do harm to and cheat the enemies. Book 1 of Plato's *Republic* contains a classic discussion of why justice and care should be universal, not limited to one's in-group. Jesus's Parable of the Good Samaritan makes a similar point. Of course, a person does have special relations with those in the in-group, and so loving and being just mean different things in the context of relating to different groups. The ancient debates between the Mohists and Confucians on the nature of universal love illustrate the complexities of the growing conception of justice and compassion for everyone. The South Asian civilizations broadened the community deserving love and care to include all sentient beings, not only human beings. This vastly extended the community to which we belong to insects, demons, and gods, but it sharply separated the community of sentience from nonsentient nature, a separation never made so strongly in East Asian and West Asian civilizations. The Axial Age did not do away with in-group/out-group distinctions, which are still powerful today. In many respects the ideals of universal compassion and justice are still honored more in the breach than in habitual practice. Nevertheless, philosophy invented itself in part by thinking through these issues.

The third radical cognitive transformation was the development across the Axial Age civilizations of conceptions of the world as a whole. These conceptions, or images, differed from one another in astonishing ways. Moreover, the different catalogues of all the things to be found under heaven are delightfully diverse, an astonishing display of human imagination. But the most astonishing point here is the effort to conceive of the world as a whole, not just the valley of one's people, one's forest, one's island. Once people could conceive of "everything," not just this and that and some others, philosophy was on its way. Zhuangzi was so subtle as to be able to relativize and make ironic even the conception of "everything."

The fourth radical cognitive transformation was to conceive that all under heaven is somehow conditioned by unconditioned conditions, resting on one or a few fundamental "causes." West Asian civilizations favored the metaphors of persons creating, or the rational principles associated with persons creating. South Asian civilizations favored the foundational metaphors of consciousness. East Asian civilizations gravitated to metaphors of spontaneous emergence, the Dao that cannot be named, for instance. The elementary conditions created by the unconditioned conditions usually were thought of as harmonies of some sort, such as form and matter, consciousness and moving bodies (*purusha* and *prakriti*, that is), or Heaven and Earth, yin and yang. Philosophy invented itself as thinkers developed ways of understanding the multifariousness of the world in terms of such basic forces, creative acts, or principles. Many different and conflicting senses of explanation developed, but they had in common the goal of understanding the more complex in terms of the simpler. Despite the diversity of cultural ideas in the world's Axial

Age civilizations, they all developed, at about the same time, what we recognize from our perspective as philosophy.

Doubtless many social conditions were involved in the invention of philosophy on a global scale. For instance, the Axial Age was a time of great empires in all the places where many local cultures with local languages were forced together in some kind of loose unity with a common language, Han Chinese, for instance, or Prakrit, or Greek. The empires moved people about, especially the elite, so that primary identifications with clan graveyards were broken. Inter-clan warfare was nonadaptive within empires. Another factor was the rise of literacy among the elites in all those areas. Writing gives you distance on the immediate emotions, actions, and ideas written about. Not all the founding philosophers were themselves writers. Socrates, for instance, was the philosophic creation of Plato. The Buddha and Confucius have texts attributed to them from the notes of students. But the ideas associated with those founding philosophers were expressed in literary form. Another factor in the rise of philosophy in the Axial Age was a striking interaction of the world's great civilization, with travelers taking ideas and philosophical behaviors across vast distances.

PHILOSOPHY AS DISTANCE

My point is that philosophy invented itself by gaining distance on its subject matter. "Distance" means taking the long view, the high view, the perspective that allows many things to be seen together. The original meaning of the root of the Greek word *theoria* was a reviewing stand from which a king could observe his army mustering or parading by. Philosophic distance has two related conditions that have been mentioned already. One is an ability to transcend immediate perceptual and emotional reactions to the world. Of course, practical action always has to be able to engage directly. But as Eric Havelock and others showed a half century ago, the pre–Axial Age culture of ancient Greece was centered around oral/aural communication in which the *Iliad* and *Odyssey*, for instance, were recited before crowds who grasped them through mimicking the emotions of the characters. This culture was derided by Plato, who taught people to think twice and more critically about things before responding in emotion and action, which was possible only in a closely remembered, most likely written down, conversation.[2] Much of early Chinese philosophy was similar to Plato's dialogues in that it consisted of "remembered" conversations, long or short, about which there could be subsequent analysis and debate, for instance, the *Analects* or *Zhuangzi*. This condition for the "distance" intrinsic to philosophy is something like an acquired habit of mind with attending media of communication.

The second condition for distance is the development of the conceptual tools themselves that allow for the synoptic view. In Western philosophy the early genre of conceptual tools for distance was that of universal categories under which particulars might be grouped. The categories might be defined in terms of one another such that, so networked, they provide ways of seeing together what falls under them. Western philosophers today ignorant of other traditions of philosophy sometimes think this is the only kind of philosophical conceptual distance and they limit philosophy to what can be dealt with logically and perhaps mathematically, logic and mathematics being important paradigms of universal categories. South Asian modes of early philosophic thought worked somewhat differently. Instead of looking to higher universal categories, they responded to plurality by hunting for underlying conditions like substrata; beneath the plurality of selves there is *atman*, and beneath the manifestations of *atman* there is Brahman. East Asian modes of early philosophic thought were somewhat different in the ways they acquired distance. Heaven, Earth, and Dao, for instance, function as fundamental categories in early Chinese philosophy. But they are as much like particulars as they are like universals, or better yet they are great cosmic elements whose interactions explain or give perspective on the workings of the manifold of nature and human experience. When the Neo-Confucians, for instance, said that principle is one and its manifestations are many, they did not mean the principle is a universal, like the Form of the Good, and its manifestations are particular instances of principle, but rather that principle works on the plurality of processes to bring them to many kinds of unity. The underlying sense of what philosophy needs distance on in early Chinese philosophy was not things in process, as in much Greek philosophy, or processes without continuous things, as in much South Asian thinking, but rather concrete processes passing through patterns, as imagined in the *Yijing*. Chinese philosophy achieved conceptual distance by inventing the dialectical relations between concrete movement in Earth, or *qi*, and pattern or the source of coherence in Heaven, or *li*. But because the universal/particular distinction never quite fit in early Chinese thinking, that fundamental dialectic was rarely expressed as a play of categories. Rather, those "concrete" elements were discussed in ways that gave them a generality or distance that kept their concrete metaphoric base. Sometimes this depended on a heavy play of irony, as in Zhuangzi, and even Laozi. But nearly always it meant a carefully controlled use of metaphor. Those metaphors worked to achieve distance just as effectively as categories treated as universals with logical structure.

These senses of distance are essential to philosophy. They allow us to conceive of things in terms of the world as a whole, as caused or conditioned by a few elementary things, and to think of humanity and the human condition in ways that apply to everyone even when we recognize differences in human context. From this flow the inquiries into what we now call metaphysics; epistemology; ethics; politics; social theory; philosophies of science, of education, of religion, of education; and philosophical anthropology. Because of philosophic distance, we can reengage inquiries of less general or distanced scope.

PHILOSOPHY AS ENGAGEMENT

Nevertheless, the attainment of distance has not been the only ingredient necessary for the invention of philosophy. The motive for attaining distance has been the desire to find the perspectives necessary to live life better. Paradoxical as it might sound, philosophical distance is supposed to enhance philosophical engagement with the most important issues of life. In various ways, the right combination of distance and engagement constitutes wisdom. This point is vague and it has been illustrated in the history of philosophy in different ways, many of which are contradictory to one another. For instance, in ancient Greek philosophy, Aristotle thought that ethics and practical philosophy prepare the way for a steady, stable life in which the highest fulfillment consists in contemplating eternal theoretical truths, which is what he thought was the closest human beings could come to God. Plato, by contrast, said in the *Republic* that the theoretical sciences, including mathematics and philosophical dialectic, are for the sake of preparing for the practical guidance of life, the life of the state and also the life of the individual trying to be just. In the Chinese traditions the practical orientation of philosophy has never been in question. Reflective distance aims to give the Daoist sensibility an accomplished harmony that yields power. Reflective distance serves the Confucian sensibility in its concerns to acquire the sagely skills at discernment and action so as to manifest clear character, renovate the people, and abide in the highest good, as the Great Learning puts it. Legalists and Mohists were even more directly practical in their use of philosophic perspective, though in my judgment without the complexity and subtlety that was preserved and cultivated in what we know as Confucianism and Daoism.

Today our world is different from the Axial Age and the invention of philosophy. Philosophy in the West has given rise to the sciences, or at least aided and abetted their development. It has become involved with the conceptualities of organized religion, especially Christianity and Islam, and later providing direct conceptual support for a scientific view of the world that objectivizes nature and persons and subjectivizes experience and morality. Philosophy with that combination of distancing and engagement has provoked a romantic reaction that now takes the form of postmodernism. Philosophy in China developed close relations with religion, including its own various religious forms, especially when interacting with Buddhism. But more than in the West, Chinese philosophy developed in the courts of government and, in the case of Daoism, in the military. In the case of Confucianism, philosophy in varying forms of sophistication became a way of life expressed particularly in families, especially those families in touch with literacy. Even today it makes sense to say that Confucianism, with its sense of ritual arrangements and classic texts committed to memory if not to understanding, provides a background culture to a great many in China, Korea, and Japan who would otherwise think of themselves as secular, or Marxists, or Christians. Family culture in America could never be thought of as Platonic or Aristotelian, though it might be thought of as Christian or Judeo-Christian with biblical texts running in the back of the mind. (By the way, the analogy of Confucianism in popular family East Asian cultures to biblical religion in the family cultures of America and Europe is a strong argument for acknowledging that Confucianism is a religion.)

PHILOSOPHY IN THE ACADEMY

Nevertheless, in our own time the fate of the philosophic traditions of East Asia, South Asia, and West Asian (that is, the West including the Americas, Australia, and New Zealand) has been to become academic. Philosophy's home is not in government, religion, science, or commerce. It is in departments of philosophy (and sometimes religious studies) in colleges and universities. This is a global phenomenon, with the possible exception of locations for Islamic philosophy.

In one sense this academic apotheosis of philosophy is an extraordinary achievement. Philosophy is not dismissed as the rants of crazy people disconnected from the real world. Philosophy rather is admitted to the group of disciplines in which most cultures now believe their elite should be educated. Although there are indeed crazy philosophers, many of whom send us emails begging our attention, most of us enjoy organized groups of colleagues, journals in which we publish with the rigor of peer review, and societies in which we meet to exchange views and learn from the criticisms of each other. Our academic profession evolves, of course, but usually with professionally approved good reasons given for the changes. Perhaps most important is that philosophy, which has so many traditions from different cultures, exists in an academic environment within which these traditions can be brought together with disciplined comparisons, sophisticated linguistic comparisons of texts and cultural translations, communications that over time develop an history of discourse, and a living dialogue with leading figures and with disciples destined to transcend them. Academic philosophy has its own disciplined vulnerability to be true both in the perspectives of distance and the specific projects of engagement.

The negative side of the academic achievements of philosophy is this very same professionalization. A profession commonly is defined as a discipline in which practitioners are responsible to their peers within the profession rather than to those they might serve. Medicine is a profession because only other doctors can tell whether a physician's care is appropriate, even if the patient dies; law is a profession because only other lawyers can tell whether the best case has been made for the client. Cooking is not a profession because, as Aristotle said, "The judge of the feast is the guest, not the cook."

Academic philosophy is a profession in just this sense, that the judge of philosophy is other philosophers. In our academic review processes for promotion and tenure we try to base our judgments on the recommendations of outside reviewers who are professionally close to the candidates. Most colleges have administrative officers and higher review committees that include nonphilosophers, but except for judging teaching, those higher stages in the review process usually limit themselves to adjudicating among competing professional philosophical reviews. Large institutions usually try even to ensure that analytic philosophers review analytic philosophical candidates, Continental ones Continental candidates, and that experts in Chinese philosophy review candidates in Chinese philosophy. At least the preponderance of reviewing authority is usually given to those who are closest in the field. Each field within philosophy is something like a tunnel with its own standards. Its very discipline for progress and good judgment requires sticking to the relevant standards. Another way to put this academic embodiment of philosophy is to say that philosophy's public, which it addresses and to which it is accountable, is other philosophers.

This puts extraordinary pressure with cognitive dissonance on philosophy, because philosophy's disciplines for engagement and distance are supposed to issue in wisdom for the world. In this respect philosophy is more like cooking than like medicine or law. We fancy that in the good old days, everyone with a liberal education was capable of reading and learning from disciplined philosophy, even if they lacked the professional discipline themselves. But now liberal education is in decline and scientific and vocational specializations are precluding the space and time for general philosophical literacy. We fancy also that in the good old days, philosophers held themselves accountable to a wider elite public and knew how to address that public or set of publics. Nowadays, it is unlikely that many nonphilosophers would look to find wise orientation to life from professional philosophers. Moreover, in the academy itself, few of the other disciplines think it is important for their own work that they learn from the wide orientations philosophers might provide them. For all our acceptability in the academy as philosophic specialists with a tunnel of professional rigor, we philosophers have become unheeded and unneeded precisely because of the walls of our tunnel. Why get the perspective of distance on things if what we see from that vantage point is irrelevant to anything we might engage outside the academic profession? The very name of the institution that Plato founded for the development of philosophical distance and engagement, his Academy, has become a sadly ironic put-down of real philosophy in common usage. To say something is merely academic is to say that it is irrelevant. A parallel irony lies in the fact that the title of the Chinese classic I cited earlier as the epitome of engagement of the world in wisdom, the *Daxue*, has become the word for the contemporary university in China, which is just as divided into academic specialties with philosophy in its own tunnel as Western universities.

Whereas philosophy's fight in the ancient world between engagement and distance was a struggle to break the stranglehold of immediacy on engagement so that the perspective of distance could provide wiser engagement, philosophy's fight today in its academic embodiment is to be able to engage something besides professional philosophy while keeping the disciplines that come from its carefully honed distance. Philosophy for philosophers alone is not philosophy: it is not framed to provide wise orientation to life of the sort that ought to come from having the distance intrinsic to philosophical thinking. I now want to make three remarks about what Confucianism might contribute to the contemporary situation.

CONFUCIANS IN THE ACADEMY: SCHOLAR-OFFICIALS

The first remark is that it would be wise for us academic philosophers with seasoned Chinese sensibilities to take on the roles of the traditional Confucian model of the scholar-official. The "scholar" part of that role is the disciplines of philosophy that we have learned and continually are expanding, its deep historical learning, its imagination at building perspectives from which the various domains of life can be balanced and integrated, and its craft at analyzing situations to see just how the manifestations of principle are many and where. The "official" part of the scholar-official role is to minister deliberately to the institutions of life that surround us. Confucians have long known that moral relations among individuals are mediated, indeed largely constituted, by the institutions within which we live. Confucianism lacks patience with moral behavior that is not attentive to the institutional or ritualized venues within which people interact. As academic philosophers we live deeply intertwined within the nested institutional structures of the academy and the surrounding society that supports and threatens it; our salaries provide the means to live in neighborhoods with homes, family, and friends, and where the arts, sports, and other elements of high civilization are vested. As scholar-officials we should involve ourselves as much as possible in the care and nurture of these institutions. Although this is no shortcut to resolving the dilemma of our unreadiness to address those outside our profession and the unreadiness of everyone else to hear what we might say if we could say it, our resolution to participate as scholar-officials in institutional ministries can make a positive difference. That participation can train us to speak beyond the profession and our participatory presence can help others understand, so long as we bring our philosophy into the participation.

Now I'm sure everyone reading this has already thought that we have too many committees already! How can we produce the professional scholarship expected of us with all those departmental and university committees, and how can we participate seriously in our larger communities with all that the academy requires of us? Cynicism is hard to avoid. Yet this is precisely the Confucian point about the philosophic standing of the role of the scholar-official. It is an opportunity for cultivation of genuinely philosophic life in our time and academic venue. Administrative roles are not just jobs that have to be done by someone, at which we take our turn (with much protest). Moreover, administrative roles are not merely opportunities to make our institutions better, although they clearly are that in some circumstances. In some other circumstances they are opportunities to make a declining situation get worse more slowly. The Confucian point, however, is that participation as a scholar-official is an opportunity to become a better philosopher.

In Neo-Confucian language, we know that principle is one and its manifestations are many. One measure of philosophic distance is understanding principle, or coherence, or harmony. But the measure of philosophic engagement is being able to identify it in the layers upon layers of a situation, to identify its presence and also where it is absent, to discern where a certain kind of coherence makes other kinds impossible and also where valuable coherent processes and structures depend on deeper background coherences. Distant reflection on coherence will never by itself provide the practice necessary to locate it in the multidimensional realities of a concrete situation. Only practice can do that. Hence, the need exists to be an engaged scholar-official in order to understand Principle in its manifestations.

But more, genuine philosophic engagement is able to do something about what one understands in concrete complexities. Here the cultivation of the official side of the scholar-official role is the substance of learning. Confucians know that the common experiences of learning how to act in the world, particularly to act conjointly with others to accomplish multiple goals at once, are not enough. Everyone can do this to some degree. But we should become seriously adept at it. The Confucian heritage stresses the lifelong acquisition of sageliness in acting, which requires learning from the opportunities for acting. Furthermore, we know that the real tests for most of our analyses of how the coherences work in the deep layers of the social and natural environment, and also in our own psyches, is whether we can work with them. Detailed observation depends on detailed interactions. It is not that first we understand and then we act. Rather, there is a unity of thought and action, as Wang Yang-ming and others have taught, so that we learn to think by means of acting as much as the other way around. The role of the scholar-official, which I urge us to resolve to play, is thus first and foremost a set of opportunities to learn how to think and act philosophically, bringing distance and engagement together, even in an academic environment and in the social life of academics. That is my first remark.

The second remark is that an added dimension to the Confucian role of scholar-official is an expectation that there be a yang-yin rhythm of participation and withdrawal. One does not have to be engaged in a given scholar-official role full bore all the time. Some people do think the world will fall apart if they slacken, and often it seems to do that. Nevertheless, full engagement all the time is very likely to lead to burnout or cynicism. Perhaps the background for this kind of sensibility is the ancient ideal, perhaps even real historical practice in some instances, of temporary retirement from public life upon the death of a parent. The lesson is that the scholar-official's public life is not the whole of life. Sometimes it is important to make a strategic retreat. When committee work gets too grinding, change committees. Better, take advantage of the academic institution of the sabbatical, however difficult that might be in this day and age. Sometimes the political battles of one's local community or, for some people, of the larger community, are best advanced by withdrawal, by a Long March. This might seem like withdrawing from public life in an absolute sense. But in fact properly timed engagement and retreat constitute a richer, more nuanced, form of continued participation than mere unrelenting effort. Thus the role of the scholar-official offers opportunity for new dimensions of self-cultivation, those having to do with the character skilled at entering and leaving public life.

Western philosophical cultures have tended to make a sharper distinction between public life and private life than has been observed in

Confucian cultures. Indeed, sometimes it is said that Confucianism does not like privacy at all but requires a transparent sincerity, *cheng*, that makes the inmost heart public. I think rather that Confucianism sees the public life of the sage as orchestrated by a rhythm of pressing forward and withdrawal. One of the reasons this rhythm is so hard to learn, especially for young people, is that active playing of official roles has an honor attached to it. While it might seem excessive to think academic committee work to be an honor, in fact people are honored for the official offices they hold, and the greater honor goes to the more important roles as one advances in maturity of ministry to the institutions within which one lives. Many of us know, and perhaps are, young scholars who have sought out departmental and college administration, with the immediate feedback of an honored identity, to the detriment of devotion to research that will be recognized only in the long run and maybe never. Mature scholars too sometimes feel that, if they withdraw from the offices that bring them honor, they will be at a loss. Indeed, they will be. Memory is short and in fact public honor does fall away when one withdraws from public office. Yet learning to live without being honored is a deep lesson for Confucians, the Confucian version of the Socratic adage that learning how to die is the way to learn how to live. Life is not always a press to be present and death is not always a retreat toward absence, but a rhythm of both that can be mastered as we learn to be scholar-officials.[3]

My third and last remark on contemporary philosophy's problem of engagement and distance is to call attention to the importance of ritual. Everything meaningful in human life involves signs by which we interpret nature and our affairs. As the pragmatist Charles Peirce taught, signs are learned habits of behavior by virtue of which we give meaningful connection to the things involved in life. Contemporary semiotics, however, has not been as wise as the Confucian heritage since Xunzi to recognize the embodiedness of the intentionality of signs. The primary metaphors of Western semiotics, interpreting texts and performing controlled experiments, are not as earthy as the metaphor of ritual. Learning the steps in a court ritual or a temple ritual is like learning a dance in which many people dance together to accomplish something. The ritual metaphor extends to ritualized behavior in business, economics, and politics, to the ritual of speaking in some language or other, to the rituals of gestures conveyed in body language, down to the basic rituals of learned styles of moving and standing.

Whereas earlier I wrote of the sagely scholar-official learning to discern the manifestations of coherence or incoherence in a thickly textured natural and social environment, much of that can be restated as learning to identify and play in the ritual structures of that environment. The Confucian tradition, as well as the Daoist, has always seen the human as set within the social and the social within wider nature. So the famous Confucian slogan recognizes Heaven and Earth as nature, some of whose elements do not involve the conventions of ritual. The slogan also joins the Human to Heaven and Earth, recognizing that human beings cannot achieve their humanity with Heaven and Earth alone but must also learn meaningfulness by becoming ritualized, beginning in infancy. Therefore, the task of discerning coherence and incoherence in the environment can be understood also as the task of understanding what rituals are operative in the institutions with which we relate to nature and each other.

My discussion of the invention of philosophy at the beginning of this chapter can be restated as an exploration of the kinds of changes in coherence necessary for the peculiar coherence of philosophic distance and engagement to arise. Empire is necessary to allow people to abandon sheer localism and think in terms of the world as a whole, of people as human rather than only as their relatives, and of ultimate explanatory conditions transcending things explained. Literacy is necessary to allow people to abandon immediacy in action and invent the cognitive apparatus to think twice. Now we can restate even this in terms of the understanding of ritual. Life in an empire is a different matrix of rituals from those in tribal life, and the rituals of literacy are different from those of an oral/aural culture; philosophy arose as a new matrix of ritual for engagement of the world with the wise orienting perspective of distance dependent on the rituals of empire and literacy.

In our contemporary situation where philosophy is mainly confined to the venues of the academy, to understand what rituals operate there, what they make possible, what they preclude, and how they ought to be changed is truly important and something natural for scholar-officials with a Chinese sensibility. The contemporary academy consists mainly of a collection of tunnels of specialization, as I've said. These each have their excellences according to the standards of the tunnels, and this includes philosophy too in its several modes. Those tunnels should be understood in terms of the rituals that make possible their dynamic progress as well as set their boundaries. In many of the natural sciences today, the various tunnel specialties are bumping into one another. One tunnel opens onto another, and new rituals are required to make possible their cooperation and integration. Old tunnels come to dead ends. Faculty are defined by their tunnel specialties, and more and more students are forced quickly into one tunnel or another to the exclusion of others. Such is professionalization. Philosophy needs to understand its isolation and frustration at having the public essential to its pursuit of wisdom in terms of the isolating rituals that cause this situation. Moreover, it needs to invent new rituals that allow it to engage other academic specialties as well as the broader affairs of life in the world outside the academy. The problem is not merely the cognitive one of inventing categories that integrate things. Indeed, the presentation of a set of philosophical categories is likely to be dismissed as irrelevant metaphysics, no matter how good they are. The problem is to invent learned behaviors that allow the tunnels to continue in their ways but that make possible the engagement of those fields in a larger perspective. At one time in America, religion, Anglo-Saxon Protestant religion, performed that integrating ritual of perspective with distance and engagement, but no more. That religion and all the others have been turned into private tunnels insofar as they have any life in the public at all. It is time for philosophy to rebuild the rituals of liberal education. I have suggested some of the advantages of the role of the scholar-official in this task.

PHILOSOPHICAL CULTIVATION

My final point is to return to the theme of philosophical cultivation. Each of us plays roles with many others in a dense matrix of rituals, a matrix of rituals upon rituals, many of them changing, but all together required to make up the texture of life in which principle is one and its manifestations are many. Each ritual is like a dance, with broad formal steps that can be learned. When the dance is performed, the social reality it constitutes is actual. Within the broad outline of the dance steps, however, each of us needs to learn how to individuate the actual steps we take. A toddler staggers through the steps; an adolescent learns basic rules of courtesy toward parents. But maturation involves individuation. We become individuals as we individuate the ways we play our roles. Critics of the Confucian approach to rituals sometimes say that human beings are thought to be defined by the rituals of their lives, and that this is a life-draining formalism. On the contrary, what defines us is not the rituals themselves but how we play them. We are how we individuate the rituals of our lives for better or worse, including how we individuate the discernment and amendment of our rituals. When we meet other individuals in those dances, we can identify them not only by the steps they are taking but by how they are taking them. That is the recognition of *ren*, humaneness, in the ritual over and above the form.

So I recommend that we resolve to attend to how we individuate the rituals that are relevant to our engagements and on which we have philosophic distance. Philosophic life is not just identifying the rituals that constitute the pursuit of orienting wisdom. It is learning to play them well, including the rituals of entering public life and leaving as scholar-officials. Learning to play the rituals requires practice, which should remind us that philosophy is not only cognitive but a matter of cultivated sagacity for dealing with the fight between engagement and distance.

Chapter Six

William Ernest Hocking

The First Boston Confucian

William Ernest Hocking (1873–1966) is to be remembered for many diverse and unusual things. Most were recognized during his long, productive, and distinguished career. But no one could have foretold during his lifetime that he would be remembered as the first Boston Confucian.

HOCKING AS A BOSTON CONFUCIAN

Who are the Boston Confucians? you might ask. Hocking would have known Boston Brahmins but not Boston Confucians. In fact, it was not until the 1990s that the title was ever used, to my knowledge.[1] The following three points characterize the school of Boston Confucianism.

First, it claims that Confucianism is a philosophy accessible to people who are not East Asians, do not read Chinese, and are not Sinologists. This is significant because many people have believed that Confucianism is a kind of ethnic philosophy, so deeply rooted in Chinese (and other East Asian) cultural identities and family structures as not to be sympathetically comprehensible, let alone adoptable, by non–East Asians. Accessibility to Western non-Chinese readers also depends on translations of the texts into European languages and on academic travel and exchanges that bring non–East Asians into contact with living representatives of Confucianism in China, Korea, and Japan. The situation now in these respects is far more fulsome than in Hocking's day, although I shall show that he had sufficient resources firmly to grasp Confucianism.

The second characteristic of Boston Confucianism is its practice of reading the Confucian tradition intermixed with Western philosophy with all positions construed as contributions to an emerging world philosophic tradition. The other traditions of Chinese philosophy, as well as those of

India and elsewhere, are to be construed the same way. On the surface this looks like comparative philosophy. But would we say that a study of Hume and Kant is comparative Scottish and German philosophy? Some Western philosophers say that the Western is "their" tradition and that treating Chinese philosophers in connection with Western ones is bringing the alien to the familiar. But the Western tradition is "theirs" only if they make it so. Few Western philosophers who cite Plato and Aristotle read them in the original Greek; most American philosophers who discuss Kantian ethics, except specialist scholars, read English translations. If "Westerners" make the tradition of Confucius and Mencius "theirs" along with that of Plato and Aristotle, it is in fact theirs. Boston Confucians are self-conscious heirs of both Western and East Asian ancient sources and integrate them into a common tradition.

The third point is that Boston Confucianism is a form of contemporary philosophic practice, not exclusively or even essentially a scholarly tradition about the Confucian tradition. Contemporary philosophical problems lie in such fields as ethics, political theory, aesthetics, philosophy of religion, science, education, metaphysics, and spiritual matters, and in each field Confucianism has important contributions. Historical resources need to be understood in order to be used, and this is a complex hermeneutical process. But from a philosopher's standpoint, historical resources also need to be used in order to be understood: their meanings do not show themselves fully until they are properly pressed into service. Boston Confucianism is a contemporary philosophy identified by the importance it gives a certain tradition's resources; the same was true three centuries ago of Cambridge Platonism, which was not so much about Plato as about England and/or Heaven.

William Ernest Hocking was a Bostonian who, in the 1930s, wrote philosophy that exhibits all three traits of Boston Confucianism.[2] I doubt he would have claimed to be more a Confucian than a Platonist, but then some present-day Boston Confucians are other things as well. Hocking had an understanding of Confucianism, particularly that of Zhu Xi, that was extraordinary for his time and entirely respectable now. He read Zhu Xi as a philosopher alongside Kant, Fichte, and Bergson, improving upon them in crucial respects. And he took Zhu Xi to have an important contribution to make to the problem of democracy and science, a problem as central for our time as Hocking's, in Boston, Beijing, and elsewhere.

Hocking is known for his cosmopolitan sympathies and his philosophy of a world civilization epitomized in his book *The Coming World Civilization* (1956). I want to focus on a crucial example of world philosophy in his thought, a particular paper called "Chu Hsi's Theory of Knowledge," published in 1936. But first I want to comment on his background in Chinese philosophy.

Hocking, of course, is known as one of the last great systematic philosophers in the Western philosophical tradition, and for thematizing his systematic conceptions in practical areas. He wrote not only for academic philosophers but for people interested in larger issues.[3] His two main systematic topics were religion and the social character of human life, and in both contexts he had occasion to study and comment on Chinese civilization, ancient and contemporary.[4] He was, moreover, of that generation of philosophers, or "public intellectuals" as we now say, who began the great conversation of East and West, including Hu Shih, who visited his Harvard class in the 1920s. He participated with Charles Moore in the early East/West conferences in Hawaii, and he took responsible understanding of the cultures of his friends and fellow philosophers to be a part of the philosophic life.[5]

In his discussions of world religions, he spent more time on those of India, including both Hinduism and Buddhism, than on those of China. He wrote only one paper explicitly about a Chinese philosopher, the one I am about to analyze, plus a review article coauthored with his son Richard of a book by Wing-tsit Chan on contemporary culture (1953) in China.[6] Thus his mastery of the Chinese tradition—especially the difficult philosopher Zhu Xi—his ability to treat Zhu Xi in intimate comparison with Western philosophers, and his adroit use of Zhu Xi for his own philosophic purpose are all the more remarkable.

ZHU XI, SCIENCE, AND WORLD PHILOSOPHY

His own philosophic purpose in the essay on Zhu Xi was to examine how science should be conceived in a democratic society. This was one facet of his interest in the development of a world civilization. Science is important for democracy, according to Hocking, not only because its technological consequences make communication possible in ways required for democracy, but because scientific understanding is democratically available to anyone.[7] In a world of scientific advancement, he thought, nearly everyone has a chance. Modern science might have originated in the West, he allowed, but even in the 1930s it had been appropriated by cultures all over the globe that were developing it in ways indigenous to themselves. China in particular by then had moved out of the anti-scientific, xenophobic, attitudes associated with much late Ching conservative Confucian culture into active entry into the modern scientific world. What might have entered China through Western imperialism had been Sinicized and the Chinese could enter democratically, as it were, into the modern world.

But science requires a particular kind of knowing. In fact, Hocking opened the essay with the observation that "ways of knowing must vary with the nature of the objects to be known."[8] Science knows objects under the assumption that there is no mind in them, no teleology. Hocking the idealist of course was also, if not more, interested in the kinds of knowing that pick up on mental and teleological matters. But as for science, it is perfectly fit for knowing nature under certain assumptions and its technological benefits are enormous. Only if science is taken to be the exclusive form of knowing does it become scientism.[9]

As to science itself in the modern Western sense, Hocking characterized it in the Zhu Xi article as both empirical and rationalistic. The empiricism of science is a devotion to the knowledge of things, not to the knower but to the things to be known. Empiricism is a kind of denial of the self and its interests in favor of a piety before nature. Hocking sharply attacked what he calls "hearty nineteenth century pragmatism" for fudging on this matter entirely (a judgment I do not share entirely). The rationalism of science consists in its desire to integrate knowledge into a whole, to know the whole truth. This leads science to ever more general and overarching principles. Modern science has the unifying language of mathematics.

But modern science in fact is not capable of knowing the moral, teleological, mental aspects of the world that Hocking held to be so important. He followed Bergson's critique of science as failing to include what wholly empirical and wholly rationalistic intuition can tell us. The world picture of science is of a mechanism whereas reality is more like an organism, according to Hocking. He declined to go as far as Whitehead in declaring the world to be an organism, or at least to be understood in the metaphors of what Whitehead called the "philosophy of organism." Hocking's counterdescription of the universe is worth quoting, not only for understanding his relation to Whitehead but because it is so like the Chinese conception of process:

> There is more looseness among the parts of the world, more waste, wider flung oceans of emptiness, more *relative* independence than is compatible with organic unity. The inner rhythms and changes are not the proportioned movements of organic processes. What the universe seems to present is a true system of interdependent motions *within which* organic groupings take place and run their life course—the whole presenting the character of a *single environment* for the living fragments rather than being itself a total organism with no environment. What interests us is not that everything shall be living and of a mental kind, but rather that the universe should offer itself as an arena for life and purpose, an arena whose very wildness, waste, vastness, unspanned gulfs of distance, offer incentives without limit to an ever-growing mentality. Seen in this way there is a

> purpose in the purposeless aspects of the world; the personal finds use for the impersonal, the living for the mechanical, the intense focuses of consciousness for the infinitely expansive unconsciousness of mass and energy-fields.[10]

How might we attain to an alternative conception of science that is just as empirical as the modern and just as rationalistic, but also sensitive to the mental? For this Hocking appealed to Zhu Xi.

ZHU XI'S METAPHYSICS

Zhu Xi (1130–1200) is regarded by most Chinese scholars as the greatest of the Song dynasty Neo-Confucians. He synthesized the reforming thought of his predecessors, all of whom responded to the challenges of Buddhism and Daoism to Confucianism. Zhu Xi's system provided an interpretation of the classic texts of Confucianism that was to remain the basis of the Chinese civil service examinations until the twentieth century.[11] The positive affirmations of his system were both metaphysical and moral. Hocking gave a neat and very accurate summary of Zhu Xi's so-called dualism, noting the inappropriateness of the characterization of dualism. Zhu Xi developed two cosmological categories, *qi* and *li*.

Qi is often translated as ether or material force. Hocking's summary characterization is accurate: "a subtle all-pervasive quasi-material entity, capable of local variation, of degrees of density and of resistance to the pure control of the spiritual principle, Li."[12] *Qi* is what is, or should be, organized or given structure by *li*, principle. But *li* is the hard category to understand. Zhu Xi's translator, J. P. Bruce, translates *li* as law, which would be neat if it is to describe a scientific universe of matter operating under the dictates of law. But, as Hocking says,

> *Li* has a pedigree which may disqualify it. It must be understood as one of four manifestations of the Ultimate Being, these four to be taken in a descending order. They are: *T'ien*, Heaven; *Ming*, Heaven's Decree, which is at the same time the Vocation, *Bestimmung*, of the creature; *Hsing*, the nature of the thing; *Li*, the individualized embodiment of the Nature, i.e., the Life-charter of the individual being. *T'ien* and *Ming* can be regarded as the active, transmitting function; *Hsing* and *Li* as the receiving function. These functions are two aspects of the same continuous activity: for Heaven is always engaged in its decreeing of destiny; and things are always showing signs of an impressed Law, the *Hsing* or Nature of the species, contained in the *Li* or Life-rule of the individual. This activity and this

> receptiveness, taken together, constitute what we may call the life of *T'ien*, or the manifestation of *Tao*, the Ultimate Order of the World, which for Chu Hsi is a moral order.[13]

Hocking's account is extraordinarily lucid, but it does not quite appreciate the metaphysical power of Zhu Xi's conception of *li*. The Dao, for Zhu Xi, is not merely the ultimate *order* of the world, as if it were on the *li* side opposed to *qi*. Rather, the Dao is the ultimate reality of the world, its process taken as a whole. And *li* is Zhu Xi's word for the most ultimate on the order side, which is sometimes called "heavenly principle." The Neo-Confucian distinction between *li* and *qi* is its development in metaphysical terms of the ancient Confucian (and Daoist) division of reality into Heaven, Earth, and their conjunction, a set of distinctions found in the *Yijing*. It is the same metaphysical principle, *li*, that is to be found in every finite thing, giving it its order. Most particularly, *li* is the principle of harmony according to which every specific thing can harmonize itself in its environment of ongoing processes to fulfill its own unique mandate. So Hocking is right to emphasize the overall ordering principle of heaven and also to say that this single principle is manifested in unique ways for each individual. His phrase "life-charter" is apt for describing the function of *li* in each finite thing. Hocking wrote with clear awareness of the fact that the Chinese did not believe that finite things are internally constructed substances but instead are specifications of larger processes that interact with one another and attain their unity or harmony in that interaction; his own previously quoted description of the world, declining to be a philosopher of organism, is a neat statement of the Chinese view that I have attempted to unfold here beginning with the first chapter.

Zhu Xi had much of the modern scientific temper, Hocking claimed, in being both an empiricist and a rationalist. Because *li* is always individuated in *qi*, it is necessary to look at things in their material uniqueness. Zhu Xi had no sense for the modern scientific method, with controlled experiments and the like, but he did direct science outward to observation. At the same time, he also emphasized that what we find in things is their principle, or *li*, and this connects them. In principle, *li* allows things to be connected with one another and with the whole.

Now it is the nature of *li* as principle that interested Hocking, for *li* is "mental" in Hocking's sense. *Li* is whatever *would* harmonize the components of a given thing or situation, and thus it is teleological. The Chinese did not believe in an Aristotelian teleology, according to which a substance contains an end or fulfillment or completion toward which it drives. But they did believe that processes need harmonization, and any thing or situation can be understood in terms of what will, would, or should harmonize the otherwise chaotic or independently progressing processes. For human life, understanding one's *li* always takes the form of identifying what processes are going on and discovering how to bring them into harmony. Because we live in a wider world, our own processes of harmonization need to be harmonized with the harmonizing needs of nature and society; Zhu Xi and the Neo-Confucians interpreted this as the Mandate of Heaven, finding one's place, or process, within the process of the universe.

Now what is true of persons is true of other animals, and nature more generally. *Li* provides continuity from the quotidian moral concerns of human beings to the strivings of animals and the larger harmonizing processes of nature. The mind of a human being is one with the mind of the universe, according to Zhu Xi and other Neo-Confucians. And the "extension of knowledge," Zhu Xi's phrase for science, has to do with bringing this unity of mind to mind, laying out the connecting principles, and creating a kind of moral continuity of individuals with the Dao. Hocking quotes Zhu Xi's fetching remark in this regard:

> In our sense of heat and cold, of hunger and repletion, in the love of life and shrinking from death, and in the instinctive seeking for what will benefit and shunning of what will be prejudicial,—all this is common to man with other creatures. (But) the diversity of Law [*li*] is seen in the existence among ants and bees of the relation between sovereign and minister, in which there is manifested no more than a gleam of Righteousness; in the existence among wolves and tigers of the relation between parent and child, in which there is manifested no more than a gleam of love. . . . It is not the case that man, as the being possessed of the highest intellect, stands alone in the universe. His mind is also the mind of birds and beasts, of grass and trees. "Man," however, "is born endowed with the *Mean*, the attribute of Heaven and Earth."[14]

Hocking pointed out that this identifies not only a biological continuity but also the "differentia of man," which is "the *balance* which exists among his instinctive propensities, a balance which fits him for hesitation and reflection, and thus for the influence of ideas upon his behavior."[15]

ZHU XI AND BUDDHISM COMPARED

What is most interesting about Hocking's exposition of Zhu Xi is that it proceeds in a comparative contrast with Buddhism. He began the essay with a brief discussion of Dharmapāla's interpretation of change.

Dharmapāla (439–507) was an Indian Buddhist who wrote a major commentary on Vasubandhu's founding text of the "Consciousness-Only" school of Buddhism, which was popularized in China by Hsuan-tsang, who used Dharmapāla's writings. All Buddhists are concerned with the nature and soteriologically bad effects of change, and with whatever unity underlies change. Buddhism, of course, denies the reality of any entitative underlying unity, but it does indeed have to know how time flows. Hocking describes Dharmapāla's interpretation of an ideal being,

> the Tathagata Buddha, to whom this unity is evident. The Tathagata is not disturbed by transition; he understands its laws. He perceives the numerous things in the world, and recognizes their attractive qualities, but knowing also their mortality, he is not tempted to seize on any of them as his good: he is like the lotus, not disattached, not swept away by the current, and yet on the other hand not fascinated, not under illusion, unspotted by the world: he overcomes the world by comprehending it.[16]

In a brilliant paragraph, Hocking interpreted this Buddhist position in modern terms:

> Things and events are not merely additive items whose sum makes up the world; science reveals them as parts of a single system, Nature. Now "Nature" is a term of hope, rather than of scientific achievement; the final synthesis of the laws of change is never reached. Before we reach this elusive physical unity, the question recurs which in western thought we supposed we had banished—perhaps the ultimate order of things is less an order of fact than an order of meaning or value! We appear driven to assume a teleological structure in things, as a condition of completing our scientific labor. The Buddhist, never wholly succumbing to anthropomorphism, provides this teleological element by invoking a quasi-personal being as a symbol of the nature of the final coherence of things, and then develops a special branch of his theory of knowledge for the perception of this being.[17]

So far, Buddhism agrees with Zhu Xi about at least the ideal of a comprehensive understanding of the world; Zhu Xi's categories might be preferable, but he obviously learned from Buddhism. Yet he was also extremely critical of Buddhism, and Hocking elicited the most critical part. For Buddhism, as Zhu Xi interpreted it, the purpose of knowing is to find the center of the self and retreat from the world. Quite the opposite of the purported Buddhist claim to believe in No-self, Buddhism is a selfish religion, Zhu Xi thought, turning people inward, away from the world and from their responsibilities to one another, family, and society. Some Buddhists, those who have taken the Bodhisattva's vow to continue working life after life to enlighten all sentient beings, might counter the charge of selfishness. But there is a big difference between the project of enlightening all sentient beings and taking care of one's family, repairing the dikes, and nurturing people in your village—the Confucian ideal. In comparative perspective, it is not hard to see why Zhu Xi would think Buddhism selfish when it encourages people to sit in meditation seeking enlightenment for themselves so that they can escape to Nirvana.[18]

Selfishness is not merely a moral epithet for Zhu Xi. On the contrary, it is his explanation for why true knowledge is so difficult to attain. The extension of knowledge does not progress by simply looking at more and more things with the principles. It requires what Hocking called "the ethical conditions of insight." Zhu Xi knew that things are to be known *in rebus*, as Hocking said, by paying attention to them on their own, analyzing them on their own terms, discerning what principle is doing with them in their processes of harmonization. But if we are selfish, all that outward analysis is distorted. We think we are looking at the other, but we are projecting our own wish-filled images. To put it in modern terms, we are pursuing our pet theories and seeing what those theories let us see. So Zhu Xi insisted upon a peculiar kind of personal character to aid the extension of knowledge, a character made sincere and chastened of selfishness. There is an extremely elaborate program of Confucian self-development to sagehood that has, as its object, not the perfection of the self or its blissing out but its harmonizing cognitive and moral continuity with the rest of the universe.[19]

This is all a bit unfair to Ch'an Buddhism, about which Zhu Xi was complaining.[20] That school too would say that a lack of selfishness must be obtained in order to rid oneself of grief-filled attachments. Once a person has attained enlightenment, it is possible to see things as they are and without subjective bias, according to the Buddhist theory. Zhu Xi's point was a practical one: the Buddhist meditation and monastic procedures were more likely to cultivate selfishness by always focusing on the self's enlightenment than to achieve enlightenment with its subsequent moral commitments to behave helpfully in harmony with the rest of the world. Hocking recognized, in fairness to Buddhism, that Zhu Xi's strictures about attaining an unselfish approach to the extension of knowledge is more like the preparatory stages of enlightenment in the Eightfold Noble Path of an earlier kind of Buddhism than to the meditation practices of the Buddhism of his contemporaries.

ZHU XI'S LESSON FOR HOCKING

The lesson Hocking drew from Zhu Xi is complex. Being careful not to ascribe a modern sensibility to him, Hocking nevertheless found in Zhu Xi's approach a moral sensitivity that surpassed Bergson's. Hocking wrote,

> If there be in the world, as Bergson supposes, a realm of mechanism, the ashes of dead life, there intuitive sympathy would have no application: pragmatic knowledge would be appropriate. But Chu Hsi, though he has a reputation of being a dualist, has no such realm of inanimate matter: he carries his attribution of life and even of degrees of consciousness throughout the universe much in the spirit of Fechner, Paulsen, Whitehead. Hence he allows no exceptions in behalf of pragmatically interested modes of knowing. All penetration into the realities of things requires a moral objectivity whose essence is unselfishness. . . . As compared with Bergson, then, Chu Hsi has far more for his ethically sensitized intuition to perceive. And because of this he would further disagree with Bergson in his view of the nature of scientific knowledge—he would not hand science over to the "pragmatic" way of knowing.[21]

Moreover, although Zhu Xi can be called a rationalist in the senses mentioned, Hocking severely qualified the full use of that term, which had been applied to Zhu Xi and his age by Hu Shih. Rationalism is usually reductive to principles. Zhu Xi is more the empiricist.

Hocking went on to say that

> scientific method is based on the deliberate and persistent effort to escape the circle of humanistic interests, not to say class interests, in its discovery of objective truth. . . . Empiricism is itself a form of self-denial, a moral will to let the object speak for itself. But empiricism holds that if we allow it to do so, the object will speak—i.e., truth is accessible.[22]

The final lesson Hocking wanted to mine from Zhu Xi was political, namely, that true science aids the democratic process. Much of my discussion here has been to lift up Hocking's Boston Confucian argument that science needs to be conceived in such a way that the moral or teleological dimensions of its subject matter can be construed as part of scientific knowing, not the projection of personal views on top of a mechanistic conception. In this, Hocking supports Zhu Xi over Bergson. But a serious problem remains. Hocking opened the essay with the observation, "If not an axiom, it is at least a reasonable presumption in the theory of knowledge that ways of knowing must vary with the nature of the objects to be known." He then pointed out the esoteric rigors of attaining to Buddhist enlightenment about change and said this kind of knowing can get to the moral as well as the most real center of the universe in ways preferable to modern Western science. This point was expanded with Zhu Xi's account of moral knowing, and the Buddhist tendency to turn inward was corrected by the Neo-Confucian concern to address the world in a harmonizing cognitive way, letting the world speak for itself. But does this mean that the Neo-Confucian path is as esoteric as the Buddhist? If so, then science with a moral heart cannot be a fulcrum for democracy, for it would require an aristocracy of adepts.

Hocking never suggested that Zhu Xi was a democrat, any more than he was a modern scientist. But he did attempt to say that Zhu Xi's approach to knowledge is exoteric whereas Buddhism's is esoteric. One branch of Hocking's argument is that Confucians of all sorts are anti-aristocratic, claiming that anyone from any part of society can study, and those good at studying can go all the way in Confucian learning. Although Confucianism developed a family culture that nourishes learning, and therefore children of Confucians are more likely to be ready and willing to study than people from social strata of little learning, Confucianism indeed has been a force to break through social class barriers. Another branch of Hocking's argument is that Zhu Xi's emphasis on empirical analysis, and improving the self so as to be unselfish when examining things, is genuinely exoteric and learnable. Buddhism, with its use of imaginative representations of semi-personalized Tathagata Buddhas, is far too esoteric. There is much to be said for Zhu Xi's down-to-earth emphasis on study, and anyone can do it.

I doubt these arguments carry the day, however, in the claim that Zhu Xi's moral science can be a democratic leveling activity. However straightforward in comparison with Buddhism, or Christianity, Hinduism, or Judaism for that matter, the Confucian project of becoming a sage is the creation of a new aristocracy. Most people around the world are in fact selfish. Most therefore could not do science in the sense Hocking advocated and would thus revert to mechanistic science. Like Dewey, Hocking would have to say that ordinary people need to become aristocratic in their capacities for democracy. Achieved aristocracy is difficult when you are born something else.

HOCKING AND PRAGMATISM

Now there is a not-so-hidden villain in Hocking's argument here, namely, "hearty nineteenth-century pragmatism," by which he meant the theory that "knowledge is (partly or wholly) *constituted* by action." Therefore, we choose our ideas and beliefs as we choose our actions. "Our judgments about the world are instruments for guiding conduct, and are therefore to be *chosen*, rather than thought out—to be chosen for the sake of their value as instruments of living."[23] This may not be a fair understanding even of William James's sloppy pragmatism. It is exactly the opposite of Peirce's pragmatism for which learning what is worth choosing is the most important lesson to investigate, and whose methods of correcting belief are in extremely close accord with the Neo-Confucian emphasis on learning the principles in things.[24] But Hocking does recognize a kind of vulgar pragmatism that has become all the more popular in the postmodern insistence that all knowing is a display of interest and power and therefore you ought to fight for your own. That vulgar pragmatism, or late-Marxist postmodernism, does indeed insist that science be mechanistic because it wants to deny the residence of differential worths in the world.

Over against that vulgar pragmatism, which reinforces a putatively value-free conception of natural science, Hocking could only urge another vision of the world. This was, of course, his life's work. This, more than any insistence that the world is made of ideas rather than matter, constituted his *idealism*. He found in Zhu Xi, more than the Buddhist and Hindu philosophers he studied, an ally in presenting this alternative vision.

Here is now a more substantive reason to call William Ernest Hocking the first Boston Confucian than a mere citation of his knowledge and use of Confucian philosophy. The particular use to which he attempted to put Zhu Xi, and the Confucian tradition to which he gained access through Zhu Xi's writings, was the creation of an alternative world philosophy for a world civilization that was being brought into existence by modern science. This is the particular aim of the so-called New Confucian movement, of which the Boston Confucians are a part, stimulated by a generation of Chinese philosophers Hocking's age or younger. One of the most influential of these, Mou Tsung-san, coined the phrase, "moral metaphysics," for his peculiar philosophy combining Western philosophical idealism with classical Confucian themes—more of the school of Wang Yang-ming than Zhu Xi, but not different on the points discussed here.[25] Mou's student, Tu Wei-ming, has been at the center of Confucianism in Boston.

It should be noted that Hocking more than most of his Chinese counterparts understood what is at stake in developing a world philosophy for a world civilization. The world civilization itself is only slowly coming into being, and so far it is not clear whether it is more civilized than barbaric. Philosophy can be one of the civilizing forces. Hocking recognized that a world philosophy cannot be the imperial triumph of one philosophy over the others, as some earlier idealists might have thought having read Hegel. Rather, the strong thinkers in all the world's traditions need to be heard in dialogue over the issues. Hence, we should know Dharmapāla and Zhu Xi as well as Plato and Kant. The syntheses that hopefully will provide the languages in terms of which we can discuss world philosophical issues cannot be schematic charts of different positions. Rather the syntheses will come from philosophers working piecemeal with as many sources as possible at the ready to construct a world vision. Plato and Aristotle did that for their time, and because of their philosophies, the West has had a language to debate not only the issues that separated them but a great many others as well. Not until Plato and Aristotle was there a genuine Western philosophical tradition. Confucius, Mencius, Xunzi, Laozi, and Zhuangzi similarly created the Chinese tradition. Indian and Islamic traditions began the same way. One or more synoptic visions is necessary before we can begin to assess whether we have a philosophy whose terms pick up the real issues for a world tradition.

I have finally reached the overarching topic of metaphysics and world philosophy. Metaphysics in the grand tradition of the West, of which William Ernest Hocking was such a distinguished representative, is synoptic vision, a theorizing that allows us to see what things are similar and different, how they affect one another and are to be conceived together. Modern Western science arose from that speculative project. But it has lost sight, in fact precluded sight, of those questions of value with moral impact that only a fool or an *a priori* philosopher could miss. And so, the long Western historical project of vision, or knowing things for their own selves and in their connections, as Hocking would have Zhu Xi say, has come upon a series of potholes. Enlightenment skepticism evokes romantic reactions; the global political hegemony of the West in the last century fostered vain attempts to impose Western philosophies across the world. Postmodernism says that everything is a function of the interpreter's interest and thereby undermines the sense of the world's otherness and reality as capable of correcting our signs.

Hocking urged us to come to world philosophy through two preparatory projects. One is political philosophy that is comparative and that does acknowledge the differences in political realities. The other is comparative philosophy of religion, or of culture as he generally handled it; religious studies, sensitive to the perspectives of religions other than those that framed the discipline of religious studies in the first place, is a crucial device for bringing into the conversation those voices that need to be heard for a world philosophy to be possible. His own contributions to political theory and religion are enormous.

But perhaps even more telling is Hocking's capacity actually to bring a major figure such as Zhu Xi into the conversation and assess his contributions with judicious nuance. In particular, the contribution he brought from the Neo-Confucians was the missing ingredient in the Western speculative project, namely, a way to conceive of knowing that is genuinely axiological, interpreting things in terms of what they have achieved, what they might become, and what difference that makes. Only when the questions of value are related to the boundaries of imagination by which we speculatively envision the world, and then brought to the specifics of actual things whose values we can appreciate and weigh, will it be possible to work through to the lineaments of a world philosophy. William Ernest Hocking saw this clearly, a defining vision for the first Boston Confucian.

Chapter Seven

Cheng Chung-ying as a Constructive Philosopher

Cheng Chung-ying is a giant among the small throng of contemporary philosophers for whom the Chinese traditions of Confucianism, Daoism, and Buddhism are as important a resource as the Western tradition of Platonism, Aristotelianism, Neo-Platonism, and their ramifications through European and Islamic thought. His institutional contributions, namely, the founding of the International Society for Chinese Philosophy and the *Journal of Chinese Philosophy*, would be enough to establish his status, for they both stem from his giant vision of what needed to be done in the twentieth century and now the twenty-first century to bring Chinese philosophy into the contemporary global philosophic conversation. Mainly because of his inspiration and work, now many societies exist that discuss and extend Chinese philosophy in the English language, and ever more journals and edited books.[1] The thirtieth anniversary special double issue of the *Journal of Chinese Philosophy* is a testimony to his influence, as are the recent edited volumes by Xinyang Jiang and Bo Mou that feature a younger generation of Chinese scholars writing in English.[2]

Even more than his institutional contributions, however, Cheng's stature is established by his own philosophical contributions. Most scholars who think seriously about Chinese philosophy (in English at least) regard Cheng as an interpreter of the Chinese philosophical tradition. His distinctive profile is that he focuses not only on the history stemming from the classical texts of Confucianism and Daoism but on the *Yijing* and its influences through those traditions as well as others, including Chinese Buddhism. Indeed, Cheng has such a catholic approach to what counts as Chinese philosophy that he stands in remarkable contrast with most of his contemporary scholars who keep their traditions neat. John H. Berthrong has argued that contemporary Boston Confucianism (try to keep a straight face) is an advance within the Confucian tradition in part because it shakes up the canon of the acceptable "Transmission of the Way" (Zhu Xi's *daotong*, and also Mou Zongsan's alternative reading) to include anything that remotely has been identified with Confucianism and that has intellectual value for present philosophy.[3] Cheng, who admits in personal encounters to being a Boston Confucian, has established a much broader canon of Chinese philosophy than the Confucian.

The thesis of this chapter, however, is that to regard Cheng primarily as an interpreter of Chinese philosophy is misleading. Rather, he is a constructive philosopher, developing his own "system" with a heavy but by no means exclusive reliance on the Chinese tradition. This reading runs against the grain of Cheng's reputation. He has, in fact, done a traditional translation with a *Sitz im Leben* commentary in his book on Dai Zhen, written while he was a graduate student.[4] Nevertheless, his Harvard dissertation itself was on Charles Sanders Peirce and C. I. Lewis.[5] His large collection of essays, *New Dimensions of Confucian and Neo-Confucian Philosophy*, consists almost entirely of commentaries on Chinese philosophers and texts, displaying a dazzling breadth of detailed knowledge throughout the entire history of Chinese thought. Nevertheless, Whitehead and Heidegger, as well as other Western philosophers, are conversation partners throughout that collection, and most of the essays are concerned to articulate what is true about their topics, not only what some philosophers have said about them. If Cheng's corpus is read as the work of a traditional Sinologist, or of an historian of ideas, or even as a traditional New Confucian recovering the Chinese genius in light of Western philosophy, it is likely to be misunderstood and underestimated. For all his brilliance as a sensitive and erudite reader of classical Chinese texts, Cheng does not seek to establish a "consensus reading" of those texts; his interpretations are too daring, too far out.

This is not to say that Cheng is not authoritative in his interpretations of the Chinese tradition. In the recent *Encyclopedia of Chinese Philosophy*, edited by Antonio S. Cua, Cheng was selected to write the essays on "Confucianism: Twentieth Century," "Dai Zhen," "Dao: The Way," "Logic and Language," "Mencius," "Philosophy of Change," "Philosophy of Knowledge," "Philosophy: Recent Trends Overseas," "Qi: Vital Force," "Qiongli: Exhaustive Inquiry into Principles," "Ti: Body or Embodiment," "Ti-Yong Metaphysics," "Time and Timeliness," "Zhang Zai," and "Zhengming: Rectifying Names."[6] Nevertheless, writing authoritative historical essays is not his main intent, and even some of these encyclopedia entries need to be read as expressive of Cheng's own interpretive philosophy.

Perhaps the most difficult person to persuade of my interpretation of Cheng as a constructive philosopher is Cheng Chung-ying himself. He regards the heart and soul of his philosophy to be what he calls "onto-hermeneutics." Hermeneutics, of course, is the interpretation of texts in the Gadamerian line that he follows and extends, and his texts are the *Yijing* and subsequent Chinese philosophical writings.[7] For Cheng, the force of *onto*-hermeneutics is that, when interpreting ultimate reality, the deep structure of the reality interpreted is the same as the deep structure of the interpreter. This, in a way, is an old Platonic and Augustinian point, but it is also the point of the knowledge of *li* (principle) in Neo-Confucian philosophy of both Zhu Xi's and Wang Yang-ming's sorts.[8] Cheng might be hard to persuade that he is a constructive philosopher when he believes that the truth resides in the unearthing of truth in ancient texts.

That Cheng is primarily a constructive philosopher means that his primary aim in nearly all his writings is to get at the truth regarding the topic as that can be defended in the contemporary context. To this aim, the interpretation of texts is secondary and a vehicle only of the aim at philosophic truth. For Cheng, the reason to pay attention to the Chinese tradition is in part because of his patriotic desire to have the rest of the philosophic world recognize and engage his own patrimony. In far larger part, however, the reason to attend to the Chinese tradition is that it offers extraordinary resources for getting to the philosophical truth when properly interpreted. The Chinese tradition needs to be interpreted in contemporary, philosophically creative, ways, he would say, in order for it to offer its resources to the larger ongoing philosophic conversation. Indeed, I believe he would say that, left to the traditional Sinologists and historians of Chinese philosophy, tradition lies inert and unengaged: a creative interpretation is needed to bring it into play. What to some of the traditional scholars looks like a creative misreading on Cheng's part is rather the means to give life to the Chinese tradition.

CHENG'S CONTEMPORARY SOURCES

One mark of Cheng's constructive philosophy is that, when interpreting ancient and more recent texts, Cheng asks questions of those texts that they in their milieu did not ask themselves. For instance, in "Inquiring into the Primary Model," he cites Plato and Heidegger as the source of onto-hermeneutics and finds five levels of "hermeneutical formation of the *Yi* text," all of which derive in their organization from contemporary hermeneutics. Cheng does indeed find textual evidence for the five levels—he is causing the *Yijing* to answer truly—but the structure of the levels themselves comes from our contemporary questions.

More broadly, Cheng derives his philosophical questioning from contemporary analytic philosophy, Whiteheadian process philosophy and its reading of the Western tradition, and continental Heideggerian philosophy in its Gadamerian expression with its alternative reading of the Western tradition. To be sure, Cheng's own grasp of those Western traditions is affected by his reading them in relation to Chinese philosophy. I might say that he has a Confucian approach to analytic philosophy, process philosophy, and continental philosophy, although what he says about them is so wildly speculative that other Confucians might not recognize the Confucian form of thought in his reading of the Western philosophic problematic. From this Confucian encounter with contemporary schools of Western thought comes his construction of the problematic with which to interrogate the Chinese tradition.

If I might be allowed a personal note, my friendship with Cheng, which goes back about forty years, has had an influence on his formation of the problematic, because my own work draws heavily on analytic philosophy, process philosophy, and continental philosophy, though more on the pragmatism of Charles Peirce in which Cheng himself is expert. Through the years we have had many conversations and have written about one another's work with the result, for him, that he has engaged at least one example of a synthetic integration of the Western traditions that itself is oriented to engaging the Chinese tradition.[9] The point is that while he has been interpreting Chinese texts, he also has been engaging Western thinkers with their own questions about those texts, and he has endeavored to ask those questions of the texts as most of us Westerners cannot do with scholarly skills.

To ask questions of a tradition that it does not natively ask of itself is both to distort and extend the tradition. The distortion is justified if the imaginative work extending the tradition has some fair grounding in the core texts and motifs of the tradition itself. Chinese philosophy is a museum piece if it is not questioned with our own concerns and made to answer in ways new to its own commentarial tradition. This point is no more applicable to the Chinese tradition than it is to the Platonic, for instance: Whitehead's questions that made him call himself a Platonist were never asked by Plato.[10] The past lives in philosophy only when contemporary questions are asked, acknowledging that contemporary questions are asked out of respect for the tradition as well as current conditions.

SPECULATIVE INTERPRETATION

A second mark of Cheng's constructive philosophy is that his interpretations of classic Chinese (as well as Western) texts are wildly speculative (a phrase I used before). Speculation itself is a dubious enterprise today, and wildness is over the top for many philosophers. Cheng would never consider his interpretations speculatively wild, though his philosophic critics insist, pejoratively, on the point. The point should not be pejorative, however, because great imaginative leaps are required for joining the contextually alien ideas of ancient-through-recent Chinese philosophy and the current conversation formed significantly by Western philosophy. Many thinkers interested in Chinese philosophy leap to fanciful analogies to make the connection and are shouted down by serious scholars of Chinese philosophy as well as detailed thinkers in the current debate. Cheng's speculative leaps are profoundly erudite and disciplined, even if they reflect a Germanic proclivity for combining Greek-derived words to epitomize hugely complex lines of thought (onto-hermeneutics? Ugh!). When Cheng traces out those conglomerate notions, the result is a detailed interpretive map.

INTERPRETATION OF CLASSIC TEXTS

A third related mark is that the form in which Cheng embraces the classical texts is through their core symbols and motifs. This stands in contrast to the current fashion to limit philosophy to what the logicians (including C. I. Lewis) call "well-formed formulas." I would express Cheng's grasp of the texts to be in the form of what Peirce and others call "vague categories." A vague category can be defined precisely in relation to other categories at its same level, but itself allows of being specified by versions of the category that contradict one another. For instance, both Zhu Xi and Wang Yang-ming affirm the centrality of principle (*li*) yet have competing accounts of that: a vague category would say what they suppose in common prior to their differences.

Cheng's interpretation of ancient texts, particularly the *Yijing*, is vague. It deliberately acknowledges the underdeterminedness of the text and preserves that. The themes or motifs of thought that he derives from that text can then be specified in many different, perhaps mutually contradictory, ways in the subsequent tradition. Nominalists would not like this procedure, for they want definiteness in all things. Yet the realists are right, I believe along with Cheng, that vague "common natures" (to use Scotus's term), are present, however contracted, in real things. Thus Cheng can romp gleefully through the Chinese tradition, taking the myriad schools all to be expressive of fundamental themes that they would not agree on articulating. Cheng usually provides the textual evidence in the cases he cites.

A vague category is hardly helpful by itself. It needs to be specified by instances, and Cheng easily provides instances of his categories from the long history of Chinese thought and across a wide array of Western traditions. Specification means not only identifying instances of the vague category but elaborating the instances in the language of the vague category. For instance, "being" and "value," two of Cheng's favorite vague motifs, can be illustrated with many instances of Western philosophies that use those words in different senses and also with many instances of Chinese philosophies that do not use close equivalents of those words. The result of Cheng's elaborate discussions through his long career is that the vague categories have become filled in with enormously rich interpretations. The categories are vague enough to represent the instances fairly, and yet they are made specific enough that eventually it is possible to see just where the different philosophers agree and disagree, at least on Cheng's interpretations.

Of course Cheng's interpretations reflect his own interests and biases. They need to be set alongside alternative interpretations, made vulnerable to correction from them, and then argued out. The problem in our situation is that he has very few peers who provide alternative readings of similar scope and depth. Most comparativists are historians who do not readily press the questions of truth in the positions compared. Furthermore, most comparativists, philosophical and otherwise, usually restrict their work to a very limited field of comparison, with the result that only a few figures or instances of ideas are brought to mutual specification. Cheng therefore has few dialogue partners. Those who engage him on specific interpretations of texts or figures usually do not have the hermeneutical horizon that contextualizes and orients his interpretations.

Cheng and I were educated in the last generation of thinkers to appreciate philosophy in the grand traditions, as reflecting large ideas and learning from large sweeps of intellectual history. From then until now we have gone through a period that prizes microstudies and is hostile to large generalizations. This is true in philosophy and also the social sciences and religious studies. The contribution of the age of microstudies has been to provide new, careful editions and translations of texts and to open up new texts, fields, and questions that had been marginalized by the previous menu of generalizations. The drawback to microstudies, however, is that, by bracketing the larger questions and ignoring the other elements in the field, their own assumptions and biases are not made vulnerable to criticism. Even when a published microstudy begins with a statement of the author's social location and a listing of apparent suppositions, the dialectical analysis and critique of the location and suppositions are missing from the study. The reading public is at the mercy of the author's own methodologically uncriticized sense of self identity. The advantage of philosophy in the grand tradition, with generalizations that map the whole, is that all the issues of bias are made internal to the dialectic of the philosophy itself.

A delicious irony has shaped the fashion of scholarship in philosophy (and other disciplines) during the last forty years. The period began with the rousing popularity of Martin Heidegger's reading of the history of

Western thought, concluding that it had been dominated by a nasty onto-theo-logo-centrism that marginalized all those positions in philosophy and culture that did not register in the logo-centric scheme. Part of the irony is that Heidegger's own reading of history is a highly specific and biased story that marginalized a great many philosophical positions in the West, not to speak of all the rest of the world's philosophies. Much of the reason that Heidegger's thought is held in contempt by many philosophers is not just his complicated language but the fact that the ideas congenial to the critical philosophers do not get registered fairly, in their eyes. His caricatured dismissal of pragmatism, for instance, is a case in point for philosophers such as myself. One result of Heidegger's logo-centric story among postmodern followers is that they reject all large-scale theories because of their capacity to marginalize and delegitimize. Postmodern thinkers are masters of the microstudy and of severely contextualized philosophy. Nevertheless, ironically, most postmodern thinkers also want to make general moral or orientational claims about the importance of lifting up the marginalized and criticizing the oppressiveness of master narratives. These general claims, of course, cannot be made from microstudies alone. They require a logo-centric master narrative like Heidegger's. And so we seem to be coming to an end of the age of microstudies to find a better balance that allows the generalizations to be made vulnerable to criticism from the microstudies and also the microstudies to be made vulnerable to criticism from the more contextualizing considerations framed by generalization.

A new dimension of the value of vague categories is apparent now. In making an interpretive philosophical claim that involves comparison, as Cheng has done so often, he is always vulnerable to someone claiming that his theoretical frame excludes fair consideration of some alternative view. The proper response to this charge is to ask whether this in fact is so. If it is, the theoretical frame has not been shaped vaguely enough to be fair to what had been left out. Vague comparative categories are not fixed at the beginning and then filled in with specifications. On the contrary, as the specifications are worked out, the vague categories need constant reformulation to make sure they are vague enough to be fair. This constant reformulation of the vague categories has been a longtime theme in Cheng's work. His preoccupation with what look like general ideas but in fact are carefully crafted vague ideas framed to give fair readings of positions under comparison has determined his rhetoric in important ways. Critics sometimes complain about the vagueness of some of his language, yet they usually miss the point about what is going on, the correction of the formulation of the categories so as to be properly vague and expressive of the true range of positions to be compared.[11]

SYSTEM

A fourth mark of Cheng's constructive philosophy is that he has constructed a system of sorts. His is not the sort of system that has a precisely expressible theory at its center, with a list of categories that can be used to show how all things are expressions of them. Whitehead has that sort of system. Cheng's rather is a system of core texts and motifs, interpreted historically, carefully crafted to show what is true and valuable at the nodes along the way. Imagine, if you will, an understanding of the history of philosophy that begins with the most ancient core texts, for example, the *Yijing*, and motifs of thought, for example, the distinction between yang and yin, and traces their development as shaping diverse and competing schools of thought, for example, Confucianism; Daoism; Legalism; the Yin-Yang School; Chinese Buddhism; Neo-Confucianism in Zhou Dunyi, Zhu Xi, and Wang Yang-ming, their encounter with Leibniz and their subsequent career in the West. (Leibniz recognized that the mathematics of yin and yang allowed for the expression of any numbers and any alphabet in combinations of long/short or off/on marks and tried to invent a computer based on that language, a technical feat that had to await the twentieth century; through Leibniz's reading of Chinese thought, *Yijing* notions of organicism entered the Western tradition, taking crisp shape in Whitehead's philosophy.) Such an understanding would explain at each juncture why each school reinterpreted or reembodied the core texts and motifs the way they did, with an analysis of what is gained and lost in that move. The study of philosophy (and religious thought) could then abandon artificial boundaries between schools and move more naturally with the causal influences of the ideas in their ramifications and branching around the intellectual world. Cheng's interpretation of the history of philosophy East and West has consistently traced the core texts and motifs through their important changes and developments. His juxtapositions of historically distant figures from East Asia and the West are natural elaborations of this methodical approach.[12]

Cheng's system is a vast collage of interpretive moves that weaves together the major figures in Chinese and Western philosophies. The system is by no means complete. To my knowledge Cheng does not deal in depth with South Asian or Islamic philosophies, and there are positions in the West particularly that he has not brought into his story. Cheng's system is not a logo-centric story like Hegel's that has an inner dynamic that makes the story run, the dynamic of negation. Rather Cheng simply has sought out the positive and negative connections that might be made among philosophers to lift up the importance of what they say for the purpose of getting at the truth. I cannot imagine any contemporary philosophic conversation into which Cheng could not enter with the erudition of his vast system, constructed over a long career, as an enriching contribution. This brings me to the final mark of Cheng's constructive philosophy.

PHILOSOPHIC TRUTH OVER INTERPRETATION

The fifth mark is Cheng's constant passion for the philosophic truth. His concern to interpret philosophers rightly stems from the fact that something true can be learned from them (or errors to avoid). The passion for truth operates at many levels, of which three should be mentioned.

Cheng takes ancient texts such as the *Yijing* to be primal embodiments of truth. They are not hypotheses developed to solve problems, nor are they philosophic positions as such. Rather they are something like poetic expressions in which some fundamental aspects of reality come to voice. To use religious language, the texts are revelations, primary witnesses. They are not so much interpretations of other texts as the primal acts of imagination that allow fundamental traits of reality to register in human consciousness. Of course those texts are many other things than primal expressions of reality. They are historically contextualized documents, and they usually do have a prehistory. What philosophy does, however, for Cheng, is to interpret the philosophically important traits of reality that come to expression in those texts. This is why he calls his work onto-hermeneutics: the voice those texts give to the realities they express cannot be heard until they are interpreted philosophically. The texts themselves are not philosophy; they become philosophy when they are interpreted. The interpreter, for example, Cheng, can say what is true in the texts about the realities they imaginatively conceptualize.

Philosophers in the more obvious sense—Confucius, Mencius, Zhu Xi, Whitehead, Heidegger, among others—already are interpreting the poetic expressions of primal traditions; they are self-interpreting, and they invite the interpretations of others that assess where they have improved the expression of philosophic truth and where they have missed something. Cheng appreciates the extraordinary creativity of philosophers, adding to, refining, correcting, and sometimes corrupting, the heritage that reaches them. He constantly lifts up insights in the history of philosophy, and his statement of those insights is a reembodiment of them. The analysis of philosophers' arguments, including an assessment of their validity, is a practice Cheng shares with most other contemporary, historically oriented, philosophers.

Cheng's comparisons are usually not to the point of laying out historical influences. Rather, he asks what philosophers learned that is true from one another. And he works hard to relate philosophers who themselves are unrelated in order to show how the emphasis of one reinforces or corrects the emphasis of the other. He rarely argues that philosophers are mistaken. He argues instead that they give expression to this insight or that, with this or that force, picking up on aspects that others' expressions lack.

The plain intent of Cheng's constructive system is fourfold: to bring to life truths given expression in the history of philosophy, primarily the history of Chinese and Western philosophy; to do so in a vocabulary of multifaceted comparison so that a wide range of other philosophers can engage him in a common public; to engage the problems raised across the range of present philosophy, using the historical ideas but reexpressing them for the current context; and to present a philosophical construction that speaks in a coherent fashion to the main topics of philosophical inquiry that relate to the intellectual epitomes of civilization—metaphysics, epistemology, ethics, art, science, religion, law, and politics. That Cheng Chung-ying has accomplished so much of this fourfold intent means that he is a genuine world-class philosopher. And what he has accomplished is a rich, constructive philosophy.

CHENG'S CHALLENGES

My last set of considerations is to reflect on the larger meaning of this fourfold intent behind constructive philosophy, focusing less on Cheng's own accomplishments and more on what remains to be done.

1. The task of bringing to life in our time truths given expression in the history of philosophy is far from complete. To be sure, other thinkers than Cheng have worked hard on the classic philosophic and religious texts of South Asia. But few have entered the contemporary discussion with a retrieval of the core texts and motifs of Islam, or of the motifs of orientation of so-called "primal traditions." Moreover, even those who have studied all these traditions as ancient witnesses or primordial imaginative expressions have usually not done so with the onto-hermeneutical thoroughness pioneered by Cheng.

The importance of doing so is not merely to enhance the scale of our resources for philosophic thinking, although that is always a good thing. The importance rather relates to the respect with which cultures in our day ought to engage each other. Many events in the last decades, especially the tragedies of 9/11, have shown the limitation of imposing the cultural (and economic and military) agenda of the West on the rest of the world. The globalized economy seems almost unstoppable now, despite growing awareness of its bias to help the nations already rich while impoverishing the poor ones and to destroy the economic cultures of peoples who do not compete naturally in the global market. For a global economy to become just requires it to reflect the differences among the fundamental motifs of thought and value to be found among the cultures it embraces. And for that purpose it is necessary for those fundamental motifs to be brought to life within the contemporary conversation.

2. The creation of a public discourse about the fundamental ideas from all traditions is necessary for the same reason. Perhaps individual geniuses such as Cheng can do the spadework necessary to bring each tradition's ancient witnesses to life, but that by itself does not bring them into conversation with one another. Cheng also has done much comparative work, as I've spoken about earlier, that integrates East Asian and Western philosophy. He has shown how this requires a new vocabulary, arising from each tradition asking questions of the other that are not native to the other. But his work can only be a first step, because it is idiosyncratic to his own vision, as is true of any individual comparativist. What is needed is a long-term dialogical discourse with many thinkers from each tradition engaging in the process of developing vague categories and specifying them as previously described. Over the long run, a new vocabulary will emerge from the dialogue itself that is not the creation of any individual. As expressions are debated, comparative hypotheses proposed, and objections dealt with by modifying the objectionable elements of the hypotheses, the public for mutual understanding will become steadier and more reliable. To be sure, we should always expect fundamental revisions as new genius exposes hidden treasures. Nevertheless, we are very far today from any kind of reliable, publicly accepted set of comparative categories for expressing the primary insights of ancient traditions to the contemporary heirs of one another. Even those of us who have spent a lifetime working with China and the West are aware of very basic disagreements among respectable scholars as to what is important in a comparative perspective. Cheng Chung-ying needs dialogue partners with whom he can work so that his own comparative onto-hermeneutics does not seem idiosyncratic.

3. The third element in Cheng's constructive intent is the elaboration of the dialogue among traditions across the wide range of philosophic questions that press the contemporary world. That is, the discussion needs to move from comparing ancient ideas to elaborating them with contemporary viable expressions so as to engage our real-world issues. No settled agenda of contemporary issues exists. Each of the great philosophic traditions, including those of the West and China, has been brought up short by suddenly emerging contemporary concerns. Let me mention four.

The first and most commonly recognized is the family of issues raised by our sharply emerging ecological science and cultural consciousness. These include ethical concerns about the environment and larger philosophic concerns about what it means for human beings to be at home in a universe now understood to be more connected and fragile than was thought before.

A second new concern has to do with distributive justice that now has a global scale. Whereas before philosophers could contemplate distributive justice within a community or region, now we understand that actions in one part of the world affect distribution of wealth in many other places, often without direct contact. Because of the successes of social sciences, we can now imagine a global economy and need to understand how that can be made just.

A third concern is differing habits regarding individuals and communities as these become focused through putatively universal human rights. Americans and Chinese are notoriously, if mistakenly, at odds over the relative weighting of individual and communal interests. Yet both acknowledge that the protection of the rights of individuals is a burden that falls on communities, not merely other individuals, and that the advancement of the interest of a community as a whole needs to be supported by individual actions, often sacrificial actions.

A fourth new concern, hard to state succinctly, has to do with the Internet and the effects of almost instant worldwide communication available to nearly everyone on authority structures. Most of the world's cultures are accustomed to training elites to monitor, supervise, and vet high-level communications. Traditional ways of structuring the critical assessment of knowledge, and the critical massing of power, are being undermined by the unsupervised cornucopia of ideas on the Internet. Professors are frustrated by their students' lack of taste in the opinions they download for term papers. Political campaigns are now conducted in the United States with strong appeal to potential voters who have no affiliation with political parties or traditions. How is this to be understood philosophically? The Internet will likely give a new meaning to democracy.

Couple new topics such as these with the old topics from the various world traditions of philosophy and the enormity of the task of developing a global dialogue in which the ancient philosophic witnesses have contemporary life is apparent.

4. To present a global public dialogue is not enough. What is needed in addition is the construction of positive philosophies that speak coherently to the problematics that arise from the fundamental achievements of civilization. I mentioned earlier metaphysics, epistemology, ethics, art, science, religion, law, and politics, to use the Western words. Although the boundaries might be drawn differently in different cultures, all those problematics are covered and reflected in the civilized traditions of philosophy. The point is, a contemporary philosophy fit for a global public needs to be able to give a coherent account that ranges through these fields. Because our thinking is so primitive regarding the first three elements of the intent of constructive philosophy, we are a long way from a genuinely global full-fledged philosophy.

Measured against this wildly speculative and idealized program for philosophy in a global context, Cheng Chung-ying's constructive philosophy can be appreciated for the giant step it is. Perhaps he has not integrated Islam into his understanding of China and the West; perhaps his language is idiosyncratic because it has not had long public testing; perhaps the agenda for contemporary philosophy is still too unsettled for him to have addressed all its major points; perhaps his constructive thought needs more systematic expression across the major fields of civilized experience. Nevertheless, his accomplishments in these areas are truly astounding.

CHAPTER EIGHT

Wu Kuang-ming as One of Three Stooges

ONE OF THREE STOOGES

A long time ago there were three stooges who made money and gained fame as comedians in the movies. After that, but still a long time ago, there were three other stooges, Kuang-ming Wu, David Hall, and I, who had a traveling road show of intercultural philosophy making presentations at colleges and conferences. We did not make much money or gain fame but we did work out the roots of the different intercultural projects each of us has pursued since. In this chapter I want to reflect on some of these differences.

The best of us was David Hall, whose death has left us all the poorer. Our collaboration with David was before his much more famous and productive collaboration with Roger T. Ames. Their volumes—*Thinking Through Confucius*, *Anticipating China*, and *Thinking from the Han*—have decisively shaped the public conversation about intercultural comparison. Much of the philosophy in those comparative volumes, however, was the elaboration of ideas in Hall's earlier work that was contemporary with his role as the roundest of the three stooges, namely, *The Civilization of Experience*, *Eros and Irony*, and *The Uncertain Phoenix*. In *The Civilization of Experience*, a study of Whitehead's philosophy of culture, Hall claimed that philosophy really is philosophy of culture, for Whitehead and himself. "Philosophy of culture" he defined as the expression of those things that are important in a culture. A philosophy expresses the epitomes of what bears value and importance in a culture and thus is valuable to the extent it expresses the important rather than the true in the sense of what a culture ought to value. For Hall, philosophy reduces, or expands, depending on your point of view, to philosophy of culture, and is a descriptive enterprise.

In *Eros and Irony* and *The Uncertain Phoenix*, Hall elaborated a complex of ideas distinguishing logical order from aesthetic order. Logical order imposes a single form organizing chaos into a cosmos. Aesthetic order recognizes each item in chaos to be a world unto itself and a perspective on the rest, with priority thus given to chaos, and claims to cosmic unity or intelligible order declared to be fictions. Hall and Ames would go on to develop the notion that aesthetic order is what they call "first problematic thinking," characteristic of some of the pre-Socratics in the West and the dominant view in ancient Confucian and Daoist China. Logical order, or "second problematic thinking," became dominant in Western philosophy with Plato and Aristotle, which Hall and Ames viewed as a bad thing. By writing about their Chinese sources, Hall and Ames hoped to revitalize the otherwise marginalized first problematic thinking for the West. Hall's comparative philosophy, with Ames, thus emphasized large cultural contrasting themes that capture the different shapes of what is important in different cultures. Not denying that there are exceptions to these themes in the cultures studied, those exceptions can be ignored as philosophies because they did not sustain themselves as important for those cultures. Philosophy of culture is not a respecter of cultural underdogs. Some of us find it ironic that Hall's great preference for the cultural underdog in Western philosophy—first problematic thinking, aesthetic order, or what he sometimes called philosophical anarchy—was the spur that set him to the analysis and appreciation of Chinese culture where he thought the Western underdog was the top dog. Let me label Hall's approach to intercultural philosophy as "thematic philosophy of cultural contrasts." Hall would call it Daoistic.

WU'S DAOISM

Kuang-ming Wu's intercultural philosophy, however Daoistic, is in many respects opposite to Hall's. Or might we hope that they complement each other? For Wu, the heart of Chinese culture is to express important things indirectly through concrete or particular images. I would call his intercultural philosophy the "poetical evocation of singular importance in defiance of systematic abstractions." His phrase "body thinking" is given precise formulation in his book that includes that phrase in its title: *On Chinese Body Thinking: A Cultural Hermeneutic*. But it expresses a more general point for Wu, namely, that Chinese philosophy and culture handle their most abstruse ideas through particular stories and very concrete images. Never does Wu claim that Chinese thought has no general ideas. On the contrary, the point of each of Zhuangzi's stories is something of very general significance.[1] Nevertheless, Wu would never admit that Chinese thought can say in universal terms what those stories are supposed to mean. The interpretation of the stories is with more stories and concrete—might I say "bodily"—images. For him, Chinese thought is allergic to abstractions, and even more so to systems of abstractions. He has been dumbfounded for over forty years that I have gotten as far as I have with Chinese philosophy while still being a systematic philosopher!

Wu has been far more appreciative of Western thought than Hall, however. His *Cultural Hermeneutic* volumes, *On Chinese Body Thinking* and *On the Logic of Togetherness*, speak as much about Western thinkers as Chinese, and they show a deep appreciation of the continental tradition in particular. Yet he agrees with Hall that Western thought has centered on abstractions, even when talking about bodily matters, say, in the philosophy of Merleau-Ponty.[2] Wu's fundamental conviction, I believe, is that reality is ineluctably singular, though also significant. Therefore, any attempt to describe reality in universals is misleading if not plainly false. Furthermore, the Chinese tradition is fundamentally right, Wu believes, although much is to be learned from the universalistic and abstract concepts of the West by means of which we can manipulate reality. Wu is very nervous about manipulating reality, however, and he thus picks up on nature-romanticism in Daoism.

Both Hall and Wu develop in their unique ways the basic distinction made by F. S. C. Northrop, that East Asian cultures develop "concepts by intuition" whereas Western culture develops "concepts by postulation."[3] Wu diverges from Hall in the implications drawn from this distinction. For Hall, the distinction demarks contrasting broad themes that define who is central and who marginal in the respective cultures. For Wu it is necessary immediately to come down to particular cases. Although Hall claimed to be a default nominalist, what his philosophy recognized were contrasting abstract cultural themes. Although Wu agrees about the virtue of nominalism, he does not resort to literal universals to make the point. His arguments are by means of analyses of specific thinkers.

Wu's work is nearly always second-order philosophy, commenting on philosophy, philosophers, and their modes. *The Butterfly as Companion* is an extraordinary extended analysis of a relatively short text, using many methods of analysis from philology to philosophical speculation. Wu does philosophy by commentary, not by himself producing master narratives, or even petite narratives. He has a brilliant literary imagination and develops many striking images, or plays on Chinese images. But they are rarely first-order philosophy. They rather are second-order images of first-order images and theories. Hall's philosophy of culture is largely third-order philosophy, commenting on the ways second-order philosophers thought about first-order philosophy. Thus Hall is reduced in his final claims to large thematic comparisons, while Wu delights in detailed comparative discussions of many philosophers, ever more subtle and nuanced, ever more celebrating the indirect.

CONFUCIAN SCOTISM

At this point let me introduce the third stooge as a Confucian Scotistic realist. I am a Scotist in the sense that I believe that things are concrete particulars, "thises," or "haecceities," to use Duns Scotus's word.[4] Nevertheless, concrete things contain universals or "common natures" within them. Singularity is the mark of existence, and yet sometimes the common natures, such as being human, rational, and deserving of dignity, are more important than the fact that one person's thisness is different from another person's. I follow Charles Peirce in saying that most of the errors of medieval, Renaissance, and modern Western philosophy come from unconscious (and sometimes conscious) commitments to nominalism. So I see Hall and Wu both as miscreants as regards their nominalism. (For stooges, to be miscreant is a happy combination of delight and folly.)

Now it should be said quickly that, for Wu, concrete particulars have meaning and signify something. Peirce would say that most nominalists recognize this point but fail to do anything about it, such as recognize common natures. Wu does not recognize common natures or universals as anything but mental abstractions. Thus, if applied literally to real things, they are false, however they might be turned into helpful metaphors. Instead he believes that the significance of singulars can be adduced through a poetic language that mothers indirection. To put the point another way, Wu believes that meaning can be shown through poetic speech but cannot be said prosaically. By carefully following a story or a nuanced critique of a train of images, Wu would hope for an emerging intuitive grasp of singular importances. These singular importances can include comparative contrasts between philosophers in different traditions.

For Hall, the proximate end of comparative inquiry is a kind of educated intuitive aesthetic grasp of the different things that the compared cultures take to be important. His aesthetics is the celebration of high-level abstractions about the importance of particulars. For Wu, the proximate end of comparative inquiry is a different kind of educated intuitive aesthetic grasp of differences and connections between singular things with a cultivated non-dependence on universals and abstract systems. For the third stooge, the proximate end of comparative inquiry is not intuitive at all, but permeated with a feeling-tone of fallibility. The entire process of comparative inquiry is aesthetic, from beginning to end, but still is fallible.

COMPARISON: DAOISM AND CONFUCIANISM

I would argue that comparative inquiry has three moments of hypothetical work.[5] The first is to articulate vague comparative categories that define the respects in which the different cultures' ideas are to be compared. This is extremely tentative. The second moment is to see how the different cultures specify the comparative categories differently. That the comparative categories are vague, in a logical sense, means that they can tolerate specification by ideas that contradict one another. Once one sees how the cultures diversely specify the comparative category, it is possible to trace out where they agree, disagree, overlap, and so forth. Comparison requires saying how the different specifications are related. These statements of comparison are all tentative too. But then the third moment is to see whether the attempt to specify the vague categories reveals that the comparative categories themselves are biased. Do they privilege one culture's ideas over others, marginalize some, distort ideas? Only after much work has been done to compare cultures in the respects identified for comparison is it possible to go back and check for bias in the formulation of the comparative categories. So in comparative inquiry, the conclusions have as much to do with ending up with steady comparative categories that have been made vulnerable to criticism and tested as thoroughly as possible as they have to do with stating comparisons according to the categories. We should expect the advancing community of intercultural philosophers to change and supplement the large-scale theories of what should be compared as much as to fill in details of comparison.

As brilliant comparativists, Hall and Wu actually practice what I preach. That is, they continually revise in dialectical fashion the overall structures and conceptualities of their comparisons as well as develop comparisons within them. But their comparative philosophies make it hard for them to recognize this. Hall's willingness to sacrifice exceptions within a culture to what is dominantly important in that culture means he cannot correct his thematic comparative categories by what they leave out, and it commits him to the large abstract themes as the real stuff of comparison. Wu's allergies to abstractions make it in principle difficult to focus on correcting the comparative categories actually being employed. Because the proximate end of comparative inquiry for Wu is a kind of educated intuitive grasp of singular importances, he does not build in a deliberate process of making the comparative categories vulnerable to correction. In fact, he sometimes writes as if there are no comparative categories; but then things would not be compared in any respect.

My companion stooges object to my approach for what I believe is their perception of its Confucian character, which is a bad thing from the standpoint of thinkers who believe it is important to call themselves Daoists. That Confucian character, relative to their perspectives, has two main points, the importance of being a scholar-official and the importance of ritual. A scholar-official takes the intellectual life to be intimately tied up with administering social processes, and my conception of comparative inquiry, with at least three stages of fallible work in need of constant correction, finds its home in collaborative work. One needs institutions of colleagues to do comparative work that not only is vulnerable to correction but actually gets corrected. For this reason, I worked out the Boston University Cross-Cultural Comparative Religious Ideas Project as a paradigmatic medium of comparison. Moreover, I developed the series at SUNY Press in which several of my fellow stooges' books have been published. And I've been an academic administrator all my life, in contrast to my colleagues who have been more peripatetic loners. My Confucian heart is suspicious that the Daoist love of unattached freedom is a fantasy that leaves one dependent on flashes of intuitive insight rather than refined and well-tested hypotheses.

The point about ritual is subtler than the point about intellectuals as scholar-officials. The Confucian conception of ritual, especially as in Xunzi, says that nearly all human activity and interaction is semiotically structured by learned gestures, words, movements, enjoyments, and shared feelings. A ritual structure is vague and requires that it be specified when it is played. Experienced ritual players individuate their ritual activity in subtle and decisive ways. Ritual structures are also modified as they are played, the way comparative categories ought to be modified as they are employed in comparison. Confucian philosophers are critics of ritual, showing where the rituals at hand are inadequate, demeaning, or otherwise deficient in making possible the human relations that should be humane and civilized. The making of intercultural comparisons is the creation of a ritual that allows comparativists to dance across the cultures. These rituals include tentatively formulating comparative categories that allow different specifications to be tried out and related to one another. This is the part of intercultural comparison that David Hall mastered so well, the brilliant leap to articulate ways or categories in terms of which cultures are different. The rituals also include the intellectual practices of playing with the specifics compared, testing articulations of them, inquiring whether they are rightly represented within the comparative categories, and so forth. This part of the rituals of intercultural comparison is the genius of Kuang-ming Wu, the subtle, sensitive, demonstration of the singularities of things brought into comparison. Intercultural comparative rituals ought also to keep both of these moments in a state of continual correction of one another and of themselves. This is the part of comparison to which Confucians aspire.

Neither of my companion stooges has much tolerance for system, in comparison or any other part of philosophy. For Hall, system privileges logical over aesthetic order. For Wu, system employs abstractions that falsify the singularities of reality. Yet how else can one present one's philosophic ideas for judgment unless one makes them vulnerable to correction from as many angles as can be imagined? Without that, philosophy is arbitrary, even when it is convinced that its conclusions have become intuitive. What is system in philosophy but the attempt to look at things from all the angles from which they might be examined and the interpretations of them subjected to correction? The abstract categories used in systems are the constructions needed to relate things so as to make them vulnerable to correction by one another. The explicit formulation of abstract philosophical categories is being honest about this, and making the categories themselves in turn vulnerable to correction. All systems are themselves hypotheses that are more or less warranted. To conduct work with a system as the overall guidance structure is like playing a ritual that itself is corrected in the play but that also allows for focus on all levels of abstraction from the metaphysical to the singular. Someone who emphasizes the honesty that comes from system building is likely to be less brilliant at intuitive comparisons of large themes than David Hall, and less subtle in recognizing the singularities of things and their significance than Kuang-ming Wu. Nevertheless, I am confident that the first two stooges need the third for balance.

Now as to the matter of the Daoist label, I suspect that Daoist sensibilities about the connection of all nature and the nesting of human life within nature tell against Hall's supposition that Daoism supports a chaos within which each thing, each culture, each project, is a world unto itself. I suspect also that Daoism's emphasis on non-action as an effective form of action tells somewhat, though less harshly, against Wu's supposition of indirection in knowing and speaking. Daoism is rather friendlier to Confucianism than either Wu or Hall might like, and is critical of Confucianism only when the latter's rituals become rigidified so as not to require singular specification and thereby themselves change in their being played. Confucians and Daoists alike emphasize knowing the roots and branches of things, and both look for those moments of equipoise where a small spontaneous action can make a big difference in what follows. For the classical Daoists, the rhythms of causation that open onto opportunities for spontaneity are those of nature. For the classical Confucians, the rhythms most important for us to know are not only those of nature but also those of cultivating social institutions, the rhythms of family growth and generations, of governmental formations, of cultural enterprises. Academic Confucians look at the rhythms of the semester system, knowing that the setting of reading lists and syllabi are the opportunities for spontaneous change. Systematic intercultural comparison has its rhythms, and these are often best noticed from the standpoint of philosophic systems.

I will never persuade Kuang-ming Wu to love systems as well as singulars. But it is great fun to bop him over the head with them as stooges are wont to do.

CHAPTER NINE

Spiritual Foundations of Chinese Culture

INTRODUCTION

I am deeply grateful for the opportunity to address this conference on spiritual foundations and Chinese culture and will take the opportunity to treat the subject as seriously as I can. Both "spiritual foundations" and "Chinese culture" are ambiguous phrases and my intent is to sort some of the most important ambiguities.

To begin with "spiritual foundations," the phrase can refer to the many foundational conditions for spiritual life that themselves are not especially spiritual. Among these are having a sufficiently settled life with food, safety, supportive companions, and a reasonably intact culture within which to articulate spiritual matters. Most of us can take these things for granted, but if we lived in Darfur right now, we would not expect much subtlety or depth of spiritual life because the foundational conditions are largely absent: we would be praying just to get through the night. I will say more about the nonspiritual conditions for spiritual life in a moment, with illustrations from Chinese culture.

"Spiritual foundations" also refers to the conditions for ascending to greater heights of spiritual development, for getting deeper into the spiritual and its mature forms. Proximate levels of spiritual development are foundational for more nearly ultimate ones. Here the languages, practices, and scriptures of a tradition are themselves spiritual but are really foundational for deeper levels of spiritual development. Most religious traditions, including the Chinese and Christian, mark stages of spiritual development, each of which is foundational for the stages subsequent to it. Some forms of Buddhism distinguish fifty-two *bhū mi*s, or stages of enlightenment!

Finally, "spiritual foundations" refers to the role that various forms of spiritual life function as foundations for other things, such as the arts and high culture, even for vitality in a whole society. Many people in the West complain that Western societies have lost their spiritual foundations and hence are more than usually unsure about the ground of obligation, about what human integrity means, about attitudes toward others, about the meaning of life, and about the life-and-death contingency of existence, collapsing into nothing more profound than consumerism.

The phrase "Chinese culture" has analogous distinctions to be made. What are the conditions within historical Chinese culture that make the specific cultures of Chinese spirituality possible? Confucius complained that they were absent in his time and he tried to rectify that. The Marxists in the Peoples' Republic complained that those conditions were too powerful, keeping China in an unjust feudal state justified by bad spirituality, and they tried to eliminate those aspects of Chinese culture that supported traditional spirituality. Chinese culture has also been fertile "foundational" soil for the "foreign religion" of Buddhism, which was the dominant Chinese spiritual culture during the Dang dynasty. Some sociologists believe there are 130,000,000 Christians in the People's Republic today, making it one of the largest Christian nations in the world, even though Christianity is still a small percentage of the overall population.

"Chinese culture" secondly can mean its specifically spiritual dimensions as developed in Confucianism and Daoism with shamanist and Buddhist influences and manifested in popular Chinese religion. Chinese spiritual culture, in ways I shall articulate shortly, is extraordinarily complex and multidimensional. The question of the compatibility of Chinese spiritual culture with Christianity has been an issue since the days of Matteo Ricci. Surely, for Chinese Christians, Chinese Jews, and Chinese Muslims, their own spirituality is a special version of Chinese culture, however much it also contains different historical roots as well.

Third, "Chinese culture" includes those aspects of culture in China that themselves depend on various spiritual dimensions of culture but that are not themselves particularly religious, such as art, moral practices and ideas, and many other things made possible by religion. Because of the suppression of religion for so many decades by the Communist government causing religion to take disguised forms, it is difficult to assess these aspects of contemporary Chinese culture that are not themselves religious but that depend on other dimensions of culture that are religious. But there are many examples from earlier periods. The most famous examples are those instances of Confucian moral and political policies that justified, to a limited extent, the claim that Confucianism is not a religion at all but only a moral way of life. Wang An-shih (1021–1086) was famous and influential as a political thinker even though he was somewhat distant from the spiritual dimensions of sageliness and the cultivation of Heavenly Principle associated with Neo-Confucian spirituality.

Fourth, Chinese culture also refers to the influences and continuities of Chinese culture outside of China, and that in two senses. First, Chinese spiritual culture became very important, even dominant, in Korea, Japan, and Southeast Asia, whose native cultures including racial ethnicity and language roots were very different from that of the Han Chinese. What was there in the native cultural foundations of Korea, for instance, that made it particularly hospitable to the Neo-Confucian spirituality of Zhu Xi, whereas the cultural foundations of Japan made it more hospitable to the Neo-Confucian spirituality of Wang Yang-ming? The mixture of Chinese Buddhism and Confucianism that went to Japan gave rise to the deep spiritual and martial code of Bushido, but very little like that happened in Korea where Chinese Buddhism and Confucianism were equally important.

I have offered these illustrations of nonreligious culture providing foundations for spiritual culture, of lower levels of spiritual culture providing foundations for higher levels, and of spiritual culture providing foundations for nonspiritual elements of culture to distinguish three meanings of "spiritual foundations" and how they might be exemplified in the Chinese case. Now I want to offer a more formal model of how to think about these things and then return to discuss them each.

AN ECOLOGICAL MODEL OF RELIGION

The basic model for considering spiritual foundations in the three senses mentioned comes from biology, and it works for most although not all of what needs to be understood. Consider this analogy. Suppose there is a pond in the woods. The pond is a complex biological ecosystem containing, among other things, the bacteria and other microorganisms in the water; the plants growing on the bottom and on the shores (that line being variable with the water level); the fish, frogs, leeches, and other animals living in and under the water; and the insects of many kinds that live on and about the surface, feeding on things in the water and reproducing on adjacent plant life. Each of these species is what I call an "ecoharmony." A living ecoharmony has members with life cycles of their own that reproduce and carry on their various activities in the larger pond ecosystem. Every ecoharmony has two kinds of components in terms of which it needs to be understood. First it has "conditional components" that consist of all that the individuals in the species need and receive from the larger ecosystem. For instance, fish need not only to have food in the larger ecosystem but also the right conditions of temperature and water chemistry, places to breed, and so forth; different species of fish in the pond might need different conditional components. Second, every ecoharmony has "essential components" that make the species what it is; we usually think of DNA in this regard. Many different species can exist in the same pond because, although they have many of the same conditioning components, they have different essential components. Not all the species of fish eat the same things, however, or reproduce in the same places, and so differ with regard to their dietary and reproductive conditions. I call these eco*harmonies* because each species is a harmony of its essential and conditional components. Prior to modern biology, Aristotelian science was inclined to think of species in terms of their essence alone, making the conditions for them secondary. Now we should reject substance thinking and consider things to be harmonies with their conditional components relating them to their environment being just as important to them as their essential components.[1]

I've been speaking of the species as an ecoharmony, but each individual within the species in the pond is also an ecoharmony; for the moment we can neglect this distinction. We should note that each component in an ecoharmony is itself an ecoharmony. The little fish and the plants eaten by big fish are themselves species with ecoharmonic structures even when they function as conditional components in the big fish. Each species of fish has an internal organic structure with substructures, each of which is an ecoharmony down to the molecular structure of the DNA. Put the other way, each species is a component of the larger ecosystem of the pond. The pond itself is an ecoharmony. It has its own "essential components" of the various species within it, but exists with the conditions of being in the terrain it is, with the chemical and biologic runoffs from the wider environment, depending on the chemistry and wildlife of the forest in many ways, and on the larger geology and climate of the area.

The pond itself can be called a complex ecosystem, an ecoharmony with some integrity of its own, containing conditions from beyond the pond but also containing many ecoharmonies within it. The ecoharmonies within the pond are more or less compatible with one another to the degree the pond's ecosystem is stable. Each ecoharmony is dependent on some other ecoharmonies in the pond but perhaps not all; some ecoharmonies can disappear without all the others disappearing. The asymmetries in the dependence relations are what are of interest when using the biological ecosystem as a model for understanding what is foundational about spirituality in the larger culture. The best way to understand the asymmetries is through the evolutionary dimension of the ecosystem.

Imagine that a long time ago the pond was formed when a retreating glacier left it as a pocket of water over mainly bare rocks. Initially, the pond water contained only primitive microorganisms that could have survived under the glacier and also in a warmer climate. The microorganism ecoharmonies that required the cold of the glacier died out. Grasses and grass-feeding animals moved into the surrounding area and their decayed remains and droppings entered the pond. This changed the chemistry of the pond water so that more species of microorganisms washed into the pond found the conditioning components they needed to survive as ecoharmonies, and their presence provided conditions for yet more things. Spring flooding allowed fish and other marine animals and plants to wash into the pond, insects from neighboring ponds flew in, and birds dropped new seeds. The forest developed where there had been only grasses, and more species of animals with their droppings and decay surrounded the pond. Most of these adventitious new pond ecosystems did not find the conditions they needed but some did, and the pond grew in biological complexity. More particularly, within the pond sports arose with slightly different DNA than typical in their species. Some of these found the conditions they needed to survive and so a new species emerged. This new species provided new conditions for yet other new species to survive and so some species unique to the pond evolved. With the new conditions in the pond, some of the ecoharmonies that previously flourished could no longer survive and died out. The other ecoharmonies that depended on them also died out. So the pond was constantly changing its internal ecosystemic complexity with some old ecoharmonies dying out and adventitious or emergent new harmonies coming in.

Adopting this model for understanding spiritual foundations and culture, we can say that human societies and individual life are rooted in nature, a point Chinese culture has understood far better than Western cultures that think nature is made for humans to use for their own purposes. At any given time, human life is set within a vast complex ecosystem including the conditions of geography, climate, the flora and fauna local to specific places, some of which are necessary conditions for human nutrition, the kinds of social ecoharmonies necessary for human survival and flourishing, all nested within one another, and the cultural systems, religious traditions, economic conditions for material life, food production systems, educational systems, and systems of the architectural milieu. Please supplement this list with your favorite systematic conditions necessary or important for the flourishing of your spirituality. But don't think of your spirituality only on its own terms. What you are likely to bring to mind as your spirituality's own terms are only its essential components. Its conditional components, all those other ecoharmonies on which it is dependent all the way down to basic biology and climate, are just as necessary to its identity as the essential components. Your spirituality's true "own terms" include all those conditions systematically functioning in the complex ecosystem of life as well as the essential features by which you would ordinarily identify it.

Now a crucial distinction needs to be made about the ecoharmonies in the complex ecosystems of human life. A given ecoharmony is dependent on certain conditions in its environment and not on others. Some other ecoharmonies can cease to exist and the given ecoharmony can still flourish so long as the conditions on which it depends remain. Therefore, relative to other ecoharmonies, a given ecoharmony can be dependent or independent. For instance, human beings evolved in equatorial Africa, dependent among other things on that climate. But without changing their DNA they could migrate to colder climates by inventing warm clothing, snug dwellings, and the like. The colder climatic conditions, however, allowed for the evolution of new balances of DNA, such as reduced melanin in the skin. So we would say that the human species is dependent on a range of climatic conditions but is independent of any one of them given the means to adapt. In matters of religion, the great missionary traditions always need some culture to inhabit but are independent of any one of those cultures in the sense that they can find other inhabitations. Buddhism, for instance, even died out for centuries in India, its birth culture, while flourishing elsewhere. Of course, those other cultures allowed for all sorts of new forms of the religion and, in fact, required some new forms for the religions to penetrate deeply into the new cultures. It is an interesting question whether the religions changed their "essential components" when migrating from one indigenization to another; many people argue that Confucianism cannot migrate because it is too much defined by its East Asian roots—though I have argued to the contrary in *Boston Confucianism: Portable Tradition in the Late-Modern World* and in this volume.

As is obvious in the biological examples, ecosystems of ecoharmonies are dynamic and constantly changing, with different forms evolving to take account of changes in their conditional components. The same is true of religious practices including those associated with spirituality, although we frequently entertain the romantic notion that we are preserving the "ancient" or "pure" or "original" forms.

RELIGION AND SPIRITUALITY DEFINED

My argument cannot move farther without paying attention to how to mark off religion and spirituality within the great ecosystem of human life. Defining religion is extremely controversial today, and I am going to offer only an heuristic definition, that is, one that is useful for making distinctions appropriate to talking about spiritual foundations and culture. *Religion is the human symbolic engagement of ultimate realities in cognitive, existential, and practical ways.* By cognitive engagement I mean the gamut from myth and legend to sophisticated theology and philosophy, in many different forms in different cultures. By existential engagement I mean how individuals' ultimate identities are formed in relation to what is ultimate in reality. By practical engagement I mean all the practices, both communal and personal, by which relations with what is ultimate are expressed and steadied.

The heart of the definition, of course, is the reference to ultimacy. Let me quickly present my hypothesis about this, though without much defense. The ultimate reality is an ontological creative act that creates everything that is determinate. No matter what you or anyone else believes the world is made of, from yin-yang vibrations to atomic particles, and no matter who turns out to be right, it has to be determinate. Anything determinate is contingent on being made together with anything else with respect to which it is determinate, which is what requires the ultimate ontological creative act. That act is not determinate in itself apart from its creating the world. It has been symbolized in the West with metaphors of the person, from the frankly anthropomorphic imagery of some of the Bible to transcendent concepts such as the One beyond any determinate distinction and Thomas Aquinas's notion of God as the pure Act of to Be. South Asian religions similarly stretched metaphors of consciousness creating its content to symbolize the creative act. East Asian thought developed metaphors of spontaneous emergence such as the Dao that gives rise to a determinate world made up of yin-yang configurations or changes. I'll quote the basic text because it is so important for Chinese spirituality. It is from Zhou Dunyi, the eleventh-century Neo-Confucian.

> The Ultimate of Non-being and also the Great Ultimate! The Great Ultimate through movement generates yang. When its activity reaches its limit, it becomes tranquil. Through tranquility the Great Ultimate generates yin. When tranquility reaches its limit, activity begins again. So movement and tranquility alternate and become the root of each other, giving rise to the distinction of yin and yang, and the two modes are thus established. By the transformation of yang and its union with yin, the Five Agents of Water, Fire, Wood, Metal, and Earth arise. When these five material forces are distributed in harmonious order, the four seasons run their course.[2]

The point is, from that which has no character of its own, the Ultimate of Non-being and the Great Ultimate, arise all the things that do have character.

The notion of an ontological creative act that creates everything determinate is very abstract, but also fruitful theologically. Any determinate thing has to be determinate with respect to something else. Therefore, for there to be a determinate world there has to be a multiplicity of things. Each thing is a harmony of components that relate it to the other things with respect to which it is determinate and the components by virtue of which it integrates these into its unique self. The former components are conditional and the latter are essential. We've seen examples of this in the discussion of the conditional and essential components of ecoharmonies. Every determinate thing is a harmony of components with four traits. The harmony has a form or pattern in which the components are arranged; it has the plurality of components themselves that have to be fitted together; it has an existential location relative to the other harmonies with respect to which it is determinate and from which it gets its conditional components; and it has the value-identity of getting these components together with this form in this existential location. Let me emphasize again that there could be nothing determinate, no world at all of any kind, that does not have form, components formed, existential location, and value-identity. These four are ultimate conditions for any world and for the ultimate ontological creative act: there could be no creative act without creating something determinate. So there are five ultimate realities: form, components formed into a harmony, existential location, value-identity, and the ontological creative act.

Set aside the complete generality of this picture and consider the world from the standpoint of human beings, acknowledging that there are many different cultural ways in which that world has been symbolized with considerable pragmatic truth. Human beings face the ultimacy of form in the guise of alternative possibilities with respect to which we have some control and among which we must choose. Often these possibilities differ in value and we lie under obligation to choose well, creating our moral character as we do so for better or worse. Every religion has the complex problematic of moral righteousness, deliberation, choice, failure, guilt, punishment, redemption, and the like because facing possibilities of different value is an ultimate condition of human life.

Human beings face the ultimacy of having components in making up the overall patterns of their life insofar as this involves coming to terms with the important components and integrating them in ways that respect their integrity. The ultimate ideal with regard to components is wholeness. Suffering and brokenness in body and spirit are the result of problems in finding wholeness. Because life is a complex of things needing integration, the quest for wholeness is a problematic developed in every religion.

Human beings face the ultimacy of being existentially located with respect to others who also are creatures of the ontological creative act just as much as themselves. From a selfish point of view, and with regard to evolutionary adaptive advantage, it is tempting to regard other people and the natural environment only in terms of how they help or hinder one's own advantage, or that of one's in-group. But the Axial Age religions all agree that because "all are under heaven," to use the Chinese slogan, all should be respected for what they are. All religions have the problematic of compassion and justice for all things, however diversely they interpret the implications of that and however imperfect the practice of universal love and justice is.

Human beings face the ultimacy of having value-identity insofar as they cope with their nearly always ambiguous value in light of what life is supposed to mean or add up to. How do human beings fit into the larger picture of creation, given their value-identities? Sometimes this has manifested itself as the quest for security in existence, framed in terms of immortality or reincarnation. In more modern times this problematic appears as the search for meaning in a cosmos that seems to have none. All religions have some problematic of the meaning of value-identity.

Human beings face the radical contingency of existence on the ontological creative act in the shock of recognizing that contingency, as distinct from the ordinary contingencies within the flow of life, a shock often associated with the encounter with death. In one way or another the deep ultimate question is whether to affirm this existence or deny it, to be fundamentally grateful or fundamentally hateful. In some terms or other, most religions advocate consent to being in general, gratitude, and union with the act of creation and its radically continent product, however filled with suffering and death.

I have now listed five ultimate boundary conditions for human life that both separately and together in various combinations establish the problematics of religion: lying under obligation, the quest for wholeness, engagement with others, the search for meaning, and the question of consent to being in general. Every religion has socially constructed categories for engaging these five ultimates, and to this extent historicism is true. The religions by no means say the same things regarding these engagements. But the ultimate conditions to be engaged are part of the nature of reality, necessarily characteristic of any world within which human beings might live, any world that is determinate in any way. Therefore, religion is just as much a response to reality for any culture as its response to its climate; the responses differ, but that to which they respond is real in what it is.

You might have been amused to find that, when you ask a sociologist what religion is, the answer is a set of functions within society, as in Durkheim's claims about legitimation of solidarity. Ask an anthropologist and religion turns out to be elements of culture that can be passed down. Ask a psychologist and religion is a coping mechanism for psychological problems. Ask an historian and religion is a major category for the continuity of identity of a group through time. Ask an evolutionary biologist and religion is what does or does not contribute to genetic adaptive advantage. Each of these disciplines has as its subject matter certain ecoharmonies that serve as conditions for the engagement of ultimacy. Religion always has a social setting and takes social forms, even for hermits. Religion always requires cultural elements as venues within which it pursues the five religious problematics. Religion always arises within psychological states and in turn modifies them. Religious engagements are always parts of larger stories. Religions affect adaptive advantage for better or worse. But I recommend that we bear in mind that the religious dimensions of society, culture, psychology, and the rest are only those that involve the engagements with the ultimate realities. The fact that a society has institutions that have functioned to engage ultimacy does not mean that those institutions always do so, and when they do not, they should be understood simply in social, not religious, terms. Cultural traditions such as Confucianism and Christianity can have powerful social effects and be of historical interest even when they are religiously dead and are not venues for engaging ultimacy. All these things can be potential conditioning components of religion, but when the engagement of ultimacy is lacking, the essential components of religion are missing and those potential conditions are to be understood on their own, nonreligious, terms. Nevertheless, when considering religion, it is not to be understood in terms of its essential components alone but also in terms of all the conditioning components that make it possible, such as society, cultural traditions, psychic makeup, and the rest.

I'm sorry to have burdened you with such a quick sketch of a whole theory of religion. But such is needed to make much progress toward understanding how Chinese culture, or any culture, can be a foundation for spirituality, how a culture's spirituality has more and less foundational elements, and how spirituality itself conditions the larger culture. Fortunately, spirituality is not the whole of religion. Rather, spirituality as that term has been used in the West refers mainly to the problematics of the quest for wholeness and union with the ultimate creative act itself. To be sure, the issues of righteousness, engagement of others, and the quest for meaning bear upon spirituality and vice versa. But spirituality most prominently means one or both of two things, getting oneself together in the quest for wholeness or giving oneself over to engaging the ontological creative act itself.

I want now to discuss how Chinese culture provides foundational components for these two senses of spirituality, wholeness and union with the ground of being. I shall discuss both Confucian and Christian forms of spirituality relative to these Chinese foundations, focusing on the Confucian to the neglect of other Chinese religious traditions. And I shall deal first with the Chinese cultural foundations when they are intact, and then when they are in disarray.

CHINESE CULTURE INTACT

Like all mature religious cultures, Confucianism has elaborate ways of dealing with all five religious problematics. Regarding the ultimate condition of lying under obligation, Confucianism has both the metaphysics of *li* or principle as manifested in each thing as a kind of coherence or harmony, and complicated ways of learning discernment and perfecting action on the basis of learned choice. Regarding the ultimate of engaging others, it has a complicated theory of "love with differences" and the ideals of *ren* or humaneness. Regarding the ultimate of the meaning of value-identity, it has the problematic of finding the Mandate of Heaven.

With regard to the two spiritual problematics, the greatest emphasis in Confucianism is on the quest for wholeness, which it has elaborated as the life of the sage. The sage is required to make a commitment to self-transformation that goes through stages. Although obviously involving the discernment of righteousness, cultivating the most effective love of others, and fitting in with a sense of Heaven's Mandate, the sage focuses rather on the integration and perfection of the self into what Roger Ames calls a "consummate person." Emblematic of this is Confucius's perhaps most famous and oft quoted statement: "At fifteen my mind was set on learning. At thirty my character had been formed. At forty I had no more perplexities. At fifty I knew the Mandate of Heaven. At sixty I was at ease with whatever I heard. At seventy I could follow my heart's desires without transgressing moral principles."[3]

What are the cultural conditions for the spiritual discipline of Confucian sagehood? Among the most important are two: family and a particular ritual structure. By family the Confucians did not just mean the nuclear biological family but an extended family with three or perhaps four generations. Moreover, the family was understood to be in a village where the related families also lived, the in-laws of every generation, so that just about every possible relation is exemplified. In this context a person grows up being loved in just about every relational way, and learning to love back. This is an important and perhaps necessary set of conditions for a person to conceive of the task of becoming a sage. In Confucian spirituality, the quest for wholeness finds its most important setting in a person's being loved and learning to return the love in a wide range of human relations. Without this family setting, in one guise or another, a person would not have the conditions necessary for undertaking the self-cultivation necessary for the spirituality of sagehood. The Confucian family thus is not merely in the family of direct touch, but also in its ancestral history. The loving virtues inherited in the family today come from the achievements in virtue of the ancestors. This solidarity of family sacrality has resonance in any culture in which family or tribal identity is important, but it is developed very deeply with little dependence on tribalism in Chinese culture. Filial piety is an important condition of being spiritually alive in the world.

As to ritual, many layers of social life are dependent on rituals that habituate behavior so as to carry out everyday moral decision-making and relating to other people. But rituals are like formal dance steps that interweave people's activities so that new levels of social reality emerge. Most social realities are not possible without the rituals that are their conditions. Regarding spirituality, the contents of the rituals are not particularly important except when the social realities themselves are spiritual. But how one plays the rituals, how one individuates them, how one makes them one's own is indeed a matter of ultimately gaining integrity in a complex social situation in which hundreds of rituals are being played at once. Apparently, most of Confucius's teaching was instruction in rituals and how to invest oneself in them. Having important rituals to play is an important kind of condition for the spiritual task of learning to invest oneself in the matrix of life's rituals with integrity. A sage is a ritual master.

Although sagacity, a prominent Confucian theme, is the Confucian ideal for the spiritual ultimate of the quest for wholeness, no equally prominent theme exists for the Confucian approach to the spirituality of union with the ontological creative act. The ancient Confucians, especially Xunzi, commented with awe at the inexplicable majesty of the heavens, but there seems to have been little spiritual focus on addressing that majesty in the ancient world. With the development of Chinese Buddhism, however, Confucianism learned the vocabulary and practices of meditation. You will remember that the Chinese metaphors for the ontological act of creation have to do with spontaneity of things arising from nothing, from emptiness. The Neo-Confucians stressed this kind of meditation a great deal, although generally in ways critical of Buddhism. Buddhist meditation on emptiness led to complete vacuity, the Neo-Confucians thought, which in turn led to quietism. The Neo-Confucians meditated on the Ultimate of Non-being that spontaneously gives rise to the determinate world and, in the human case, to action. For the Neo-Confucians, what I have called union with the ontological act meant identification of that act as the inner heart of oneself ready to move into action. For the Confucians of all periods, the ultimate ground of things is to be found already in the human heart. To be in touch with the ground of being meant, not the Buddhist retreat from the world into monasteries for the contemplation of Emptiness, but rather the enhanced readiness to act.

So much for now for the Chinese cultural roots of Confucian spirituality, however briefly outlined. Reflect now for a moment on the Chinese cultural roots as foundational for Christian spirituality. Christian spirituality is different in a great many ways from the Confucian. But

Matteo Ricci, the great sixteenth-century Roman Catholic missionary to China, recognized the great potential of Chinese cultural roots for Christianity. He saw the Confucian spirituality of sagehood with its roots in family and ritual as being a close analogue to the educated Christian aristocrat. So he learned Chinese, dressed as a Confucian literatus, and engaged the Confucian intellectual circle as a quite respectable sage. Such success as he had came in large measure from the fact that he was respected as a sage. Ricci also thought that he found a Chinese cultural condition for union with God in the ancient Chinese concept of Shang-di. Shang-di was a storm god, the high God of the earliest dynasties with anthropomorphic properties rather like the early renditions of Yahweh. Here Ricci was less successful with the Confucian literati. They knew that the anthropomorphic conception of Shang-di had been given up for the most part in sophisticated Confucianism for the nonanthropomorphic notions of Heaven and the Ultimate of Non-being and the Great Ultimate. Ricci's mission failed in the long run, however, not because his Chinese version of Christian mysticism did not catch on, although that was a problem. The real problem was with Rome, which rejected the Chinese dependence on the family as a condition for virtue and sagehood. Chinese veneration of ancestors was taken to be idolatry incompatible with Christian monotheism, and Ricci's missionary strategy was forbidden. In actual Chinese culture, the veneration of ancestors was never taken to be incompatible with meditative engagement of Heaven, the Dao, or any of the other symbols of the ontological act. Rome never saw the irony in the analogy between Chinese veneration of ancestors and Christian veneration of saints, angels, and the Blessed Virgin, a condition of Roman Catholic piety that Protestants at the time did believe to be incompatible with the spirituality of monotheism.

CHINESE CULTURE NOT INTACT

Step back for a moment and reflect with a critical eye on the spiritual ideals of Confucianism and Christianity and their relation to the Chinese cultural traditions that are their conditional foundations. I've spoken of spiritual ideals because the ideal is so rarely achieved, either in Confucianism or Christianity. And the reason for that is usually that the conditions required for them rarely obtain. If the problematic of becoming a sage depends on having a family of great extension and close connection with ancestors worth venerating going back generations, then the fact that most families are dysfunctional makes the project of spiritual sagehood seriously unrealistic. And is it not the case that most families are dysfunctional, especially if you look beyond the immediate nuclear family to others who might be influential? Psychotherapists will tell you that families that function with the ritualized authority structures advocated by Confucians and many Christians are common covers for traumatic abuse. Too many relatives are criminals, or moral failures, or seriously incompetent at playing the idealized roles required. Confucian culture idealizes an ancient time when it was imagined that families stayed on the family plot of land for generation after generation. But in fact such peasant cultures suffered frequent dislocation. The times of genuinely stable government in all the world's cultures have been infrequent and brief. In the United States most of the population is descended from immigrants who left their ancestral families behind; a significant minority are descended from slaves whose families were almost wholly broken. The Native Americans were mainly nomadic and generally at war with one another. A family seriously intact for more than three generations is very rare indeed. In ancient China the very motivation of Confucius's work was to respond to what he took to be a serious breakdown in civilization, including government and the economy but also the family and the required ritual structure. Although he appealed to the past, that was a fiction and in fact he was inventing the future. Irony of ironies, for Confucius, it required sages to rectify conditions so that family life and harmonious rituals supporting the institutions of high civilization would be possible.

One of the most important differences between Christianity and Confucianism lies in their attitudes toward families. Whereas most Second Temple Judaism out of which Christianity was born shared the Chinese sense of identity being formed by kinship relations, Jesus said only negative things about families. He required his disciples to leave their families, even when they should be attending to mourning the dead; he said he came to bring a sword to family relations, not peace; when his own family members were ashamed of him and tried to get him to stop healing and teaching, he said his true father was God and his true siblings were believers, not blood kin. When Jesus was on the cross, he told his mother to take the Beloved Disciple as her son and asked him to take care of his mother, even though he had plenty of siblings to do that. The early Christian communities were not built up out of kinship groups but focused much on the widows and orphans, the outcasts, those who had no families. Congregations became substitutes for families, and other family-substitute social organizations such as monasteries and religious orders developed because you could not count on families. After all, Adam, Eve, and their children were not an auspicious beginning for family life. Despite what some religious conservatives say today, Christianity is a religion that is explicitly independent of family functionality, whatever other social orders and conditions it depends on. Therefore, Christianity has great appeal in East Asia today, where traditional societies that understand themselves in terms of being tied to land and extended generational families find themselves at a loss. In China people are being moved from the country to the cities en masse. Modern technology makes jobs dependent on merit and mobility. Therefore, Christianity has great appeal in China because it offers an alternative to a deeply eroded if not always fictional family structure. Islam is likely to offer the same thing, because it too creates an alternative to the family. Buddhism offered the same thing a millennium and a half ago in the chaos between the Han and Dang dynasties.

It therefore becomes an interesting question whether the relative success of Christianity and other non-family-oriented religions in China would develop forms of social life that in turn can become conditions for something like the Confucian sage. Certainly within Christianity there have been saints who look something like such sages, although much careful comparative work would have to be done to establish how similar they are.

Functional rituals are also crucial for a Confucian sage, as well as for many of the institutions of high civilization. We live, as did Confucius and Jesus, in times of great cultural pluralism, where the rituals of any one group could hardly be generalized beyond that group and few intergroup rituals existed. Most forms of Christianity that are now flourishing in China are of the conservative sorts that foster Christian in-groups. But Christianity also has an anti-in-group strain of hospitality to all. In fact, the original Christian paradigm shift, manifested in Saint Paul, was the transformation of the promises God made to Israel in the Sinai covenant to be applicable to all the Gentiles as the New Covenant. This means that, if conditions in China stabilize, partly through the emergent contributions of Christianity, perhaps some saints/sages will emerge who can shift in-group Christian defensiveness to a more liberal hospitality that develops rituals for engaging larger segments of the population. I personally believe that would be a more authentic form of Christianity.

One more comparative point needs to be made here, although I obviously have already simplified an extremely complex ecosystem of spirituality in culture. In traditional, intact, idealized Confucian culture, it is supposed that Heaven or the ground of being, the ontological creative act in my language, is within us as our motivating heart. Therefore, people do not need saviors from the outside, only sagely models, usually ancestral, to motivate spiritual efforts toward either personal healing and wholeness or union with that ground. Christianity has a vague analogy to that Heaven-centeredness in its idea of the image of God in each person, but in the ordinary Christian worldview this is rendered impotent by original sin, and therefore an external savior is necessary. In Christian spirituality, the more advanced one is, the more the conditions are right for the next steps in spiritual maturity, the more internal God in Christ is seen to be. For Augustine, for instance, God is discovered to be closer to us than we are to ourselves, rather like the Confucian model. But where the conditions for higher spiritual advancement are missing and the culture or one's personal psyche is in disarray, the appeal of an external savior is very great. Perhaps that accounts for the current appeal of conservative Christianity in China, which offers an external savior who can help the helpless. If that contributes to more highly developed and stable cultural conditions, then perhaps the more internal divinity strain of Christian spirituality will become common, as well as the Confucian spirituality of sageliness.

I hope I have argued persuasively for the following points:

- Religion is not just one thing, such as the simple pursuit of salvation, but at least five: the pursuit of righteousness, wholeness, compassionate engagement of others, ultimate meaning, and union with the act that creates all determinate things.
- Spirituality focuses on the second and fifth of those, namely, personal wholeness and perfection on the one hand and union with the ground of all things on the other, often both at once.
- Every stage or level of spiritual achievement is an ecoharmony that depends on certain other conditions obtaining for its conditional components. Therefore, we can ask what cultural, social, psychological, and personal elements are necessary for each kind of spiritual achievement to be possible.
- Within spiritual development itself, there are stages that are conditions for one another, often in some kind of hierarchy of achievement. Higher stages of spiritual development might depend on new nonspiritual conditions, such as a newly stable society, as well as prior spiritual achievements.
- Spiritual achievements themselves become conditions for new achievements in culture, society, and so forth.
- Whereas it is tempting and traditional to think of high civilization and high spiritual achievement on the model of a hierarchy of stable conditions, in fact all the conditions are in flux. Therefore, the biological model of an evolving ecosystem is better, articulating as it does how any given ecoharmony, say of a spiritual sort, is dependent on some conditions and independent of others, constantly adapting to flourish or perish.

I hope to have illustrated all these point in discussing the spiritual foundations of Confucianism and Christianity in the cultural conditions of Chinese culture. Abruptly leaving the discussion here illustrates the dynamic complexity of an evolving spiritual ecosystem.

CHAPTER TEN

Selfhood and Value

Pragmatism, Confucianism, and Phenomenology

EXPERIENTIAL FRAMES AND PHENOMENOLOGY

The American pragmatic tradition that I espouse and work to extend regards human experience as interactions of persons with their environments.[1] This is a fundamentally different frame for experience than the transcendental frame common in most forms of European phenomenology, as will become clear in what follows. It can rather neatly be mapped onto many themes in Confucian approaches to experience, as Roger Ames and David Hall have argued.[2] Experiential interactions are interpretive in the sense that they employ signs to grasp the environmental elements in certain respects.[3] Hence the interpretations are always triadic, taking the signs to represent the objects interpreted in the respects as interpreted by the interpreter. As Peirce said, the basic form of interpretation is that the interpretation takes the object to be as represented by the sign in a certain respect, as in interpreting a barn to be red in respect of color.[4]

The selection of the respect in which to interpret the environment is always a function of valuation, taking that respect to be the relevantly important one.[5] The valuation might be significantly biological, as in the quick flight that interprets a rustling in the bush with the sign of danger: the interpretive flight precedes analysis of the sound or even consciousness of the potentially dangerous situation. Such biological valuations have evolutionary adaptive value: persons who flee first and inquire second stand a better chance of living to pass on their timorous genes than those who look first to see whether the noise was made by a tiger and don't live to pass on any genes.

Most human experience is guided also by values built into the culture and made into habits of daily life, indicating what is important to notice and respond to in typical environments, shaping the quotidian day. These include interactions that are more responsive as well as those that are more active and directed. Some of these come to consciousness, but most do not unless the interactions are misguided by the habitual signs. For instance, we usually do not notice the furniture when walking through a familiar room unless something is out of place and we bump it.

Much of human experience is guided by values that involve explicit purposes that are more or less conscious. Sometimes we greet friends not only out of habit but with sincere interest; sometimes we purposely seek for a strategy to act in order to deal with a difficult person or situation. Sometimes we sit down to write papers and organize our hours around intellectual inquiry. Sometimes we move vigorously in order to get exercise. Most of the time, we are making many interpretations all at once, with shifting phases of conscious attention. A short time ago on my morning walk I was reflecting with good, nostalgic feelings about being on this panel with my old friends, Ed and Chung-ying (I also was thinking about Linyu, but she is not old!). These reflections were interspersed with wonderings about what I should say, and what they were likely to say, a kind of easy musement that shifted among the intellectual and personal elements.[6] Then I got to the big hill and suddenly became aware of my heavy breathing and concentrated on raising my heart rate. Until then, the interpretive habits of my walking engagements of the environment were pretty much unnoticed. All through the walk I was taking appreciative stock of the beautiful neighborhood near my home, admiring the trees and many of the houses, and nodding to an occasional neighbor. Simultaneously, I was interpreting the aesthetic qualities of my neighborhood, walking for the sake of exercise, attending to my body's needs and habits, thinking about philosophical issues, reflecting on the different paths my friends and I have taken, and delighting in the memories of friendship.

Different values, and values of different sorts, guide the multiplicity of congruent interactions involved in my walk. Among the most important are those that parse the "environment" into foreground and background elements. The foreground elements are the objects of an interpretive engagement, but objects always as set within backgrounds. Each of the interpretive interactions on my walk identifies my environment differently regarding foreground and background. Moreover, the configurations of foreground and background are constantly changing. Sometimes the changes are caused by arising attractions and repulsions. Often, however, they are caused by interruptions, something the pragmatist Charles Peirce called Secondness, a kind of brute opposition that interrupts the continuous operations of habits that will be described later. Conscious attention is highly sensitive to interruptions.

On this pragmatic model of experience as multileveled and dynamic interpretive interactions and engagements, value plainly is involved in the environments as well as in the interpreters. On the side of the interpreter, value is involved in the selection of respects of interpretation. At the same time these personal valuations are good or bad insofar as they recognize what is important in the environment. The real value resides in the environment in correlation with what human beings can apprehend and respond to. A tiger in the rustling bush is really bad for the slow-to-flee interpreters and their potential progeny. An environmental disaster would make my walk through town horrific. The structure of the environment is what contains the values we more or less relevantly learn to recognize, and our experience is shaped by signs that are more or less in accordance with the "affordances" of the environment to fit our valuing habits. "Affordances" is a term introduced into psychological thinking by J. J. Gibson to mean the ways by which environments are structured in complex ways that afford being interpreted with the resources and interests of an interpreter's semiotic system. The walker in the jungle interprets the whole situation of noise in the bush at once. The value in the interpreter's intentional sign-filled interpretation is matched more or less by the structure of the environment. People, of course, want to develop value-laden interpretive structures that pick up on what is important in the environment.[7] Nathaniel Barrett is developing pragmatic models for cognitive science employing the notion of affordances, although the point would have been recognized by Peirce and the other pragmatists.[8]

This pragmatic valuational experiential model is different from the dominant model of phenomenology in continental philosophy, from which both Cheng and Casey pick their major cues.[9] Broadly speaking, the continental tradition follows Kant in supposing that experience is what is in consciousness and its subconscious layers and that this makes possible the project of describing consciousness. Phenomenology is the description of experience for this tradition, description deep and multilayered. No one has explored the subtleties of consciousness in a descriptive mode more than Ed, and Chung-ying is looming large with a phenomenologically descriptive ontology from the *Yijing*!

My pragmatic trajectory says rather that experience is not especially a matter of consciousness but of interpretive interaction. Peirce argued, conclusively to my mind, that there is no such thing as intuitive consciousness, but rather that what we think we see and hear in consciousness is a matter of inference when you come down to it. He showed that our sense of the seemingly continuous visual field fills in inferentially all the spots that don't register where the optic nerves enter the eyes and no rods and cones can pick up anything.[10] Nothing is simply given, only selectively taken in a complex environment of multilayered interpretations with a lot of corrective interruptions or Secondness thrown in.

Because consciousness is a vagrant and often ephemeral aspect of experience, pragmatic phenomenology cannot be something controlled by ideals of description. Hegelian phenomenology described the appearances of the rational advance of consciousness through the dialectic of Spirit (*Geist*). Value or importance, for Hegel, is defined by the place in the dialectic. Husserlian phenomenology bracketed claims to say what is real and important in order to describe accurately the forms of consciousness. If things appear in consciousness as carrying one value or another, this is just a matter of their form and indicates nothing about what is really important. Later phenomenologists such as Maurice Merleau-Ponty recognized the limitation of the consciousness model and worked hard to articulate experience through the body.[11] Two students of Professor Casey and me have developed this even further. Drew Leder's *The Absent Body* is an important defense of body-thinking in critical dialogue with the Cartesian tradition. David Strong's *Crazy Mountains: Learning from Wilderness to Weigh Technology* develops a bodily sense of perception of value that goes so far as to engage mountains in climbing. The point about perceptual experience through the body places these phenomenologists close to William James. But whereas James held to a metaphysical "neutral monism" according to which the neutral experience stuff can be organized either according to subjective selves or according to logical structures in the environment, with the result that the self is just as much a contingent construct as a mountain viewed from many angles, Merleau-Ponty, Leder, and Strong treat the body as a medium for a self to engage objects of appreciative perception. Heidegger was aware of transcendental philosophy's hidden commitment to construing the world as a function of the self's synthesizing activities, and he struggled to define phenomenology as the world "coming across the open" to us (Dasein). But he never escaped the priority of Dasein as the subjective condition for experience.[12]

The pragmatic model of valuationally ordered interpretive, interactive engagement is radically different. The self and its first-person perspective is just as much a *product* of ongoing interpretive interactions as any representation of the world engaged, not the *a priori* or transcendental condition for the interpretive interactions. On this pragmatic model, phenomenology, in Peirce's use of the term, is not description but rather classification of things engaged or interacted with, including the "interactors," according to basic categories. Peirce argued that all things encountered or supposed in any way can be classified in one or several of three categories.[13] For Peirce, all things have an immediate character, perhaps as experienced but always as simply being what they are. The immediacy of qualities is included here. This is Firstness. Because the Firstness of things is in-itself or immediate, qualities or things as Firsts do not differ from one another because they cannot be compared. We can never interpret something as a First without mediating it. Secondness is the oppositional quality of things, their in-itself-ness and resistance to being absorbed into others. One of Peirce's examples is the feeling of someone pushing against you on the other side of a swinging door; interpreting this as opposition is more than Secondness, but the opposition itself is a Second. Another of Peirce's (more fanciful) examples is the experience of floating in a hot air balloon above a city in the dead quite of night when a shrieking factory whistle goes off; interpreting it by jumping is more than Secondness, but the shock is a Second. Secondness is the source of reality's correction of our bad signs and habits. Peirce's criticism of Hegel was that the latter swallowed up Secondness in interpretive Thirdness, losing the sense of reality over against all interpretation; I think he would make the same criticism of signified/signifier semiotics. Thirdness is the mediation of things so that they are brought together in some respects, related while maintaining their differences. All signs are Thirds, for Peirce. They have their own-being, Firstness, and their oppositional differences from other things, their Secondness. But their Thirdness consists in their mediating functions. Only things that are Thirds can be interpreted. Indeed, only things that are Thirds can be determinately what they are and different from other determinate things in some respect. There can be no Firsts alone, or Seconds alone, or Firsts and Seconds together, although Peirce speculated that an evolutionary metaphysics might move from Firsts to Seconds to Thirds. If there is anything determinate, it is a Third that is what it is (its Firstness) over against something different (its Secondness) in some respect (its Thirdness). Experience as interpretive interaction is primarily a function of Thirdness, although the realities interpreted have their corrective secondness and all experience has the qualitative immediacy of Firstness.

INTERACTIVE EXPERIENCE AND RITUAL: THE WESTERN CONTRIBUTION OF CONFUCIANISM

Contributing to this conversation with Casey the continental phenomenologist and Cheng the Chinese philosopher, I want to say that Confucianism supposes experience to be very much the ways the pragmatists, especially I as a late pragmatist, affirm. Human life is interactive and responsive, grasping things as having value and responding valuationally, appreciative in positive and negative senses and struggling to improve interpretive reactions. I have focused my discussion so far on Peirce because he had an explicit "phenomenology," to which I will return shortly. But James and Dewey have even more detail about experience that resonates with the Confucian tradition. Moreover, Whitehead too can be counted as a pragmatist and he leads to even more comparative connections with Confucianism. Those points are for another time. Buddhism, with its many approaches to interpreting consciousness, is much closer to Husserlian phenomenology, and I am willing to give Buddhism over to the continental phenomenologists as a friendly conversation partner. When we get to issues of ordering life, where the millennium-old debates between Buddhists and Neo-Confucians take shape, we would need to look at the approaches to morals that relate continental and pragmatic approaches, which is another topic.

Now, however, I want to pick up on a specific kind of interpretive interaction that is most profitably understood in terms of the Confucian tradition of ritual analysis. Although ancient beyond accounting and anticipated articulately in Confucius's *Analects*, Confucians understand ritual in a fundamental ontological sense to supplement the material forces of nature (*qi*) and the ordering principles of Heaven (*li*). The classical slogan hails the ontological "Trinity" of Heaven, Earth, and the Human. Xunzi pointed out that people have bodies with many material capacities and also emotional and intellectual capacities deriving from the source of coherence and intelligence.[14] Moreover, we have a psychophysical governing capacity that can take control of our actions. But neither the material forces of physical properties nor the naturally given capacities for emotional response can tell us what is worth hating and loving, emulating or fleeing, fearing and trusting. The biological capacity to control our actions does not by itself, without education, tell us what to control and for what purpose. In addition to Heaven and Earth, Xunzi gave metaphysical primacy to humanity, by which he meant the development of conventional ritualized meaning with cogent signs. These conventional interpretive rituals are habits, as the pragmatists say, and include, among many other things, learned ways of standing and moving, gesturing meaningfully, talking in the semiotic structure of some language, habits of family and personal interactions, as well as more obviously ceremonial rituals.[15]

Not all rituals are plays among people. Some of our rituals focus mainly on the natural environment exclusive of human beings and social institutions. When gravity causes us to fall, that by itself is not a ritualized interaction with nature. But as soon as an infant learns to interpret the pull of gravity and develops habits of throwing his toys high and attempting to stand, the interactions with gravity are ritualized. Most rituals are learned with some kind of imitation. Infants imitate their elders' ways of standing. For instance, most East Asians learn to stand with their feet parallel, whereas Northern Europeans stand with their toes a bit angled out. When a cancer starts growing in us without being noticed, that is a nonritualized interaction with nature. But when we interpret how we feel as sickness and go to a doctor, thus discovering the cancer, the interaction with the cancer is ritualized. Cultures differ in the ways they ritualize illness. When the tiger in the bush did not make a telltale sound and simply pounced on someone for dinner, that person was not ritually interacting with the tiger. But the tiger perhaps was hunting with ritualized habits; perhaps tigers in different families ritually hunt differently. If the person were walking by the bush on the alert for tigers and failed to escape because the person's rituals for jungle-walking don't pick up on wholly silent tigers, the person still was ritually engaged with the tiger.

A great many of our interactions inclusive of people and social institutions are ritually shaped for better or worse. Among the most important things in our natural environment are other people and all the social institutions and organizations of our lives. The Confucian tradition has always seen human individuals and social realities as interacting parts of the environment, specifications of nature while also being of human composition. What is especially striking in the Confucian understanding of ritual is that nearly everything we do is made possible by learned, that is, ritualized behavior. Talking with friends, we are already engaging in rituals of balance against the force of gravity, rituals of greeting, rituals of language speaking, and rituals of conversational interaction, all at once. That we speak in a common language does not tell us exactly what to say, though we might also have rituals that direct the conversation to certain topics. The rituals that are explicit ceremonies, say in politics or religion, themselves are made possible only by the vast web of rituals in which the ceremonies take place. We Confucians focus (with marginal success) on being in healthy ritual interactions with other people at all levels of civilization.

The Western intellectual traditions tend to distinguish between individual actions, institutional operations, and natural things that behave according to nonpersonal laws of nature. Modern Western thought has sometimes been attracted to mechanistic conceptions of nature apart from institutions and human intentions; since the nineteenth century, mechanistic thought has been replaced by statistical senses of natural causation. Some early modern thinkers such as Thomas Hobbes have attempted to give mechanistic interpretations to social institutions and even to human choice. Max Weber's notion of the ideal type tries to predict human behavior as if behavior moves according to what would be predicted in a rational system. Neither continental phenomenology nor any Chinese philosophy of which I know has attempted to treat human institutions and individual behavior in a mechanistic way, although of course both give great encouragement to predicting the future.

In contrast to the Western modernity and postmodernity, both pragmatism and Chinese philosophy see individual human action and interaction, through the web of rituals internalized and connecting individuals to other things, to be interpenetrated by ritualized institutions and all other forms of causal interaction. Nature, institutions, and individual agents are not three distinct spheres but overlapping and interpenetrating layers of different kinds of natural processes.

THE SELF

Rituals of all sorts are somewhat vague forms that need to be made specific in order actually to be played. This is somewhat like the distinction prominent in continental semiotics between a language and actually speaking in the language, which would be like the distinction between a ritual as a complex of habit-potentials and actually playing the ritual. Rituals are like dance steps: they are vague patterns and within each pattern there are many different specific ways they can be played. The vagueness (a technical notion in Peirce) of the steps means that they can be specified in different ways, perhaps even contradictory ways, by different players or even by the same player on different occasions. A person learning a ritual, like one learning a dance, can play the ritual many different ways at first, perhaps not even noting how different the specifications are from one another.

As a dancer becomes more expert, however, the different specifications within the pattern become less random and more individuated. In time, the dancing becomes this individual's way of dancing the pattern, distinct from and likely recognizable in contrast to the ways other dancers dance the steps. Likewise with rituals. Though the ritual can be played by any individual in many ways, as they mature individuals individuate themselves more and more. The mature individuating of ritual playing is a large part of how we become individual selves. A small child can learn some large set of role-plays for treating mother and father. But by late adolescence most people can play those ritual roles so as to relate to their own specific mother and father, and do so as to express their own individuated ways of playing those roles that might be played quite differently by siblings.

A significant part of the human self, although not the only part, is the individuating of role-playing. (I'll introduce another part shortly.) A mature individual is involved in playing a gazillion ritual roles all at once. Each self is a matrix (read yin) of ritual intersections and also the extensions of activity to play rituals overlapping within that matrix that individually reach out to interactions perhaps far distant from other rituals within the matrix (read yang). The rituals for relating to colleagues at work overlap those for relating to family members, but they also extend out in non-overlapping ways. Confusions about this can be embarrassing, if not disastrous. My wife once said in a fit of pique, "I am not your secretary!" And I have known colleagues (not Confucians, surely) whose secretary has said, "I am not your wife!" I am playing a host of rituals on this panel. Ed Casey and I have been friends since we were college classmates; for a while we both taught at Stony Brook, where he was my department chair. All these relations have a ritualized substance that he and I are playing together now. Chung-ying and I have been friends almost as long, and he graciously has developed rituals that moved me into the community of Chinese and American Confucian scholars, publishing many of my papers and setting me up to play scholar-official roles. He and I have shared many more panels than Ed and I and have a very rich set of mutually supportive academic performance rituals. I have known young Dr. Gu a much shorter time, but two of her major doctoral professors, Steve Odin and Joseph Grange, were my own doctoral students, and so she thinks of me through the rituals of me being her academic Doktor Grossvater.

One of the most important things to recognize about rituals such as these is that when people play together in rituals, they can relate to both others and themselves as equally being role-players. Instead of the modern Western primacy of self-and-other, the basic Confucian sense of self is to be related to other players of ritual roles as one among the many selves playing. We can regard ourselves as being one among many players in any given ritual. Or to put it differently, the concrete reality is the rituals being played and ready at hand for play. Human beings conceive of themselves as ritual players among and with others, if they are alert to the rituals as such. We can conceive of the other players as themselves matrices of multitudes of rituals, just like us, but unique in their own bevy of rituals and playing reciprocal roles to ours in the ritual at hand. We see the others as working through the individuations of their ritual play, just as we are, becoming more mature. From the perspective of the ritual play itself, not the conscious perspective of any subject-self within, all the players are viewed as players, including ourselves with the others. The fundamental frame is not me facing the others but rather all of us playing together. This is the first part of the Confucian sense of self that I want to stress.

A second basic pragmatic Confucian part of the self comes from the observation that each of us has at our core a capacity to perceive and respond to the value-laden things around us, to the Ten Thousand Things, as Confucians call the world. Each individual is a continuum from the inner elements of response through bodily functions, postures, and actions to being able to perceive and act across space and time to connect with the other things.[16] Those abilities require the individual to develop language and other sets of symbols for parsing out the objects in the foreground of their environmental background, as well as interpretive knowledge, skills at moving through the natural and social environments, and many other things. Confucians emphasize the very great importance of learning so as to be able to perceive distant things through helpful theories and practical habits, and to act well. Sometimes Western phenomenologists think that the perceived world is simply given, "there" in consciousness or in experience to be analyzed. Think of how anyone from any culture can listen to Bach and find it interesting, perhaps pleasurable; someone from the Chinese musical tradition would find it less comprehensible than a Westerner who recognizes its harmonies; then note that someone with a highly refined musical education in Bach would hear much more than those of us whose musical education is at the entertainment level. It is not that the musicologist hears the same thing as us amateurs and can analyze it better. The musicologist actually hears things we amateurs miss. Perception is an achievement that requires learning. In many ways, becoming a mature self so as to relate well and responsibly to the Ten Thousand Things is like becoming a martial artist, learning to sense and bear the eddies in the *qi*.

The importance of ritual here is that my own personal self includes all the rituals I learn to play. Because the rituals, including speaking my language, intrinsically include the other people and things who reciprocally play them, the others are part of my own individual self. I am all sorts of rituals shared with others: in many places in my life, I am We. All the things playing ritual roles with me are in various senses components of my personal continua of connections with the things of the world. So, the Western ideal for the individual, to be a subjective self over against and in relation to objective Others and the world is hard to register on my Confucian model. Western sociologists and anthropologists often think that East Asians put the group or community ahead of the individual. But that simply is to misread the Confucian metaphysics of selfhood.

Yet a third part of the Confucian self is what the tradition calls "sincerity" or *cheng*. Sincerity is the educational ideal of becoming transparent through all the layers of the continuum each person has with the things of the world. It means eliminating selfishness that might distort perception and response. But it also means untangling our emotions that hide our motives from others and ourselves. It means practicing ritual play that relates properly to the ritual components and situation. It means learning how to be "present" to others in ritual play and elsewhere. It even means dressing right to indicate what you honestly think and feel about others and yourself. For some people, how they dress is a device to protect themselves and deceive others. For other people, how they dress is meant to "express" themselves. But for Confucians, how we dress is an attempt to be deferential to others and to ourselves, openly showing our regard with sincerity. Because so many relations are ritualized, often dress is coded for the ritual, and dressing according to code shows whether one is conforming or not and thus showing sincerity in engaging the ritual as such. But even more, how we dress is an attempt to be respectful and vulnerable at once, without hidden agendas.

The English word "sincerity" often has the connotation of expressing oneself honestly, not holding back our feelings, "letting it all hang out," to use a phrase that for some signifies a virtue. The Chinese word *cheng* that is translated "sincerity" has a slightly different structure. It means first having developed the skills to appreciate other people for who they are, our institutions for the good they make possible, and surrounding nature for its many worths. Then it means clearing up the continua of interactions that connect us with those others so that we can respond appropriately. Confucian sincerity is a clarity or transparency between the Ten Thousand Things and our inner heart with its natural openness to appropriate response. Becoming sincere means working on oneself, but the ground for this is not oneself but rather the nature and values of other things with which we interact. Sincerity in the Confucian sense is not expressing oneself without disguise but rather making oneself appropriately responsive to the things in the world whose nature and value need to be discovered and appreciated.

Sincerity is the deepest existential virtue for us Boston Confucians because it is so very hard to attain and failure in it is a form of existential self-contradiction. The ancient fault of Confucianism, for which it has been criticized by Daoists from the beginning, is that the emphasis on ritual can degenerate into mere formalism. When sincerity is lacking, that is what happens. An insincere person can even individuate much role-playing, or at least develop an individuated style. Sometimes such phonies can deceive many people, though we usually can detect a bad smell.

Confucian rituals historically have been criticized for being oppressive, men degrading women, the rich oppressing the poor, mothers-in-law enslaving their daughters-in-law, as we shall discuss at greater length in chapter 15. This should be impossible if the men, the rich, and the mothers-in-law were truly sincere as they played the rituals with their potential victims. In each of these instances, sincerity requires true respect and appreciation of the others involved in the ritual, and ritual play that cannot be played sincerely ought not be played. But who can completely purge selfishness, straighten out their emotions, play rituals rightly, always be humanly attentive, or afford a proper wardrobe? We can always make progress; the Confucians say this potential for progress lies even in "small people." But almost inevitably, failure blunts selfhood.

Confucians thus have a deep sensibility of tragedy. Partly this is because sincerity is so hard to attain, and even then seems to be a vagrant and ephemeral trait. This is only part of the reason for the Confucian tragic view, however.

The other part is that many of the rituals we play are corrupt and bad. Many of the traditional Confucian household rituals have such unevenness of power that women simply cannot be respected sincerely, the poor cannot be related to by the rich with sincerity, and mothers-in-law cannot run the families of their daughters-in-law with true sincerity. Those rituals need to be changed. In our own time, think of all the rituals that carry on racism, or worsen a dysfunctional family, or sabotage a social institution, or promote war, or desecrate an environment, or keep certain people in oppressive poverty. In so many places there is an obvious need to change the rituals we have. Confucius and Xunzi were right that, without appropriate rituals, children cannot be reared, family life is impossible, and the body politic is a chaos of the strong against the weak. So Confucius said we need to recover the rituals of the sage emperors of antiquity that made high civilization possible in the first place. But once we have some rituals, this does not guarantee that they are the right rituals. The right rituals are those that can be played with sincerity. Sincerity is the touchstone for judging rituals. We need to remember that sincerity requires learned appreciation of the Ten Thousand Things, particularly other people, and the cultivation of one's own sagehood of transparent appropriate behavior in the environment.

The need to change our rituals for the sake of sincere deference for all involved is at the heart of Confucian morals. To be sure, Confucian ethics includes learning some moral virtues in order to be sincere. The recent emphasis by Roger Ames on "role ethics" rather than internal virtues appreciates the pervasiveness of rituals in the Confucian understanding of the self and others. But I believe that even more important than these well-recognized themes of Confucian morals is the imperative to engage in active ritual analysis and the correction of bad rituals. Better than most cultures, Confucianism is sensitive to ritual and can point out how our lives operate by rituals that need to be understood as such. Whereas many cultures think social relations, including power relations and class distinctions are "natural," we should understand them as being ritualized all the way through, although of course not reduced to rituals alone as some "social constructivists" are likely to say. So we can learn from Confucianism to put great emphasis on analyzing and reconceiving our global societies in terms of their ritual structures, and judiciously criticizing them from the standpoint of their justice. For this, Confucians need to lighten up on their attention to the past, intent on recovering a great history after a century of suppression. Instead we need to look outward and to the future to facilitate an appreciation of our institutionalized rituals with an eye to changing them.

But changing rituals is difficult. We late moderns hope that changing laws will do it. But the experience in America of changing the civil rights laws shows that this has helped the African American middle class but has done little for the underclass, who are still in bondage to rituals of self-hate, economic self-destructiveness, substance addiction, and dysfunctional civic life. It is those deeper rituals that need to be changed. Confucius thought in his own time that presenting the rituals of the sage kings could help the problem; most scholars today believe he just made them up, his protestations of merely passing on traditions notwithstanding. Through much of Chinese history, it was believed that emulation of a wise emperor, or a good grandfather, could develop improved rituals. Sometimes it seems that the most helpful models to emulate are athletes. Can we not do better? The great Confucian contribution for our time needs to be the invention and deployment of rituals that make for peace, freedom, resolution of conflict between genuinely contradictory interests, and human flourishing. Strange, this sounds like John Dewey, does it not?

Even when we have to play what rituals we must, our play should be oriented to changing the rituals themselves. Yet so often we seem to be forced to reinforce the bad elements. Perhaps most tragic is the fact that we do not now have the rituals that allow us and our nations to interact peacefully and resolve disputes without war, injustice, economic suffering, or pitting the strong against the weak. One of the great advantages of many rituals is that they allow people who have directly conflicting interests and who hate one another to cooperate in the ritual dance so as to get something done, for instance, run an economy or a household. You don't have to like your ritual partners in order to play the ritual that accomplishes something. Our world, like Confucius's, simply lacks the well-practiced rituals that allow for the settling of large economic, political, and military disputes.

Pragmatic Confucian phenomenology of Peirce's sort is not a descriptive examination of consciousness but rather an analytical classification of the kinds of things that need to be harmonized for high civilization. The value of those classes is that they point out some of the tasks of ritual formation, as well as the difficulties of harmonizing what we simply cannot imagine how to fit together. Nevertheless, some things can be fixed. The Confucian approach to tragedy, like the pragmatist, is to feel it in the heart as sincerely as possible, lament what has happened, and then get on and try to do better next time. Pragmatic Confucians do not expect victory, only the opportunity to do the best we can on our watch, educated to appreciate both the vast and deep values as well as the pervasive injustices in our environment. Philosophy is not just for description but for learning to appreciate and renovate.

Chapter Eleven

Individuation and Ritual

My aim in this chapter is to complement a current approach to Confucianism in two ways. First, there has recently been an emphasis on personal "character" in Confucianism. A character is something that can be attributed to a person the way a property can be attributed to a substance. The underlying background metaphors of substance allow many fruitful connections with Western discussions of ethics, now often phrased in the language of virtue ethics. There is a contrary pull in Confucianism, however, that treats individuals as defined in significant ways by their participation in networks of rituals. In an important sense, for Confucius and most in his tradition, no one "has" a character as such but rather "is" an identity shared with others that includes complex ritual play. The point about ritual is not in opposition to the study of character, but is a balancing complement.

Second, many contemporary philosophers trace their Confucian lineage mainly through Mencius, to the neglect of Xunzi, the great theorist of ritual. This is an orthodox line that runs explicitly through both Zhu Xi and Wang Yang-ming. But Xunzi is receiving renewed attention these days, and I represent part of that emphasis. Again, this is to complement and enrich our appreciation of the complex Confucian heritage.

In this vein I shall develop in this chapter some contemporary Confucian philosophical comments on ritual and individualism. I have developed a contemporary theory of ritual in other writings that will be summarized briefly here.

The general polemical context for these reflections is the old commonplace that Confucian societies are organized around group identity, whereas other societies, particularly Western modern meritocracies, are organized around individualist behavior. This context has many facets, only a few of which will be addressed here. The more particular polemical context is a reaction to *Ritual and Its Consequences: An Essay on the Limits of Sincerity*, by Adam B. Seligman, Robert P. Weller, Michael J. Puett, and Bennett Simon.

This chapter (1) summarizes my (contemporary) theory of ritual drawn from Xunzi and pragmatic semiotics, noting that much of that theory has been introduced in earlier chapters here. It then (2) develops certain points about how people individualize rituals and through that individuate themselves, a point alluded to in the previous chapter. Part of the process of individuation is to come to appreciate the fragility, vulnerability, and perhaps plain falsity and injustice of the rituals with which one is involved. Sincerity (*cheng*) is not to be understood in contrast with ritual, despite the tendency to do so in Fingarette's classic *Confucius: The Secular as Sacred* as well as in Seligman and coauthors. Rather, sincerity and ritual should be construed as culturally and dialectically involved in their mutual definition. Then (3) I shall argue that rituals played by individuated persons provide an extraordinary approach to addressing the Other as Other, something problematic for Western approaches that find it hard to treat the Other as not reduced to what can be experienced by the subject. In ritual playing, the Other is not a function of the subject's experience but is simply another player. Of course, (4) we need the right rituals, or at least adequate ones, and properly individuated players for this deep respect for Others to find embodiment and practice.

RITUAL AND XUNZI

The basic Confucian themes about ritual are most efficiently developed through some of the categories of Xunzi, although he was not the first Confucian to address ritual nor the last.[1] Xunzi argued that the biological and psychological natures that human beings receive (from heaven or nature) as their natural endowment are radically underdetermined.[2] We have capacities for many emotions, thoughts, and will concerning self-governance, as well as for bodily actions.

> Love and hate, delight and anger, sorrow and joy, are stored within—these are described as "the emotions given us by nature." The eye, ear, nose, mouth, and body each have the capacity to provide sense contact, but their capacities are not interchangeable—these are termed "the faculties given us by nature." The heart/mind that dwells within the central cavity is used to control the five faculties—it is called "the lord provided by nature."[3]

But there is no natural endowment for fitting the emotions to their appropriate objects, or for thinking coherently in communication with others, or for disciplining ourselves to do the right things. So Xunzi said that ritual was needed to bring all these things together. By ritual he meant any meaning-bearing learned or learnable behavior that helps accomplish some purpose, from cultural styles of standing and walking, signals for showing respect in eye contact, the use of language, to rituals in the sense of more commonly recognized ceremonies. Without such rituals heaven and earth (or one's natural inheritance) cannot give rise to the human. The human requires rituals to bring the natural endowment to the human level, which is why Confucians take such pride in the trinity of Heaven, Earth, and the Human.[4] A contemporary way of recognizing this point is to note that what distinguishes human beings from the other "high" animals is the human's advanced capacity for semiotic behavior, where the use of signs allows for complex patterns of communication and interaction. The Western approaches to semiotics have focused mainly on words and language as the paradigm ritual behavior. The Confucians generally have taken a broader view in which learning how to stand and bow, what to wear so as to be respectful, and the steady rehearsal through ceremonies of the bonds of human relationships are as important sometimes as speaking correctly. If Western semioticians from early on had construed language use to be among a much wider range of ritual behaviors, there would have been nothing unexpected or new in Searle's discovery of the "performative."[5]

Most but not all rituals involve several people interacting in a ritual pattern like in a dance. Most rituals contain sub-rituals and themselves are part of larger ritual structures. Different rituals sometimes intersect in certain episodes, bringing together the players of the separate rituals who otherwise would not interact. Confucians have found family rituals most instructive, a complex interweaving of husband-wife rituals; parent-children rituals; brother-sister rituals; older–younger sibling rituals; nuclear family–grandparents; aunts and uncles, cousins, and distant relatives' rituals. The early formation of Confucian rituals was in the context of rural life, a context that has changed many times in Chinese history and that is very different from modern urban life. Family rituals are implicated in rituals of friendship, neighborliness in one's town or apartment building, employment in various kinds of economic activities, governance at the local and most distant level, and so forth. Ritual patterns are not steady, especially when the rich implications of rituals with other rituals in changing circumstances are taken into account.

One of the most important elements of ritual that needs to be added to customary Western theories is that rituals allow for the cooperation of people whose purposes and interests might be very much opposed and in competition. Playing a ritual together accomplishes some social or personal purpose, whether it is greeting other people, putting the children to bed at night, or getting along with the neighbors. The things, behaviors, creativity, and appreciations that constitute high civilization are possible only when there are rituals, the playing of which performs the civilization. With rituals of greeting, people who hate each other can still get along for a bit, though without greeting rituals they would have resorted to violence immediately. In a competitive world where great social stakes ride on people's behavior, ritual makes possible the accomplishment of enormously important activities that otherwise would not take place because people's interests are in competition. You don't have to like your fellow workers, but if your work is properly ritualized, you can work together and get it done. The rituals of diplomacy are a hedge against war and often the alternative to war is better rituals of competition. Patterns of dancing together for the sake of the dance allow the dance to take place, even when the dancers hate one another.

Rituals are patterns of meaningful behavior, most often involving more than one person and more than one role. One common approach to ritual analysis is to focus on the pattern of roles itself and how that pattern constitutes or allows for a certain kind of social reality or function. Certainly Western cultures would benefit from being more alert to the ritual patterns that make up daily life than they customarily are, compared with Confucian cultures. Only recently have Western cultures become aware of the ritual patterns of social maladies such as racism, discrimination against ethnic minorities, diminished social expressions for women, and bigotry against gays, lesbians, and other sexual minorities. The usual Western reaction to such social maladies, when recognized, is to try to find a villain. Michel Foucault—for instance, in *The Order of Things*—and his followers have done enormous service in pointing out how so much of what is perceived to be obvious and commonsense truth is a function of the structures of special discourses. "Discourses" are a thin and anemic slice of ritual behavior, abstracted out from the richer social reality; analysis of "discourses" seems an easy way in to the issues for people whose only paradigm of ritual is language. If Foucault were to be read as analyzing ritual rather than discourse, his contribution would open up many more lines of important inquiry. Foucault shares the Western disposition to find a villain for social maladies, and for him it is the struggle for the power to control the discourses, which in turn he says reflects the parochial interests of those who seek that power. For Foucault, like Marx before him, the villain is not individuals as such but social class in a dynamically structured social situation. Surely he is right that there are important instances in which particular social interests with power determine discourses and thereby determine what roles people have to play and what happens when those discourses are played out in society. Nevertheless, rituals, including their manifestation in discourses, have an inertial power simply because they are the social habits by virtue of which life goes on. Rituals can remain in force long after everyone's interests have changed and no one benefits from them. As the building blocks of social life, even when they are bad, rituals have staying power until they are changed: changing rituals puts the social fabric at risk. In some instances, rituals have an inertial staying power stronger than the powers behind the interests of any of the current stakeholders in the society. The Confucian approach to rituals, I believe, has far greater potential than Foucault's for discerning the natural joints and places for change in the social fabric.

INDIVIDUATION

Nevertheless, the Confucian approach to ritual has focused less on analyzing the patterns of ritual behavior than on how individuals come to play the rituals. Babies learn ritual behavior by imitating parents and older siblings. But the ritual patterns are vague roles, not specific or completely determined. Like in a dance, the ritual roles are broad steps of interaction, and they need to be played in individual ways. A small child learns to walk, for instance, by stumbling forward; anything counts as walking so long as there is forward motion on two feet. Slowly the child learns to control the lurches and develop smoother ways of walking, indeed ways adapted to the child's own body type. Cultural elements also help to individuate the walking: Chinese children learn to walk so as to put the toe and heel down almost simultaneously, whereas Western European and Anglo-American children learn the walking style of first heel, then toe. To exaggerate the cultural differences, the Chinese way is almost like shuffling, the Western way almost like a goose step. Before long, children develop individuated ways of walking so that they can be recognized by their gait alone; this individuation continues to deepen throughout life.

Walking can be done alone, although it is learned through imitation, trial, and error. Dancing, however, usually involves partners, and here the individuation is more complicated because a person learns to dance differently with different partners. What begins by struggling to get one's feet and hands in the right place at the right time relative to others becomes a more personal and individuated style of dancing. The ritual outline of the steps is the same early and late, but the dancing becomes individuated to each person's style, and that relative to the styles of the others.

The rituals most frequently in focus for the two and a half millennia of Confucian tradition are those associated with family life.[6] As I mentioned earlier, these rituals are complex and overlapping, defining behavioral roles among different family positions and different functions such as economic, educational, life-care, and political. Among the most important Confucian rituals are those of boys toward their fathers, collectively constituting filial piety. At an early age, these are taught as rather abstract duties and symbolic gestures and postures of respect. But even early on, filial piety has to be individuated to this boy having to deal with his particular father. Boys slowly learn that other children's fathers are different from their own and that they are rightfully treated differently. Even more slowly, boys learn that they themselves are different from their friends and thus have different capacities for relating to their fathers. Moreover, the content of filial piety changes with stages in life. For small children, very much of filial piety is obedience to parental dictate and learning to discern when the father or mother is pleased or displeased; it also involves learning to appreciate and bask in the father's and mother's love. Beginning with adolescence and moving through many stages, filial piety comes more and more to be taking on the skills, work, knowledge, adult social roles, and virtues of the father (and mother). In traditional Confucian households it is important for a young man to become a father so as to learn how his father did it and to prove that his father has taught him how. Later in the filial relationship, the son comes more to take over from and to take care of the father (and mother and others of the older generation). The popular image of filial piety is the grown son taking care of aging parents who have become dependent. In our time, the male gender orientation of filial piety of course is broadened to include women, and families of filial care are rarely a single household.

The point to be stressed here is that an individual comes to be his or her own individuated self through individuating the important rituals of life, according to the Confucian sensibility. A boy comes to be more and more himself as he individuates his ritual, that is, semiotically meaningful, relations with his father (and his mother, siblings, aunts, uncles, cousins, friends, classmates, fellow workers, neighbors, etc.). This individuation is always a dual process. On the one hand, it involves orienting oneself to whom the others are in the ritual, one's father, for instance. The complication here is that the other is always changing in reference to oneself, as the father individuates himself as father: the other is a moving target. On the other hand, it involves the invention of the specificities of one's own self in the ritual relation. Westerners often think of this as "discovering" oneself, as if one's character were already made up waiting to be discovered. Indeed, Westerners often suspect that the ritual forms impose strictures and limitations on one's true self that needs to rebel against them in order to find oneself. Rebellion is an important part of ritual behavior, but not at this point. Rather, Confucians see the rituals as providing the form for the having of a self if the individual can only individuate specific ways of playing the ritual.

So individuals have to develop and transform themselves into people capable of playing the family rituals well. The rituals themselves enable friendships, work relations, community roles, and the rest. Looked at from the standpoint of the individuals, this is the problem of developing character where character is defined as competence at playing the important ritual roles of life, as Roger Ames has articulated. Whereas Westerners are likely to look upon the development of such character as a function of developing individual virtue, Confucians look upon it rather as defining character in relation to others as mediated by the various ritual patterns with roles for the individual. In a very important sense, one can never develop one's character as if it were one's own property. Rather, it is developed in relation to other individuals developing their characters as connected by the dense fabric of ritual roles.

Individuation in role-playing is not merely a matter of getting specific within the general outline of a ritual role. All experience in the Confucian view is shot through with *value*, and there are two kinds of norms in particular that are important for individuation in ritual behavior, sincerity and probity.

Sincerity (*cheng*) can be understood as the state of having all the layers of one's inner intentions, feelings, and outer actions so aligned with one another that one's heart is transparent in one's actions. And vice versa: one's actions follow without inhibition or deviance from one's heart. For the Confucians, this kind of sincerity, which is so important for playing ritual roles rightly, is vastly more difficult to achieve than sincerity as so often intended in the West. Westerners sometimes think that one can become sincere simply by ceasing to dissemble or by developing the courage to speak and act out of one's inner convictions and passions.[7] Of course, these things are involved in the Confucian ideal, but many other things are involved as well. For instance, one cannot be sincere in one's responses to things unless one has learned to perceive them properly and then to understand what one has perceived. And one cannot act out of the responses of one's heart unless one has learned to organize oneself so as to be able to accomplish what one intends, a rare virtue. Ritual behavior has many levels or layers moving from the heart to the external actions. The Confucians love to point out that how one dresses is crucial for revealing one's heart in respect to the others with whom one plays important rituals! One's clothing and demeanor are part of actions with reference to other people, not mere expressions of personal idiosyncrasy. Deep education is required for this complicated sincerity, although Confucians admit that some people take to this education more easily than others.

The "big problem" for sincerity on which Confucians have pondered since the beginning is selfishness. Selfishness takes many forms, distorting one's perceptions, perverting intentions to play the roles well, and distorting our actions even when based on good intentions. In the Confucian project of properly individuated ritual behavior, the cultivation of sincerity thus has two kinds of drives. One is the positive drive to become competent at making the passage from heart to outer action continuous and transparent. The other is the negative therapeutic drive to discover and eliminate the usually hidden roots and branches of selfishness.

The other kind of norm for individuation in ritual roles is probity, by which I mean a capacity to discern and act on the values expressed in one's situation, especially in the people and the social structures. The Neo-Confucians, as I argued in chapter 1, elaborated the technical conception of principle (*li*) to indicate how being a thing in the natural (and social) world is to have value, and how that value is also a function of the environing things, and of the environment itself. In *Sagehood: The Contemporary Significance of Neo-Confucian Philosophy*, Stephen C. Angle has written about how that might be understood in contemporary terms and develops an understanding of *li* as "coherence." ("Principle," the received translation of *li*, does not say much of anything.) I prefer "harmony" to "coherence," although there is another Chinese word, *he*, that is usually translated harmony. Whatever the metaphysics, the Confucians have believed since the beginning that value is a characteristic of things of the cosmos and that human society is to be conceived as constituting elements within nature. Moreover, value is not taken to be a property resident in things, like predicates in substances, but rather is a function of things as they are related to other things in their environment. The beauty of the eagle is in winging down the mountainside. The virtue of the warrior includes his place in the battle line. The value of the father is in his roles in the family (and elsewhere). Things are valuable in context.

The other side of the Confucian approach to value is that human beings are hardwired to appreciate value when it is encountered, although they have to learn how to activate that appreciation. The tradition of Mencius has emphasized the importance of preventing this natural appreciation of value from maturing and unfolding. The tradition of Xunzi has emphasized the importance of positive learning, especially through learning to play rituals, to find out what is valuable when it is nonobvious. Both sides emphasize the importance of learning and erudition in order to discover what the world is like. The ideal of the sage is to become adept in seeing and responding to the values of things in appropriate ways. So often this means discovering deeper grounds for harmony or coherence than appear among the array of warring factions.[8] The Confucian tradition has emphasized the continuity of value (*li*) in things with its presence in structuring the inner heart and its responses. Probity is the virtue of connecting these so that actions can be moral.

Individuation in probity thus raises the question of right action. Ritual roles are defined in ways that make actions possible and give them form. But what happens if one's probity reveals that a certain ritual behavior stands in the way of moral action? Confucians have been preoccupied with the problem of what happens when one's father, or the emperor, demands obedience in a wrong cause.[9] What one should do, of course, is to "remonstrate" with the authority. Remonstration is a clear part of filial piety and civil obedience. But when should one disobey if one's remonstrations are dismissed? Go into exile? If your father commits a crime, should you turn him in to the authorities (a question asked also by Plato in the *Euthyphro*)? Confucius was hesitant. If the emperor is incompetent or wicked, should you rebel (Mencius said, Yes).

Individuation in ritual behavior is never just playing the roles in a style suited to oneself but includes also playing the roles with probity. Therefore, the ritual behavior is enormously complicated by having to navigate the individuation with the moral judgments to which one's probity gives rise. The ritual pattern by itself does not answer the questions of how to individuate the rituals with probity.

Sincerity and probity together are two crucial ingredients in becoming a true person. They would have little or no content if the person were not in a nexus of ritual role-playing positions. The rituals provide the environment in which the person can become a true individual in the sense of being individuated in interpersonal relations. Because of the need for sincerity, ritual should never be mere role-playing, as if one's heart were not in it. In fact, when one plays rituals insincerely, that is a deep vice, according to Confucians. The common criticism of Confucianism as mere formalism, indeed a formalism that rigidifies hierarchical authority relations, is first to be made by Confucians themselves. One of the deep predicaments of the human condition, according to the Confucians who appreciate the social functions of rituals, is that it opens itself to insincerity and with that the loss of the true self. In this respect, Confucian culture, to the extent it is true to its philosophic roots, is individualistic, not communalistic. Of course, because of the communal character of so many of the rituals that make possible high civilization, people are never thought of outside of social relations and so often it is the ritual structure of the fabric of relations that needs moral attention. But the human meaning of ritual playing is the development of individual character, which is the individual's responsibility. The probity side of this individual commitment to playing the rituals well places extraordinary demands on individuals to become competent and unselfish at learning what is at stake and to play the rituals so as to be observant of the norms and values at hand.

This leads to a powerful sense of the tragic and to an underlying vexation at the ambiguities and compromises of life. The Confucian claim that ritual constitutes the fabric of individual life with others commonly is thought to be personally and socially painful because the rituals restrict freedom. Instead of being obliged to play ritual roles, sometimes individuals want to shuck them all and be free. What would they do if they were free? They would go "on the road" and wander like Jack Kerouac's hippies. The Confucian model for this is self-imposed exile and it stands as a complement, not a corrective, to the model of ritual role-playing. This popular view of ritual as constraining the free spirit does not pick up on the most important sense of tension and disease in Confucian culture, namely, the ambiguities and tragedies of not being able to individuate roles with coherence in accord with probity. Probity is both an extraordinary achievement and a deep burden.

The Confucian virtue of humaneness (*ren*) is far more complex than sincerity and probity, but it involves them both in high measure. Rituals by themselves can be played by people without humaneness. But this is a grievous fault that prevents robust individuating of the ritual roles. And this in turn prevents the development of the individual, which is what usually motivates insincere ritual play in the first place. Two more topics need to be explored to bring home this point, the role of the Other and the importance of having good rituals—not any old rituals will do.

OTHERNESS

I said earlier that rituals allow individuals to cooperate in whatever work the ritual accomplishes while having opposing, competitive, or even contradictory interests. One of the ways to tell a good ritual is by determining whether in fact it allows for conjoint actions among people with radically different interests, a point to which we shall return later. Now, however, the element of ritual to notice is that understanding the human situation in ritual terms allows for understanding Others in ways that vex some Western modes of thought.

The problem of the Other in European philosophy comes about in this way. European philosophy (and here I mean to exclude the American philosophy of pragmatism) has seen the human epistemological situation to be that of interdefined subjectivity and objectivity. Experience is the activity or property of human subjects who look out onto a world. The things of the world are conceived to be objects within subjective experience; a whole host of problems that have preoccupied modern European philosophy, both continental and analytic, follow from this, which have to do with how we, from our subjective perspective, can know things as they are in themselves. Can we know them only as they appear to us?

The powerful Kantian stream goes so far as to define objectivity in terms of the conformity of outer things to the forms of the human mind, to our modes of receptivity, and categories and synthesizing activities for organizing experience. An "object" is what conforms to our experience and whatever in the object does not enter experience on our subjective terms is somehow unreal, or unknowable at least. The scientific tradition has elaborated this Kantian point, which has had many variations, to say that its objectivity consists in its reduction of claims about the world to claims about what the world amounts to when expressed in the various sciences' categories, theories, instruments, and research agendas.

Needless to say, something is wrong with this. Other people are not only what they are in our subjective experience. They have an interiority and external reality of their own. They have a value and dignity of their own that might not be registered at all in the ways we experience them. Nonhuman nature is the same way, not merely a construct of our subjective experience. Experience itself bluntly shows this to be the case. We experience people as not being reducible to our experience of them. They have a resistance to being defined in our experience; they exude a sense of the More. Emmanuel Levinas and others have sharpened this point into a major philosophic project.[10] But even the most detailed phenomenological description of other persons and their Otherness is still only a description of our experience. It is of the Others as part of us.

Frustrating as this is to mere philosophers caught in the subjective/objective orientation to the world (usually blamed on Descartes), this orientation is culturally disastrous in its treatment of people. People are turned into mere objects in the experience of the people with power and are brutalized often by being treated as nothing more than what serves the interests of the powerful. Medicine has objectified patients. Colonized peoples have been reduced to the judgments made about them and their cultures by the colonizers. Enemies are reduced to people who should be eliminated because they oppose the interests of the powerful. The people lacking power do the same thing to those who have the power. No remedy for this exists so long as we understand others to have no reality except in our experience. "Our experience" can be defined as transcendentally as one might please, as in Husserl's phenomenology, but the point still holds: things are reduced to the actual or possible experience of them.

Confucians recognize something of the structure of the subjective/objective distinction, the self and world. This often is expressed in terms of the polar continuum between the inner heart and the Ten Thousand Things to which individuals relate. Although Confucians insist on continuity from the inner heart to external actions on real things, a continuity that should be sincere and activated with probity, they do not see the situation as defined by the subjective/objective contrast.[11] Rather, they see it as constituted by a natural standpoint within which individuals interact, most often in ritualized, meaningful, roles. An individual understands herself or himself to be one among many individuals in the dance of a ritual. The other individuals are also players in that ritual pattern. I see the Others to be players in the ritual just like myself. Moreover, I see myself to be a player in the ritual just like the Others. The fundamental reality of the ritual, or nexus of rituals, makes players of us all. Certainly, each player needs to individuate the playing, and individuation has all the dimensions already mentioned and more. But I see my individuating to be part and parcel of the ritual reality, just like the individuations being cultivated by the others.

To be sure, my own playing of a ritual has a subjective perspective as I try to play the roles well, individuating my performance, cultivating sincerity, struggling with probity and its consequences. But that subjective perspective is not the only or even the primary frame within which I understand and behave. Rather, the ritual itself is the frame within which I understand my own subjective struggles. And it is also the frame within which I am oriented to the Others who, of course, are understood to have their own subjective struggles. In the ritual play, we are all Others to one another, and this is the way each of us understands our own subjective issues of individuating the rituals well.

This is the truth in the common observation that people in Confucian societies identify with the group before they do with their own individual concerns. However, this contrast is too superficial. It is not that Confucians identify with the "group" first, but rather with the rituals that include the Others as well as oneself and within which everyone works out individuating personal identities. Exerting oneself to play the ritualized fabric of life well is just as much an assertion of self as it is an assertion of the group, because the very self-constitution of the self has to do with becoming humane in the very particularized contexts of one's array of rituals. The group/individual contrast reflects the Western assumption that individuals are primary and collectively make up groups. The Confucian affirmation is that individuals are already constituted by the rituals connecting them and that the questions of life have to do with learning to play those rituals well with sincerity and probity and to work through their ambiguities and tensions.

One benefit of the Confucian ritual approach is that all the players enter the ritual activities with their whole being. They are Others to one another in their mutual play, but they are not reduced to the roles they play in the rituals. To the contrary, precisely as players they are individuals individuating themselves in the roles, coping with the integration of many rituals, and suffering through the ambiguities and tragedies that come from living with some degree or other of probity and sincerity in their ritual matrix. Of course, a given ritualized interaction might be merely instrumental and superficial; but the Confucian ideal is to treat Others within our ritual engagements as themselves players individuating themselves in all the ways involved with their own "subjectivity," as Western thought would have it. The common observation that Confucian businessmen begin a meeting by drinking tea together and talking about their families before they "get down to business" illustrates the point. (Someday the anecdotes will include business women, but perhaps not for a generation!) Paradoxical as it might seem from Western assumptions, Confucian ritual practice makes it part of the ritual to treat others not as mere *role*-players in the ritual but as *players* who come to the ritual roles as human subjects individuating themselves through a stretch of life with many ritual interactions.

The result of this is a kind of profound deference to the Other that quasi-automatically colors Confucian ritual behavior. By treating Others as players, one does not treat them as reduced to the roles in the rituals that are part of one's life. To be sure, there are always difficulties in getting to know other people—a conversation about families over tea is sufficient only in a homogeneous society. Also, often there are pressures just to "get down to business," and these pressures occur among Confucians as much as busy Westerners. But the orientating frame of Confucian ritual playing is filled with respect and deference for what the Other might be as a player in the other's matrix of ritual connections.

RITUAL ABUSE

This idealized picture of the Confucian ritual approach to individuals and their treatment as Others needs a reality check. Confucian rituals have been very abusive in some situations, especially regarding women (as we will discuss in chapter 15). We have already seen some reasons for this. The players in the rituals might be relatively un-individuated stumbling novices, obsessed with the ritual roles rather than the players because they have not mastered the roles themselves. Or the players might not be very sincere and therefore cannot bring themselves into their roles with much transparency, let alone look for that in the other players. Or the players might be lacking in probity, looking at the roles only habitually or instrumentally, not being critical, not trained to look for what is good and bad in the overall context of the ritual behaviors. But an even more important factor in the abuse of Confucian ritual culture is bad rituals.

That a rich matrix of rituals within which to live makes high civilization possible is an important observation. But that same matrix might contain ritual structures that habituate limitations to civilization or encode evil and oppression. That the rituals of Confucian economic life place the power and principal roles in the hands of men to the relative exclusion of women is a bad thing. We are finding out now that rituals that discriminate between people on the grounds of gender distinctions are very often bad: they might enable economic activity but do so unfairly when they define participation on grounds of gender rather than, say, productivity, skill, and other criteria relevant to business. In the American context, the rituals that habituate racism are similar: distinctions according to race are rarely genuinely important to encode in rituals involving neighborly living, economic and political activity, friendship and domesticity. The same thing is true for rituals that encode differences in sexual orientation for the various ritualized structures of society.

An extension of probity in Confucian ritual culture is the critique and amendment of the rituals at hand. In his day, Confucius was a radical critic of his culture, arguing on the one hand that it lacked many of the rituals necessary for high civilization, having descended into violent barbarism, and on the other that some of the rituals that in fact were in place were counterproductive, rewarding the unworthy. For our time, a great work for Confucian moral philosophy is, first, to point out where our society is ritualized; second, to analyze how the rituals work, what they enable, what they prevent, and how just they are; and, third, to develop new rituals in place of the old.

Coming to understand that the rituals of many cultures are unfair to women, to outsiders of different races and ethnic communities, and to sexual minorities, leads to the important task of developing new rituals in these regards. But the situation is more complicated than this. Social and economic conditions are shifting dramatically, and the rituals that fostered justice, communication, and respect for the Other in the olden days often are not relevant in the new circumstances. New rituals are needed and they need to be seen as transitional, always in modification as changes continue. How can you share tea and stories of families through internet transactions, especially when they are automated? A new vision is needed of engaging players in rituals as themselves individuals individuating themselves with hoped-for sincerity and probity as well as skill. Perhaps there is some merit in complaining about the Internet and what it does to face-to-face communication between players of the important rituals. But the virtue of complaining seems to be that one feels better afterward, not that it does much direct good. Rather, the merit lies in investigating new ritual possibilities that do for our changing world what the Confucians did in their best of times.

Perhaps the most immediate challenge for Confucian moral thinking today is to understand how violence might be mitigated by harmonizing rituals. Rituals allow people who otherwise are in serious conflict to work together in the ritual pattern. Just as greeting rituals are needed to make possible peaceful encounters, so diplomatic rituals are needed to enable economic and cultural conflicts to be negotiated peacefully. Of course, there are limits to what rituals can do in this regard: all parties need to be persuaded that more is to be gained by playing the rituals together than by going to war. Part of this persuasion is the exhibition of the possibility of greater harmony behind the conflict. But then, the heart of Confucian moral theory is the cultivation of the means to discern the harmonies in the heart, in things, in situations of conflict among things, and in the background in which all things, including oneself and one's culture, have value.

Chapter Twelve

Authority in Social Institutions, Accountability, and Credibility

I think of myself as both a Christian and a Confucian and lay claim to both heritages. As an individual, however, I am not a representative of either civilization. I am not a Christian in general, but a particular kind of Christian—liberal, Protestant, philosophical, and mystical. Nor am I a Confucian in general, but a particular kind of Confucian, leaning on Zunxi more than Mengzi, on Wang Yang-ming more than Zhu Xi, and most importantly, an Anglo-American Boston Confucian rather than a Chinese, Korean, or Japanese one. For me, Confucianism of a certain sort is a viable way of life in Western civilization.

This complicated sense of personal identity calls attention to the great generality in the project of elucidating the engagement of Confucian and Christian civilizations. Confucianism is by no means the only way of life in the history of China, taking into account the Daoist, Mohist, and Legalist schools, the millennium of powerful influence from Buddhism, and the later Western influences, particularly Marxism. But probably it is true that all those other schools, especially the ones originally from outside China, have been Confucianized to a large degree, and that contemporary Confucianism has internalized them to some degree. Therefore, it is appropriate to speak of China generally as having a Confucian civilization.

The case with the West is a bit more complicated because from the ancient period it involved an interesting symbiotic and yet competitive relation between Semitic religious roots and Greek philosophical roots. Christianity from the first through the fifteenth centuries combined them but then, with the Protestant Reformation, set them in opposition to one another. Judaism adopted many elements of Greek philosophy but never with the enthusiasm or thoroughness of Christianity, and therefore it can be said to be a Semitic religion with Greek influences. Islam adopted a much larger share of Greek thought than Judaism but never institutionalized the critical skepticism of Greek philosophy to the degree that Christianity did from the earliest days. Nevertheless, in a general sense Western civilization can be called a Christian civilization because of the dominance of Christianity over both Judaism and Islam in Europe and the Americas. Islam, located from Morocco to Malaysia, is not to be regarded as just part of Western civilization, but it defines its own sphere in which it is dominant in various places over Christianity, Judaism, Hinduism, Buddhism, and Confucianism.

A greater complication is that Christianity and Confucianism are world religions, with cultural representations in several civilizations. It is estimated that 130 million Chinese today are Christians, making it one of the largest Christian countries in the world, even though that is a small percentage of the overall population of China. Do those Chinese Christians represent Christian civilization, or rather Christian religion within an overall Confucian civilization? Similarly, with Confucianism in the United States, some of whose members, such as myself, are ethnic Anglo-Americans: Do we represent Confucian civilization in Boston or rather a Confucian cultural influence on the modes of life in the West as embodied in Boston?

SINCERITY IN AUTHORITY

Noting these qualifications about the complexity of distinguishing and relating Confucian and Christian civilizations, however, I would like to address the question of the role of sincerity in the credibility of those in authority in social institutions, a question of great importance in all civilizations but to be discussed here in terms of Confucianism and Christianity. Both Confucianism and Christianity have placed great value on sincerity, on making the heart pure and transparent, albeit with different ways of contextualizing sincerity. For both, only sincere people are credible, and people earn credibility when they prove they are sincere in their promises. Also, both civilizations at times if not always have linked sincerity with leadership and with the exercise of authority and responsibility. The Confucian approach is based on the family model of parental authority, which Tu Wei-ming aptly names a "fiduciary community."[1] The Christian approach is much more diverse, historically, and has adopted models of authority from many sources—from the Roman family model (much like the Confucian), from the ruler as representative of God (or Heaven, in its Confucian parallel), and from democratic models that sometimes invoke the blessings of deity on the procedural bodies of democracies.[2]

What happens, however, when the constituencies of the authorities, the social organizations within which they exercise authority, are diverse and impersonal, and have competing interests? In a small unit, such as a real family, rituals of courtesy might make it possible for the authority to explain and justify to all within the constituency why decisions are made that are favorable to some and harmful to others. In this case, those to whom harm is given can still believe in the sincerity and credibility of the authority even if they dislike the decisions. In larger units, such as a large community, a business, or even a nation, those to whom the authority's decisions cause harm find it difficult to believe in the sincerity and credibility of the authority because the authority is thought to be accountable for the good of all, including those to whom harm is given. In point of fact, the authority is accountable *for* making decisions for the good of the whole constituency, which might mean harming some, even when the best attention is paid to harmony. But the authority is accountable *to* the whole as well, which includes people for whom the authority is no longer credible. So my question is how Confucian and Christian civilizations have dealt with the problem of accountability without credibility.

The answers to this question depend on circumstances, of course. At the national level, for instance, both Confucian and Christian governments have at times had to resort to force to compel obedience from elements within their constituency who deny them credibility and legitimacy. At the same time, within Confucian governments has been a long tradition of remonstration against the authority, with those in opposition being willing to sacrifice something and then at a certain point withdrawing in retreat. Because of the very great importance of credibility, however, when pressures become too great, the Confucian authority collapses and the government turns either to chaos or to totalitarian, nonaccountable, and noncredible, rule.

Christian governments in Europe and America slowly evolved toward democracies that attempt, through various checks and balances, to build the redressing of harms from the government into the government itself. In democracies, credibility suddenly becomes relatively unimportant in principle. It can be assumed that authorities are biased or corrupt, but they are also accountable to a political process that corrects that. The issue of credibility reemerges with great force in democracies, however, when the political process itself loses credibility. In the United States at the present time a significant portion of the constituent groups believes that the government simply does not work and is not accountable in any way to them. In times such as these, credibility can be regained only when a charismatic leader emerges with conspicuous credibility. But charisma can be temporary and illusory. People want their government to be credible, and when it makes decisions that help some and harm others, that credibility is put in jeopardy again. Adolf Hitler brought great credibility to the German government after the weak Weimar Republic. But that credibility was temporary and had disastrous results. Barack Obama was elected to the presidency of the United States with extraordinarily high enthusiasm all over the world for his intelligence and open personality. He was made into a symbol of hope for people across the world, in part because he represented an American electorate that could rise above racism and selfishness. But he has been hampered by an economic situation no miracle could cure and by a resistant racism and selfishness that was cultivated and used by his political opponents so that he has lost credibility with a significant sector of the electorate.

Both Confucian and Christian civilizations have models of credibility for authorities in circumstance when they are not dominant, when they are in diaspora. During the first millennium of the common era, there were more Christians in Asia than in Europe, and they were nearly always in the minority in their social settings. In China today, as mentioned, Christians are numerous but still a tiny minority. Early Confucianism in Japan and Korea held a minority status, and also in China during much of the Dang dynasty. Confucian communities across the West grew during the twentieth century, beginning with Chinese in diaspora but coming to include non–East Asians. In conditions of minority status, lacking much political power, both Confucianism and Christianity depend very strongly on personal credibility. Personal credibility is a powerful form of opposition to hostile dominant cultures.

The crux of the question for both Confucian and Christian civilizations is how those in authority can act for the good of the whole of the institution that sustains their constituencies when their credibility depends on convincing individuals that they are working for the good of the individuals. Can leaders be trusted to serve the institution's best interests as a way of serving the whole constituency, for instance, all the people, when the best interests of the institution cause harm for part of the constituency? To do so, they must learn the art of sincerity.

In order to explore these points, the next two sections shall discuss models of communitarian versus individualistic harmony and the nature of perceived sincerity in leadership.

COMMUNITARIANISM VERSUS INDIVIDUALISM

Earlier we noted that scholars commonly say that Confucians (and other East Asians) think of themselves primarily in terms of the group that they are in, putting the interest of the group ahead of their personal interests, whereas Christians (and other Westerners) put their personal interests first and treat the interests of their groups as secondary. Obvious examples of this exist and do not need to be rehearsed. But counterexamples also exist. Moreover, pure examples of communitarian and individualistic priorities are regarded as pathological by both civilizations. Confucians could never accept a pure communitarian model because "What Heaven imparts to man is called human nature," calling for individual cultivation and the exercise of caution in the superior person, an individual.[3] The entire Confucian project begins with the self-cultivation of the sage, which is an individual and sometimes private affair, although its aim is transparency and discerning effectiveness in the community.[4] To be sure, the project of self-cultivation arises out of a familial and social context, which is the venue within which that self-cultivation needs to individuate itself. But Confucian self-cultivation is possible in contexts where familial and social conditions are very bad: that was precisely the historical context within which Confucius articulated his revolutionary ideas about how to be a good person in bad circumstances. So a person who put the interests of the group very far ahead of personal interests would be viewed by Confucians as both neglecting the primary art of self-cultivation and perhaps inadvertently supporting a very bad group whose interests are disastrous. For Confucians, an important primacy is given to making self-cultivation and the attainment of sincerity the basis on which one can trust oneself to serve the larger community.

Christians too from ancient times have been preoccupied with self-cultivation, which goes under the theological title of "sanctification." But sanctification in Christian thought is consequent to and dependent upon "justification," which usually means the individual identifying himself or herself with the Church or Christian community in which freedom from sin is to be found. What is most important in many forms of Christianity is belonging to the community within which salvation is found, and then within that community working on self-cultivation. Ironically, for Christianity the primary identification is with the Church community, although it is an individual decision, sometimes a serious existential decision, to join that community. In most practical contexts, Christians inherit their religious communities the way Confucians inherit their families, even though it is assumed the individuals affirm that inheritance at a stage in their development where it is also possible to disavow it. Max Weber argued that Protestant Christianity emphasized a kind of individualism that resonates with capitalism because of its stress on the individual concern for salvation; but then again he argued much the same thing about Confucianism in a different cultural context.

Under the effects of modernity, including both Enlightenment thinking and the development of a consumerist society, many Christians have found it difficult to be at home in their religious communities. Sometimes this is outright alienation, as in those who reject religious affiliation. More often it is the demotion of the specifically religious community from being the most important affiliation that defines one's ultimate existence to being one among many affiliations that contribute to ultimate identity and fulfillment. Modernity has been experienced differently in China, but no less decisively. The brief Western-inspired criticism of Confucianism, which was identified mainly with the overall culture of the late Qing dynasty, was followed by an increasingly Sinicized version of European Marxism that shook loose family identifications, represented self-cultivation as antisocial selfishness, and in the extremes of the Cultural Revolution attempted to reduce individuals to mere servants of the revolution with no significant identifications with affiliation groups such as families, professions, or distinctive locales. The recent resurgence of Confucian culture is repairing affiliations with groups that provide some social as opposed to strictly individual identity, or individual anonymity. The present growth of Christianity in China, ironically, can be viewed in part as the success of resurgent Confucianism that emphasizes the individuation of persons in concrete group affiliations. This is parallel in many ways to the emphasis in some parts of Western civilization on individual reconnection with families and groups of origin, including religious affiliations.

Therefore, we must be careful to not overstress the distinction between Confucian communitarianism and Christian individualism. True, from ancient times until now Confucianism has stressed that one learns humaneness (*ren*) within parental and sibling relationships, and one learns to concretize and express this in the family context. Similarly, Christianity has noted the frequent disarray and dysfunctionality of families and asserted instead that one learns humaneness within the life of the Christian community, a body supposedly animated by the harmonizing, healing, and stimulating Mind of Christ. "Taking on the Mind of Christ" is very like taking on the virtue of the ancestor.[5] But families have been in disarray in China in recent times, as they always have been, and Christian communities are in disarray in the West now as much as ever. So the model in both Confucian and Christian civilizations of group-belonging as the source and goal of individual identity does not now work perfectly, and the balance between individuals and communitarianism is rarely found: and, when it is, it is set differently in different circumstances.

The question of this chapter is not directly about communitarianism and individualism, although that is usually how it is construed. Rather, the question is about what happens to a social authority when the society contains competing constituencies and the authority necessarily has to harm some in order to help the whole; in this circumstance, the authority's decision can be interpreted by those harmed as helping the others rather than the whole. In contemporary society, East and West, those who are harmed do not think of themselves in this context as individuals. Rather, they think of themselves as within a harmed group. Farmers might think the government favors urban life. Unskilled workers might think the educational system helps only the middle and upper classes. Businessmen might think the government caters to pressures from skilled workers. An ethnic minority group such as the Mongolians or the Tibetans in China, or the African Americans or Latinos in the United States, might think the government harms it with policies that favor others; or the dominant Han Chinese or Anglo-Americans might think the government favors the minorities. Government authorities, of course, attempt to balance out in harmony the competing interests of different constituencies. Often these attempts are little more than responses to political pressures, although sometimes they are based on sound principles of balance. But even supposing that the governing authorities have found the balance of support and taxation that is most just for the whole, inevitably some groups will be harmed and others helped. Even John Rawls's principle that every political change should be aimed to help the least advantaged groups the most will result in resentment from those groups who believe they should be helped more, and who thus are harmed by the arrangement.[6]

In this circumstance, how can the credibility of the authority be maintained in the eyes of those who believe themselves to be harmed? In a small family, perhaps everyone can come to see how the authority has brought about the best balance for everyone, even those who seem to be harmed at the moment; a long-range view of future compensation can be taken. In a large country, however, or even a complex community, the reasoning behind the balance chosen is too difficult for most groups to understand because it is too diffuse. Decisions need to be made at many levels within the government, and often the top authoritative leaders such as legislative bodies and executives have to manage the results of those levels of decisions rather than the decisions themselves. Moreover, in large societies the decisions are conditioned by what is politically possible as well as by the factors about which decisions are to be made. Often only those people close to the many decision points can be aware of what is politically possible. The result is that decisions are handed down in law and policy that are opaque with regard to their internal reasoning and are perceived by each group mainly if not only in terms of whether it helps or harms them. Therefore, the credibility of the authority cannot consist very much in the various constituencies actually understanding the justice of the reasoning behind the decisions. This leads us to the final topic, the nature of perceived credibility and sincerity.

PERCEIVED CREDIBILITY AND SINCERITY

From ancient times, as expressed for instance in the Great Learning, the Confucian response to the problem of credibility in authoritative rulers has been that the ruler must be personally virtuous in ways that can be perceived and understood by the ministers who work with him or her personally. This is to say, the emperor must be sincere in the Confucian sense, able to apprehend things with the values they have and able to respond to them appropriately, with no selfishness blocking or distorting the emperor's appreciations and responses, and all the time perspicuous to those who know him or her well. Then the ministers who know the emperor personally will imitate his or her virtues in themselves, becoming sincere and perspicuous to those who work with them. The ministers' assistants themselves will imitate the ministers' virtue, and so on down to the point where the lowliest villager apprehends the virtue of the local magistrate and internalizes that as his or her own virtue. Thus the villager does not really need to understand the political, economic, and military reasoning that takes place at the higher levels but can trust, through a reverse chain of inferences of virtue, that those who make decisions at the higher levels, including the highest, have the character and skill to choose who most reasonably brings about the optimum social harmony. The villager, then, can perceive on the one hand that this village is harmed by the governmental policy but be confident on the other that those higher in the chain of decision-making have acted with a wisdom that itself cannot be grasped in the village.[7]

Of course, this is an unbelievable idealized picture. To be an advanced self-cultivated Confucian sage is very difficult and rarely achieved. Emperors are subject to very many distractions and temptations to selfishness. Middle echelon bureaucrats are even more caught up in webs of corruption, in systems of distortion and traditions of biased judgments. To expect the transitive imparting of virtue actually to work from the emperor step-by-step through dozens of layers of social authorities down to the ordinary villager is to expect the impossible. Chinese history is filled with stories of corrupt bureaucrats being exposed. Mencius even said it is legitimate to revolt against an emperor who has "lost the mandate of Heaven."[8]

The nearly inevitable failure of the ideal transmission of virtue through a trickle-down effect does not mean that the Confucian ideal fails to define the conditions for the credibility of the authority, however. The failure only accounts for why it is so difficult in Confucian society for authorities to have proper credibility. They can be acknowledged as legitimate in their defined authority, at least up to a point, even when they are not credible as acting for the good of the whole society. At some point, however, even that legitimacy can fail and parts or the whole of a society can descend into relative social chaos.

Western Christian cultures in ancient and medieval times often assumed that authorities ought to be obeyed because they were put in place by God. This was Saint Paul's view.[9] Through the centuries this developed into the theory of the divine right of kings. The credibility of the king, or emperor, or pope, came from the fact that God had put the authority in place. A frequent assumption was that God would not put a nonvirtuous authority in place. But the credibility did not come from perceived virtue, rather from divine consecration. Enough experience showed, however, that many authorities were so lacking in virtue and plainly incompetent that the divine origin of their credibility itself became incredible.

Two other undercurrents in Western Christian culture slowly came to prominence over against the view that leaders are credible because they are ordained by God. One was the Greek idea of democracy, which said that a hierarchical structure of authority is to be rejected in favor of a one-level authority structure, the people. This was expressed in many ways, and for a long time with incomplete recognitions of who the people are, often excluding slaves, women, foreigners, and so forth. The actual executives of a society receive their authority, and hence credibility, from the people, governing with the consent of the governed. Because within any large group some constituencies are harmed while others are helped, the problem arises constantly about defining the consent of the governed: By popular voting? Consent through simple majority? With what protections of minorities? The European Enlightenment recovered this Greek heritage and developed it in ways well known in European and American democracies. An intrinsic problem with democracy, relative to the credibility of the government, is determining how that government is to receive and bear the credibility that comes from the people when the people themselves are divided against one another.

Another strain from the ancient world was the Roman conception of the aristocrat, the paterfamilias, in many ways very much like the Confucian notion of the gentleman or the sage. The aristocratic Roman "father" was so cultivated as to define as his own interest the interests of those under his care. For such an aristocrat to be "selfish" was for him to work for the good of those who depended on him and whom he identified as his own. This was transformed into the feudal hierarchy of the European Middle Ages but remained as an ideal after that careful medieval social crafting of dependent/responsibility relations collapsed with the rise of modern commerce. By the eighteenth century, a class of people had developed who were defined in large part by their sense of civic responsibility. Among the most famous of these were the American aristocrats, who directed the American Revolution against Britain and then organized the country around the constitution defining checks and balances of power, people such as George Washington, John Adams, Thomas Jefferson, Alexander Hamilton, James Madison, and James Monroe. Although all these people had their own private interests, they were able again and again to put these interests aside in favor of the interests of the nation as they saw them.

These two strains, Greek democracy and Roman aristocracy, came together in the original conception of the American democracy. The credibility of the government derived from the fact that the people who were to be elected to the legislatures, to the judiciary, and to executive office were themselves aristocrats of civic responsibility. These aristocrats might differ radically among themselves concerning policies about economic and military affairs, and they were elected by competing constituencies. But their perceived virtue, very much like that of a Confucian superior person or sage, was sufficient to give credibility to the process, not to the governmental decisions themselves necessarily but to the process by which they were reached. The American "founding fathers," as they were called, were careful to be cautious about treading on the rights of minorities, although of course they were dismissive of many rights for slaves and women.

This Western story about the credibility of the government arising from the credibility of civically responsible representatives to act with the consent of and for the good of their constituencies is another idealized picture. Even the founding fathers of the American government were often not as virtuous as they seemed. By the presidency of Andrew Jackson, whose followers proclaimed, "To the victor belong the spoils," meaning that the majority winning an election could serve their own interests without regard for the losers, the assumption of civic responsibility in a representative was deeply shaken.[10] In fact, people did act for their own personal self-interest instead of the interest of the whole. This was taken to be in fact an advance in democracy, with each villager empowered through the vote to press for his or her own advantage. Politics became the art of compromising with others so as to gain sufficient support to achieve what was most in one's own self-interest. Political rhetoric became less about what is good for the whole than about how to interpret issues so as to gain most support for one's own interests. What was traded was not one good for another, but power to achieve one's own interests. Or so the political process came to be understood by many of the electorate in America and in other democracies. Of course the situation is much more complex than this. There have been notable heroes of civic responsibility such as Abraham Lincoln, and perhaps Theodore Roosevelt, Franklin Roosevelt, and Harry Truman, to name only American presidents. And many factors having to do with economics, immigration, imperialism and military adventures, as well as the evolution of news media and other forms of communication, have complicated these transformations.

The result has been, however, a great longing among Americans in the first decade of the twenty-first century for a new aristocrat of civic responsibility to lead the government. President George W. Bush came to be seen, rightly or wrongly, as a representative of only the very rich whose financial adventures ruined the economic life of a great many Americans and then others across the globe. He was thought to believe that overwhelming military power guarantees victory and that victory justifies war when the interests of the rich profit from the war, leading America into two morally ambiguous wars of foreign occupation. He was thought to believe that American power is so great that cooperation with allies is not very important. People looked to President Obama to be the opposite of all these things, a person who conspicuously could remedy the economic situation, call everyone (including other nations) to cooperation, and to end the wars. He was given the Nobel Peace Prize, much to his own discomfort, before he had made peace anywhere.

Of course, President Obama could not work miracles in any of these fields. He knows that resolving any of them involves pushing for compromises to bring competing constituencies together in some semblance of harmony so that progress can be made. But the people whose disastrous economic lives he did not remedy quickly complain that he has hurt them while helping the rich bankers. The people from many of the different constituencies that elected him find that he does not support their interests with a pure ideology, but with compromises they do not like. Many people are disillusioned.

CONDITIONS FOR CREDIBILITY

The contemporary American situation thus illustrates sharply the problem highlighted in this chapter: how can an authority, such as an American president, be credible when many constituencies believe his policies are harmful to them while unfairly helpful to others? Two conditions are necessary for credibility, and they are related.

The first is that the authority has to be effective in accomplishing some important improvements in the situation that is perceived to be harmful. If the leader is not effective, then it is hard to believe in good intentions and virtue because the news media cannot be trusted to articulate a person's alleged sincerity or rational good judgment. Against nearly universal opposition from the opposing political party, President Obama won a major victory securing universal health care for Americans, and a victory reforming the financial institutions that caused so much harm to many Americans and others across the world.

The second condition for credibility is a trust in personal character, very much of the Confucian sort. This trust requires demonstrated effectiveness in accomplishing something of what is intended. But it also means displaying a character that is open about its political intentions, open about the influences and pressures that move it, open to learn from anyone who has a case to make, resolute in persevering through difficulties and criticisms, willing to compromise for the sake of the greater good, and prepared to accept defeat in one area while continuing to press for progress in others. The inner core of such a credible personality is extensive knowledge, wit and intelligence, and a carefully cultivated set of habits of will, self-control, and persuasiveness. Its outer manifestation is humility, sensitivity and care for others, and a capacity for engagement. These Western Christian (and other) virtues of the hero of civic responsibility in authority are very similar to the Confucians virtues of the self-cultivated sage.

But in these days of news media hype and spin, how can the people tell about these virtues in their leaders? Political organizations attempt to project ideal portraits of leaders. They attempt to represent their opposition with vicious caricatures. The news-media themselves are often driven by their own political agendas and report what they believe supports their cases. Often news media report the sensational events, interpreting them in the most dramatic way possible. Given these distorting variables, how can people learn the subtle things about their authorities' "sincere character," the genuineness of their attempts to be open, responsive, and resolute in proper measure; the truth of their intelligence, knowledge, self-control, and cultivated will; the authenticity of their humility, sensitivity, care, and engagement?

Perhaps the best that can be hoped for is that the actions of authorities over an extended time will reveal their inner characters in which credibility might come to lie. Perhaps over time the negative projections of political groups about each other will cancel one another out. Perhaps over time the competition among news media services with different agendas will allow some truth to come out. Perhaps over time scholars and journalists will be able to sort the distortions from the truth. Perhaps over time the villagers and common people will learn to read character from actions. Or perhaps not, or not in time.

When the credibility of authorities cannot be ascertained and maintained, social hope moves to the credibility of the political process within which the authorities work, with its checks and balances. When the credibility of the political process cannot be ascertained and maintained, the political process devolves into the competition among many constituencies for the power to gain their interests. Sometimes that competition results in political compromises that sustain governments that can adjust to crises and care for institutions. But nearly always that reduction of government to a conflict of forces among competing groups hurts the small people who are protected by no one.

Chapter Thirteen

Confucianism and Toleration

WHAT IS CONFUCIANISM?

In contexts of political philosophy, Confucianism is frequently identified as a culture with a long evolving history in China, with branches in other countries such as Korea, Japan, and Southeast Asia that were amalgamated with other local cultures, and now with a broader vision of Confucian diaspora. In the diaspora, Confucianism usually is associated with local enclaves of East Asian people situated in other countries like "Chinatowns." All these parts of Confucian culture have been historically evolving and have differed from one another by how they have adapted to the other cultural contexts. But they have continuity with one another by lineages of interpretation of core texts among the intellectuals and habits of social and ritual formation, such as an emphasis on family and filial piety.[1] In these contexts of political philosophy, it frequently seems beside the point for non–East Asians to claim to be Confucians unless they "go native" in some East Asian culture.[2]

Viewed this way, toleration in Confucianism becomes an historical question. Some cultures named Confucian have been very tolerant of other religious philosophies, of diverse ethnic groups, of differing social practices concerning food, sexuality, and lifestyle issues, and of the role of women, and other so-called Confucian cultures have been intolerant in regard to such as these.[3] Some Confucian cultures have been tolerant of many variations within what counts as the Confucian culture; others have been more monolithic. Some Confucian cultures have emphasized coexistence with non-Confucian cultures, or at least with some of them, and others have been hostile or anxious to keep a cultural distance. The study of the history of toleration among the many branches of Confucian culture in this sense can be highly instructive, just as the history of toleration among Christian, Buddhist, or Jewish cultures is important to understand.

But this is a fundamentally wrongheaded way to think about Confucianism, especially in relation to large-scale ethical issues such as toleration. First of all, it is an historical mistake. Confucius and his disciples of the first several generations led a reform movement within a culture that they opposed, the chaotic and violent times of the "Spring and Autumn" and the "Warring States" periods. Most of the Confucian thinkers we remember were on the outs with their governments, or at least had testy relationships, as in the case of Wang Yang-ming. When Confucians such as Wang Chong were well received by the government, they still were vigorously engaged in trying to effect cultural change, for instance, the suppression of superstition.

Second, to identify Confucianism with a culture is to ignore, distort, or suppress the dialectical relation that it and most other religious or philosophical worldviews have with the cultures of the societies within which they live. Religious philosophies, not excepting Confucianism, take their bearings from what they consider to be ultimately important, and this generates a distinction between the situation and what is ideal relative to that situation.[4] As the Confucians would say, you need to keep in mind what is "all under Heaven."[5] The situations of Confucius's time and our time are very different, as are the situations in East Asia relative to those in the West. A religious "worldview" has to bring some integration to the various domains in the situations of the people who hold them. Because there are so many different situations for Confucianism, there are many variants on Confucian worldviews. But each of those worldviews includes what Peter Berger calls a "sacred canopy" giving some expression or other to what Confucianism takes to be ultimately significant, the boundary conditions for the world.[6] Classical Confucianism expressed these in terms of notions such as Heaven, Earth, and the Human, whereas Neo-Confucianism elaborated these in terms of principle, material force, and sagehood, topics visited throughout this volume. Although the Confucian family of worldviews involves significant variation because of the differences in the domains for which they provide orientation, they are all Confucian in that the domain of the Confucian sacred canopy has some bearing on at least some of the other domains. By "domain" is meant some concrete area of life that involves particular orientations, such as one's family, job, historical location, health, or communications system; the domains of one's life need to be related to one another by a worldview, and where they are not so related, they are relatively meaningless to one another. People in different situations have different domains and hence need different worldviews. One domain of life for most people has to do with symbols engaging ultimacy, a sacred canopy. Classical Confucian texts articulate a Confucian sacred canopy that might be common to all the variant Confucian worldviews that otherwise are very different because of variations in the domains that the worldviews need to integrate.[7] In any case, the affected domains in any Confucian worldview have a normative or ideal character that very frequently is in a critical relation to the situation where the worldview obtains.

Third, the mention of worldviews reflects an elaborate theory of religion that among other things articulates the dialectical relation between the religion and the actual situations of culture and personality within which religions are practiced. Among the variables relating religious worldviews and specific situations are six continua.[8] One is the relating of the various domains of the situation to be addressed in the worldview on a continuum from very sacred, as in a sacred canopy, to very mundane, such as preferred breakfast diet. A second is a continuum in the symbols in the sacred canopy from very transcendent to personally intimate. A third is a continuum in the interpretations of the symbols from folk religion notions to the very sophisticated ideas of philosophers. A fourth is a continuum between a sacred worldview that is highly individuated to a person and the degrees to which this worldview is shared with others; this continuum is integral to issues about religious communities. A fifth is a continuum between worldviews that are very comprehensive in orienting the many domains of a situation to one another and worldviews that connect only a few domains and leave the rest relatively meaningless with respect to one another. A sixth is a continuum of intensity, from very great to barely significant, with which an individual is committed to or inhabits a religious worldview.

To understand Confucianism, then, requires understanding how some Confucians have an operative worldview that interprets nearly all the domains of life as affected by key notions in the Confucian sacred canopy, and others limit those to, say, just family life, being no different at the office or factory from Buddhists, Christians, or militantly secular people. It is "Confucian" all along that continuum. Similarly, some Confucians symbolize what is ultimate in highly transcendent terms, whereas others neglect the transcendent in favor of terms that more directly bear upon life in the various domains. Some Confucians operate with very sophisticated notions of principle, material force, and the ideals of humaneness and sagehood, whereas others operate with folk religion versions of these, often borrowed from Buddhism, Daoism, and shamanism. Some Confucians orient themselves to others as sharing a common Confucian worldview, whereas others find few fellows in this regard. Some Confucians take their Confucianism to apply to a great many aspects of life, others to only a few domains. Some Confucians are very seriously devoted to being good Confucians, whereas others give it lip service to please their parents.[9]

Given variables such as these, it is possible to see how in one and the same social situation, even in the same family, some Confucians can advocate radical revolution against the status quo, whereas others just go with the flow and call it Confucianism. Needless to say, Confucianism is itself highly controversial within such internally diverse situations, and the Confucian tradition is replete with "prophetic" Confucians telling others they should be different.

To label a given historical culture as "Confucian" is convenient shorthand for historians but also a dangerous abstraction, ignoring, distorting, or suppressing what makes Confucianism interesting as a religion. Sometimes vaguely salient generalizations can be made about societies by religious labels. Samuel Huntington made some good points by contrasting "civilizations," defined each by a dominant religion.[10] David Hall and Roger Ames have stimulated important discussions of comparative cultures by contrasting Confucian with Western thinking. But looked at closely, the living religions are far more variable. Moreover, no religious worldview such as Confucianism at any time is pure from its founders; each is a syncretic amalgam of antecedents, often with different religious labels. Too often in the present situation, Confucianism is identified with a particular historical culture only in order to blame some presently perceived ill upon it, such as the suppression of women and sexual minorities, bigotry regarding other races, or unwillingness to embrace social change.

How then should we approach the question of toleration relative to Confucianism? Any number of ways might produce interesting results. The considerations of this section, however, suggest that we look at the present social situation, relative to issues of toleration, and ask what the sacred canopy of Confucianism might contribute to viable worldviews for those issues. What follows is not a historical analysis of Confucianism and toleration but a normative philosophical analysis of some of the things Confucianism can and should contribute in the current situation.

TOLERATION, IN-GROUPS, AND OUT-GROUPS

One way to focus the problems of toleration in the twenty-first century is to see them as issues of in-groups relative to out-groups. Relative to the boundaries of groups, the issues of toleration are double-barreled. Some have to do with the toleration of the out-groups, or some of their traits, or members, or competitive existence. Others have to do with toleration of deviations within the in-group. The notion of groups with boundaries and internal structures is itself very flexible. Biological and cultural evolutionists call attention to the ways small tribal groups organize themselves so as to be more competitive in the struggle with other groups for survival and flourishing. But groups are defined in many different ways, sometimes overlapping, such as kinship groups, tribal groups, language groups, religious groups, geographical niche groups, social class groups, economic and professional groups, among others. In our common intellectual life, it is customary to think of issues of toleration in terms of tolerating members and behaviors of outgroups different from our own in-group, and in terms of tolerating members of our own in-group who deviate in some ways from the in-group's norms. This "us versus them" is a common default framework for thinking about issues of toleration.

Confucian philosophy suggests a different default framework. We can call it a framework of "concentric circles of conditions for flourishing," although this metaphor suggests too much mathematical regularity. The center of gravity for much Confucian social thinking is the idealized family. Individuals learn to achieve personal identity in terms of relating to family members in somewhat ritualized but biologically based roles, as Tu Wei-ming has argued in his *Centrality and Commonality*. Every family depends on a larger social unit, however, within which it flourishes or not. In classical Confucian thinking society was agrarian and the family was conceived to be nested in a village, which was nested in a larger economic region, which was nested in a further hierarchy of levels of organization up to the emperor and his court. And then the empire itself had relations with foreign powers and geophysical circumstances that were conditions for the flourishing of the empire. We should be careful not to think of the family as the most basic *atomic* unit of human life in Confucian thinking, although that has been claimed. Although individuals are formed in families, their own knowledge, voluntary inclinations, and ritualized behaviors themselves need to flourish. Without those individual traits, family life is not possible; but a dysfunctional family can prevent the flourishing of an individual's inner capacities. One of the classic texts for this motif of Confucian thought is from the Great Learning:

> When things are investigated, knowledge is extended; when knowledge is extended, the will becomes sincere; when the will is sincere, the mind is rectified; when the mind is rectified, the personal life is cultivated; when the personal life is cultivated, the family will be regulated; when the family is regulated, the state will be in order; when the state is in order, there will be peace throughout the world. From the Son of Heaven down to the common people, all must regard cultivation of the personal life as the root or foundation.[11]

This passage leaves out many social steps between the family and the emperor. Also, this particular ordering of knowledge, will, and mind has been hotly debated, especially by the tradition following Wang Yang-ming that disputes the quoted ordering, which comes from Zhu Xi.[12] Nowadays, the nests of conditions for social flourishing are much more complicated than the agrarian model, and Confucians would have to analyze the levels of causal connection in order to distinguish the circles of dependency in modern social terms. Nevertheless, the principle of ordering of conditions for flourishing is fairly clear.

Relative to toleration, the principle is that anything in the wider environment can be tolerated so long as the narrower environment can flourish. For instance, anything can be tolerated in a local neighborhood so long as the families within it can flourish. But the neighborhood depends on a broader social order that keeps the peace and distributes wealth. Any such broader social order can flourish if the yet broader conditions for high civilization are present, and those conditions can be tolerated if they promote the flourishing of the social order. High civilizations interact and depend on an order of global politics, tolerating whatever is in the global political order so long as the high civilizations flourish.

The principle of toleration works from broader to narrower as well. Anything can be tolerated in the high civilizations so long as it does not prevent or corrupt a global political order. Anything can be tolerated in a broad social order so long as it does not prevent or corrupt the high civilization of which it should be a part. Anything can be tolerated in a neighborhood so long as it does not prevent or corrupt the broader social order. Anything can be tolerated by way of family life that does not prevent or corrupt the neighborhood of families. Anything can be tolerated by way of individual knowledge, inclination, and other aspects of personal life that does not prevent or corrupt the functioning of the relevant family.

The phrase "anything can be tolerated" emphasizes the potential for great personal and cultural pluralism in Confucian ideal thinking. For instance, families can tolerate a neighborhood that itself tolerates families of different cultural or racial composition, if that neighborhood allows the families to flourish. But if a family is prevented from flourishing by a neighborhood overly determined by cultures hostile to the family, the family should not tolerate that neighborhood. Similarly, if a neighborhood that otherwise would tolerate families of different cultures is prevented from doing so by some overly exclusive and prejudiced families, those prejudiced families should not be tolerated in the neighborhood.

To be sure, Confucianism sometimes has been a dominant philosophy in societies that have had "us versus them" issues of toleration, societies with feuding families, ethnic bigotry, and the like. To revert to the in-group–out-group identification is easy, especially for societies under pressure. The potential contribution of Confucianism, however, is to remind people that there are more complex ties that bind than would appear when the in-group–out-group distinction is given great weight.

This Confucian default model of concentric circles of conditions for flourishing reflects the more general Confucian point that there is value at every level of existence. This default model rejects the model that value is all selfish for oneself or one's in-group and that other individuals or other groups are valued only instrumentally with regard to one's self or in-group. In terms of human social life this means valuing the simultaneous flourishing of interconnected levels of personal and social existence. Each level has both internal and external conditions for flourishing. Understanding the complex interactions of these levels of conditions is one of the goals of sagacity. Operating with the concentric circles default model makes it hard to simplify issues of tolerance to in-group versus out-group traits because on some level, no group is an out-group to another, but all groups contribute to or inhibit the flourishing of their collective interaction. To put the point another way, no individual is individuated only within a singular in-group. True individual identity involves individuation through all the levels of conditions for flourishing. The significance of this can be seen from many angles, some of which are explored in what follows.

TOLERATION AND NARRATIVE

Another common way of understanding issues of toleration in the twenty-first century is through narratives. Most narratives are stories of conflict, of overcoming obstacles (usually other people), of warfare, feuding, displacement, religious opposition, apostasy, betrayal, competition, domination, and submission. In light of these narratives, people make judgments about what should and should not be tolerated. Many people try to make sense of their lives by reducing them to narratives.

But narratives simplify a vast set of conditions to just those elements that are significant for the story line.[13] The people and factors that do not play a role in the narrative line are ignored, dismissed, distorted, and made not to count. The vast layering of conditions upon conditions, from personal knowledge and rectification of the will through issues of family, neighborhood, society, the Son of Heaven, and peace in the world, is obscured through the force of a narrative that imposes a simple meaning on the world. Those simple meanings, usually involving conflict, often prevent clear vision of what should be tolerated and what not, building deep commitments to bigoted approaches to other people and cultures.

Confucianism subordinates narrative to a kind of cosmological vision of the world. The Chinese had their chroniclers, of course, and kept historical records. But they did not get their orientation to life from a grand narrative, such as a creation story with a fall and redemption, or a legend of a promised land, or stories of the gods that give meaning to life. The ancient East Asians believed in lots of gods and supernatural beings in their folk cultures, and sometimes those gods had to be appeased or bought off. But people thought of the gods as just different kinds of beings that inhabit the world. The Confucians were generally against supernaturalism.

The Confucian cosmology has emphasized constant change with the motive power of material force being shaped by the structures of harmony in principle, or, more anciently the Earthly changes as shaped by Heaven. Conceptions of yang and yin articulate how changes take place, and the patterns of the hexagrams of the *Yijing* mark out types of changes. But by and large these structures of change are not narrative structures. Rather, they are structures of the constant interactions of all the manifold things under Heaven, all interacting in a constant great rush. The Confucian cosmology does not tolerate the dismissal of the massive amounts and kinds of changes that would be necessary to ignore in order to take narrative structure to be very important. Social conditions are under constant change, for the Confucians, but more guided by the changes of seasons than any divine narrative. Dynasties rise and fall, and there is always a story in their arising and ceasing, but more like a natural process of emergence, flourishing, and decay than like a singularly unique story defining a people. Orientation for personal identity, for Confucians, is not to find a place in a cosmic or historical drama but to have a place among All under Heaven. One's sense of place is more determined by directions relative to other people and things than by a place in a story. Social class orientation is determined by relations with other social classes and the interactions among them. Confucian geography has five directions: north, east, south, west, and here. "Here" is a place defined by the concentric circles of conditions relating any "here" to the Ten Thousand Things in their related sets of causal connections.

Some people claim that Confucians do not have much of a cosmology or metaphysics and rather concentrate mostly on ethics. That claim is false: Confucian ethics takes its orientation from conceptions of institutionalized or ritualized life that in turn are elements within cosmic nature. The Doctrine of the Mean bases human nature directly on Heaven, not on merely anthropological notions. But the claim is right that Confucians do not base their ethics on any kind of divine intentionality or will. The closest thing to that in Confucian thought is reference to the Mandate of Heaven, but this has to do with finding what is appropriate for one to do, not with finding what some cosmic mind wants one to do.

With regard to issues of toleration, then, Confucians would direct attention away from the grudges and enmities that have their base in some real or imagined narrative of cosmic purpose, national identity, tribal or clan conflict, or personal destiny. Rather, all the elements that others might pluck from narratives to say that some behavior or some person or group of persons ought not be tolerated should be reconsidered as embedded in the vast array of circles of conditions for flourishing. Confucians would remind us that nothing takes its meaning or worth from any one story, or even from a number of stories, but from the infinite density of patterns of yin and yang changes. The structure of that density of patterns is never overall a narrative, because that narrative necessarily excludes all the other narrative perspectives. Rather, it is more like the array of overlapping circles of conditions for flourishing, from the inner heart through family, neighborhood, society, civilization, and the struggles of world order up to Heaven itself.

TOLERATION AND PERSONAL RESPECT

Central to any Confucian approach to issues of tolerance is respect for individuals. The main Confucian word for this respect is humaneness, *ren*. Very much of the whole Confucian cosmology is packed into this complex notion, of which only a few strands can be extracted here. The first thing to note is that every person is regarded as unique, only secondarily as a member of a class. Thus, equality under the law is something that makes Confucians uncomfortable, even when it is seen as necessary as a hedge against inappropriate nepotism. Emphasizing a kind of innate human capacity to empathize with another person as who that person is, the Confucian sensibility services this regard for uniqueness. Selfishness, which diminishes this innate capacity so emphasized by Mencius, amounts to reducing others to roles determined by one's own selfish interests.

The second thing to note about respect, however, is that others are attended to as playing ritualized roles relative to oneself. One learns to respect others in terms of family relations, then neighborhood relations, then the institutionalized relations of a larger society, and so on. Although every person is unique, each other person also has a ritualized relation to oneself that determines in part just how one can indicate respect, as a son respects a mother, a neighbor respects a neighbor, an official respects a higher official. When strangers are encountered, Confucians elaborate rituals of establishing ritual relations. To have no ritual relations with strangers is exceedingly problematic. Bad rituals that prevent ritual relations that respect the uniqueness of others, rituals of racial or sexual bigotry, for instances, are the object of Confucian ire.

The third thing to note about respect is that, like oneself, any other person is at the center of a vast nest of rituals defining his or her place. Everyone lives in a matrix of networks of rituals relating to others in terms of family, friends, socializing, economic matters, and so forth. Only one or a few of those rituals define a relation of this other to oneself. But the other needs to be regarded as at the center of his or her own matrix of ritual networks, as I argued in chapter 11. If the other is not your father, perhaps he is someone else's father and is in part defined by the paternal roles. This is the Confucian way of handling the point many Western thinkers make by talking about the other as a subject with his or her own perspective on the world. Respect means taking that perspective into account as defining part of the other's uniqueness.

The fourth thing to note is that, like oneself, any other person has to learn to play the roles of his or her ritual matrix, as analyzed in chapter 11. The ritual roles are like dance steps that formally define a channel of behavior relative to others. But how one plays the roles is like how one individuates the dance steps. The rituals that structure social relations are not the forms of the dance steps alone but the actual playing of them. An individual is a player of the ritual roles, not merely the possessor of them. A child can learn to speak dutifully to parents by the age of five. But it takes decades to individuate the filial roles so that it is just oneself, uniquely oneself, who is behaving like a proper child toward one's particular parents in just one's own way. All our roles, however strictly formal, have to be learned and individuated, and many roles are difficult indeed. From a Confucian point of view, many of the difficulties and struggles in life have to do with finding or inventing roles that relate us meaningfully and justly to other people, and then learning to individuate our playing of the roles so as to be sincere and mature. To respect another person, then, is to be able to address that person as someone struggling to individuate the matrix of ritual networks that constitute his or her unique position. To respect that struggle sometimes requires giving the other the privacy of not having to be fully present in the situation. When and how that privacy is possible depends on the concentric circles of ritualized conditions for the flourishing of the other, of oneself, and of the institutions involved in ritual relations with both.

To respect another person is not necessarily to approve of or like the other person, who might be one's enemy, a villain, and a disaster for all those around. Social life often means opposition to others, opposition while maintaining the possibility for respect for the other as a player struggling to individuate his or her own ritual network.

A deep and important element of toleration, from a Confucian perspective, is to respect others as individuators of the roles in their ritual matrix. This is part of treating them as human beings. If they play some roles that are bad, their playing of those roles perhaps should not be tolerated. Ritual roles that prevent or impede the flourishing of the circles of flourishing should be changed or not allowed. Even when this is so, however, the Confucian approval of intolerance in that instance needs to be consistent with respect for the other as a unique individual struggling to play the roles well.

TOLERATION AND HARMONY: THE ETHICAL METAPHYSICS OF PRINCIPLE

In the end, concerns for toleration cannot escape the issues of ethical judgment. Here the Confucian perspective focuses on the metaphysics of principle, *li*. As indicated in chapter 1, the slogan "principle is one, its manifestations are many" has been the subject of much controversy in the tradition and here is one practical interpretation of it. Principle in itself is whatever makes a multiplicity of things harmonize together. Given a specific multiplicity, it is the pattern of their harmony. Not all multiplicities can be harmonized, however; for some, there is no pattern according to which they can be together. Harmony itself is valuable.[14] A harmonized multiplicity has the value of getting these things together in the place where they are relative to other things, with this pattern rather than some other. That a thing has value in itself because of its harmonizing of its components a certain way in a certain place does not mean that it is valuable relative to other things. Flourishing germs make a sick patient. A well-organized mob can destroy a neighborhood. A skillful politician can ruin a state.

So the deepest aspirations for Confucian sagacity are the learned abilities to discern how things cohere, how coherence is impeded, how the coherence of one thing is required for the coherence of another, how the coherence of things in conflict with one another might be modified by a background coherence that resolves the conflict. Coherence as such is "one," but the things that cohere are "many." Confucianism has little to appreciate in Aristotelian substance philosophies according to which "things" are what they are by virtue of possessing properties. Substance philosophies exaggerate the sense that things have identities in themselves and thus facilitate "us versus them" thinking, according to Confucianism. Rather, things are structured processes of harmonious behavior that are possible only against the background of other processes of harmonious behavior, which in turn rest in yet other background elements, from the graceful bow in greeting to a friend to the slowly shifting rotation of the heavens. Nothing has its properties except in layers of layers of other coherent contexts. Substance thinking tends to neglect the background requirements just as narrative thinking tends to neglect what does not count in the story. To encounter another person, then, should not be to treat the person as an individual alone, but as an individual with inherited DNA, with an history of health and illness, with affectional habits derived from a particular family, with an educational background of a certain sort coming from neighborhood institutions, with an economic status determined by roles in the economic system, with an historical political background, made possible by certain conditions of geography and climate, which in turn are made possible by atmospheric conditions filtering the sun's rays, and so forth. A Confucian mother in Boston buys bananas to put on her children's cereal and sagely reflects how that simple act supposes the existence of the store that stocks bananas, the distribution system by which goods are delivered to the store, the agricultural system in tropical countries where the bananas are grown, the economic system that funds banana production and takes profits for owners who might be quite distant from the growers, the transportation of the bananas by plane from the tropics to Boston, the dependence of nonlocal food distribution on vast amounts of airplane fuel, the interest this creates in controlling countries with oil production, the implications of a tropical diet in Boston for war and peace, and the effects of climate change on continued food production. Well, she probably does not reflect on all that at once while trying to get the children fed before school. But she does know that this breakfast does not stand by itself and that it is what it is through all those levels of conditioning. Our contemporary understanding of what levels of systems to look for is quite different from what a granddaughter of Confucius might have looked for. Contemporary science has revealed a vastly more complicated personal, social, and natural world than imagined centuries ago. Who would have thought that the choice to use an aerosol rather than a stick deodorant should be affected by considerations of modification of the ozone layer?

It should be emphasized again that each of these levels of systems of coherence has its own manner of flourishing. There are good and bad diets for growing children, stores that make a reasonable profit selling healthy food and those that choose to make more money from unhealthy food, distribution systems that stock the stores efficiently or not, bananas that are ripe and wholesome and bananas that are blighted, economic systems that reward the people well and those that are exploitive, international carriers that are well run and those that are dangerous, oil production systems that work well and those that do not, a political situation that coordinates all this, economic practices regarding food and transportation that support the larger natural environment and those that are detrimental, and so on.

Rarely can all these be made to flourish together, and incoherencies abound. The ordinary situation is that all of these systems are compromised somewhat and we make do with relatively uncoordinated attempts to keep each of the systems going. Wars over oil in the Middle East are not caused entirely by Boston Confucian mothers feeding their children bananas. But luxurious expectations of Bostonians about cuisine, a cuisine that is healthy, do have an effect on economic resources and world politics.

A Confucian sensibility regarding life is to see its many levels of reality as implicated in patterns of coherence and incoherence. No action affects only one thing. When something prized fails to flourish, the cause may not be in its own incoherence but in the incoherence of conditions behind it. Not all things can be made coherent. Some conflicts cannot be resolved except through violence with serious winners and losers. But Confucians analyze the world in terms of why conflicts arise and what might be done to resolve them.

With regard to toleration, a Confucian would say that any person, any behavior, any culture or social organization has a prima facie right to flourish out of the principle of respect or humaneness. The only question of toleration is what the costs are of those flourishings to other things, where the "costs" are to be understood in terms of the nesting of conditions within concentric circles or lines of causal implications. The answers to those questions determine whether and how the prima facie right to flourish should justifiably be compromised.

SOME CONFUCIAN MORALS OF TOLERATION

The first Confucian moral is that bigotry in all forms should be rejected. Bigotry is negative thinking and behavior toward persons in a group because of a trait that obtains for all in the group when that trait is falsely believed to be bad. Racism is an obvious example. There is nothing wrong with being a particular race per se. Bigotry against sexual minorities such as lesbians, gays, transgenders, and bisexual people is another example. Unless the qualities that identify these traits can be shown to be bad per se, there is no ground for any bigotry against them and all should be tolerated, other things being equal. The Confucian insistence on respect of others is the first bulwark against bigotry. Because most forms of bigotry also define the objects of bigotry to be an out-group to the bigot's in-group, Confucianism's transformation of in-group/out-group distinctions into concentric circles of different kinds of relationship is another hedge against bigotry, although sometimes people in the oppressed group loathe themselves and thus are bigoted against themselves, as is frequently true of sexual minorities.

A second Confucian moral is that all judgments that something or someone ought not be tolerated are context dependent. The importance of flourishing stands on its own as Confucians grasp the togetherness of things according to patterns of principle, but the flourishing of one thing might cause damage to another and judgments have to be made as to how to make these things coherent if possible. The kind of flourishing that consists in pursuing one's own interest freely might not be tolerable in times of war when everyone needs to work in concert. On the other hand, war is generally a bad thing precisely because it calls for inhibiting free expressions of interests. Wars, warlike behavior, tempting abundance of armaments and the like, should not be tolerated, according to Confucian thinking, unless war is absolutely necessary.

A third Confucian moral regarding toleration is that there should be no fixed rules for what should be tolerated and what not, because what promotes or inhibits relevant flourishing is so context dependent and the context is constantly changing. Rather, constant learning is required for the sageliness to understand the shifting measures of coherence that determine what should and should not be tolerated.

A fourth Confucian moral, contrary to the thought of many scholars who read Confucianism as a version of virtue-ethics, is that sage judgment is neither following rules nor acting out of predetermined cultivated inclinations. Sage judgment rather requires becoming learned about and attuned with the shifting conditions that bear upon what should and should not be tolerated. Even the Confucians who emphasize the presence of principle in the inner heart of people say that this is good because it facilitates the recognition of coherence and incoherence in things of the world. Good judgment depends on learning the world more than acting out of some character.

A fifth Confucian moral is that we should never allow a complex social ritual, structuring important relations between classes of people, to determine by itself what should be tolerated and what not. Most large-scale social rituals do advantage some people and disadvantage others. But the Confucian sensibility says that we should constantly be vigilant about whether the rituals at hand are justified in the multiple layers of concentric circles of conditions for flourishing. Confucians know that rituals are absolutely essential for giving meaning to behavior: rituals are semiotic systems. Nevertheless, not all rituals are good, just as not all social systems that are meaningful are good. Central to Confucianism's moral vision is the project of critiquing and repairing inadequate rituals.

Confucianism is sometimes thought to be a socially conservative philosophy because its insistence on attention to and observance of rituals seems to rigidify and give support to bad social structures, such as the suppression of the flourishing of women or sexual minorities. But that criticism makes sense only when we have come to see that the rituals at hand do in fact suppress rather than enhance flourishing. Given what we now understand about ritualized cultures that suppress the flourishing of women or sexual minorities, Confucians in most circumstances should be radical feminists and gay liberationists, as I shall argue in chapter 15.

A sixth Confucian moral relative to tolerance is that, the more variety in a coherent harmony, the better. Homogeneity is dull; variety is better. The Confucian themes of harmony and coherence emphasize this density of differences. But variety requires often special conditions to contain cultural differences and sometimes that higher level of coherence is hard to achieve. Other things being equal, the more diversity of family cultures a neighborhood can sustain, the better. Confucianism for a pluralistic, meritocratic, highly mobile, urban culture such as obtains in Boston as well as much of the rest of the world cannot advocate the same social policies it would for a relatively homogeneous agrarian culture. This is a time for vigorous creativity in inventing rituals for making the components of a pluralistic world cohere and flourish.

CHAPTER FOURTEEN

Confucian Humaneness across Social Barriers

This chapter develops three points concerning Confucianism and spiritual traditions. The first concerns the classic Confucian notion of "love or humaneness with distinctions." The second concerns the role of ritual in Confucianism to build bridges across cultural differences. The third concerns how Confucian humaneness, *ren*, allows the acknowledgment of what some Western philosophers have called "otherness."

To preface the discussion, it is important to acknowledge that Confucianism, like the other spiritual traditions of China (and the world!), has had a long and varied history, as affirmed throughout this book. The first section of the previous chapter detailed some of the variety of ways of being Confucian. In this chapter, Confucianism shall be identified with some ancient themes stemming from pre-Han times. Those themes have been elaborated in many different and sometimes contradictory ways. But the concern here is to elaborate them in a *contemporary* way to show how a Confucian in our time might contribute to extending humaneness across rugged social barriers.

"LOVE WITH DISTINCTIONS"

The first thing to note about Confucian humaneness (*ren*) is its association with the Axial Age revolution that extended from East Asia through South Asia to the West Asian lands of the Mediterranean. The term "Axial Age" was coined by Karl Jaspers and was used to characterize the period roughly from 800 to 200 BCE, during which time philosophy was invented across the ecumene and the religions and religious philosophies came into being that we know now as Buddhism; Confucianism; Daoism; Greek philosophical paganism (Plato, Aristotle, etc.); Hinduisms; Jainism; Prophetic Judaism, from which, in combination with Greek philosophy, Christianity arose; and Zoroastrianism.[1] The elements of these religions or religio-philosophies developed slowly and in many conflicting ways within each general tradition. Yet by the end of the Axial Age, that is, by about the second century before the common era, the following themes were universal to them all: some conception or other of the world as a whole, conceptions of the ultimate principle or principles upon which the world as a whole exists, definitions of human identity as having more to do with the relations of individuals to the ultimate principles (for instance, Dao, Heaven/Earth, Brahman, Emptiness, God) than to local kinship settings, and imperatives to love everyone and to be just to everyone (not merely those within one's in-group). The general reason for the universality of love and justice is that all people are equally and most importantly related to the ultimate principles, only secondarily to special relations with each other. All these themes were revolutionary relative to pre–Axial Age religious cultures.

The Confucian theme of humaneness is a version of the Axial Age theme of universal love. In contrast to pre–Axial Age cultures according to which one should be humane to one's own people and rude or hostile to others, particularly barbarians, the early Confucians said that one should be humane to everyone, and that this trait itself is one of the ways in which a human being can become humane.

But in ancient China it would seem that Mozi's philosophy, roughly contemporary with that of Confucius, was a more direct embodiment of the Axial Age ideal regarding universal humanity. When asked whence the "harms" of the world come, he said,

> They arise out of want of mutual love. At present feudal lords know only to love their own states and not those of others. Therefore they do not hesitate to mobilize their states to attack others. Heads of families know only to love their own families and not those of others. Therefore they do not hesitate to mobilize their families to usurp others. And individuals know only to love their own persons and not those of others. Therefore they do not hesitate to mobilize their own persons to injure others.[2]

In the case of universal justice, Mozi was explicit in tying it to the ultimate principle and the common relation of all people to principle:

> Heaven wants righteousness and dislikes unrighteousness. With righteousness the world lives and without righteousness the world dies, and with it the world becomes rich and without it the world becomes poor, with it the world becomes orderly

> and without it the world becomes chaotic. Now Heaven wants to have the world live and dislikes to have it die, wants to have it rich and dislikes to have it poor, and wants to have it orderly and dislikes to have it chaotic.[3]

Mozi advocated equality for all people, and cutting back on elaborate funerals, expensive clothes, and good foods.

The Confucian objection to Mozi was complicated, involving a rejection of what was perceived as hyper-utilitarianism and an over-anthropomorphizing of Heaven.[4] But the deeper Confucian objection was this: people are *not* "equal"—they are each unique and should be respected as such. Therefore, it is not possible to love everyone by treating them the same way, as Mozi taught. Rather, humane behavior needs to make distinctions in order to treat people in the ways they should be treated given who they are and who the person treating them is. The distinctions Confucius seemed to have in mind have to do with social relationships:

> The Duke of She told Confucius, "In my country there is an upright man named Kung. When his father stole a sheep, he bore witness against him." Confucius said, "The upright men in my community are different from this. The father conceals the misconduct of the son and the son conceals the misconduct of the father. Uprightness is to be found in this."[5]

In contrast to Mozi's doctrine of universal egalitarian love, Confucianism has long advocated "love or humaneness with distinctions." In ancient times, this meant loving one's own family more than those in other families, one's own community more than other communities, and one's own empire more than the barbarians. Love, or humaneness, in this context means not only affectionate regard but also taking responsibility for those loved and deferring to them as worthy to be loved. The Confucian doctrine of "love with distinctions" does not mean that there is anyone who should *not* be loved, only that people are to be loved differently, or treated humanely in different ways, with more attentive responsibility for those in relative proximity. Other religions, such as Buddhism and Christianity, agree that everyone should be loved, that compassion be universal. But because, in practice, love is mediated by the social structures of the situation, universal love easily becomes an empty value unless it can be shaped so as to recognize distinctions in relationships. Confucianism thus has a head start among world cultures in recognizing the complexity of treating everyone humanely when people are in such different relations with one another. Many barriers exist across which the expression of humaneness is difficult.

In our own time we understand the social barriers to be much more complex than were expressed in the ancient texts. They cannot be conceived simply in terms of distance from an intergenerational family, although those barriers are surely important. We know now much more of the structures of socioeconomic class stratification, of how varied those are, of how upwardly and downwardly mobile people are within social classes, of how these are affected not only by ownership of the means of production but by technological advances, climate, and shifting markets across the world. We know now about many more of the complexities of different kinds of personality, with different learning styles, and different psychopathologies, across which love needs to be conveyed. We understand that contemporary social barriers to the expression of humaneness include ethnic divisions, and religious divisions, and civilizational divisions. We recognize that groups have different and conflicting interests centered on economic matters, or claims to land, or appropriation of resources. All these social barriers to the expression of humaneness are abundantly illustrated in the conflicts of world civilizations, but most of them are also illustrated in the internal struggles of small towns.[6] Contemporary social sciences are multiplying our appreciation of these alienating social structures at an astonishing rate.[7]

Something like the Confucian ideal of humaneness with distinctions has become a social imperative for every contemporary society. Reinforced in every major religious and cultural tradition, humaneness stands directly opposed to the dehumanizing effects of so much of late-modern economic and political interaction. How can humaneness acknowledge the differences among the people and groups to be treated humanely and find distinctive ways to address them across the boundaries? This question is not to be answered only by examining the particular kinds of boundaries on which the ancient Confucians focused, namely, those emanating from distance from family. It needs to be asked in terms of our contemporary understanding of social boundaries that make humane treatment difficult.

RITUAL THEORY

Nevertheless, the ancients were not concerned only with boundaries set in familial terms. Xunzi, the ancient theoretician of Confucian ritual, noticed that societies are stratified into social classes based on economic, political, and birthright differences. It did not occur to him that the vast differences between the rich and poor could be changed; the idea of social engineering did not become generally plausible until the eighteenth century in England with the work of John Wesley. Nowadays, we understand social justice to demand that social inequities be remedied where they can, and political philosophies from Marxism to liberal progressivism have engaged in massive social experiments in changing class structures. But some class differences endure and perhaps have gotten worse in certain economic situations. Xunzi even believed that social class distinctions were a good thing because they were necessary for organizing the economy efficiently and preserving social order. But he recognized that people in all social classes should be treated humanely by each other, especially so that those in the lowest classes would have enough to live full lives.

The problem with people, Xunzi thought, is that by nature we are selfish, like infants, thinking only of ourselves; modern psychologists call "primary narcissism" what Xunzi notoriously called the "natural evil of humanity." Moreover, although human beings have all sorts of emotional and physical capacities given in their biology (by Heaven, he said), biology does not teach them to attach the right emotions to the right objects, or to rule themselves judiciously. Actually, according to Xunzi, human nature by itself, that is, as given in biology, is vastly underdetermined. Our physical capacities need to be trained, as do our intellectual and emotional capacities. Whereas Mencius and his tradition have said that human nature is essentially good and will unfold properly if not distorted, Xunzi and his tradition have said that human nature is not complete without culture to determine its underdetermined capacities.

His answer to both natural narcissism and biopsychic underdetermination was ritual. Xunzi's notion of ritual was extraordinarily profound, referring not only to court (and religious) rituals but to all behavior that is shaped by conventional signs, as we have noticed numerous times in this book. A culture has a repertoire of signs that might be very different from that of another culture but that accomplish the same thing, for instance, standing, greeting, and speaking. East Asians learn to stand with their feet parallel; Westerners learn to stand with the toes out at an angle. East Asians greet one another with a bow and with the hands together; Westerners with a handshake. Speaking in Chinese or English is a difference in ritual, even when saying the same thing.

For Xunzi, a human being needs to be ritualized in order to make high civilization possible. Men and women can copulate and produce offspring but cannot raise them to be humane without family rituals that provide distinctions in roles and divisions of labor, especially in ways that foster mutual respect. The Confucian tradition as a whole has placed great importance on the family as the locus of learning to be humane. One learns how to be humane, in general, by being loved by parents. But it is more complicated than this. Parents find it easy to love an infant—it is almost a biological instinct. Parents have to grow in the subtlety of their love in order to love an active child, teaching the child how to develop capacities and take on responsibilities. Parents have to grow in their own love a very great deal to love a rebellious adolescent. Then parental love has even more to learn when children are grown and move away. The intent behind parental love is to raise the children to be virtuous. Filial piety is a kind of love appropriate for children to have toward parents. In commonsense terms, this has meant that children take care of parents in their old age. But in the deep Confucian terms, filial piety is becoming virtuous and demonstrating this virtue so as to free parents from the task of making their children virtuous, to show them that they have succeeded and can retire with satisfaction. How can this be done? With only a little irony we can say that it is by the children themselves marrying and having children and demonstrating their own virtue by loving their children in the appropriate ways, stage by stage. Thus parents cannot be satisfied that they have loved their children into humaneness until they see their children do this with the grandchildren. Perhaps this accounts for the very great importance of multigenerational families in traditional Confucian societies and points out the great limitations that highly mobile societies place on the closely monitored teaching of humaneness. All sorts of surrogates for children and grandchildren are possible, of course, in education and apprenticeships. All of the acts of parenting and filial piety are given meaning by the ritual conventions of culture. Without those ritual conventions, the acts would not carry humaneness.[8]

Just as families would not be possible without ritual, so friendships, organized social life, economic activity, and all the other things important to high civilization require ritual. Human biological nature, according to Xunzi, cannot be fulfilled without the rituals of conventional culture. Thus he gives very great importance to the ancient trinity of Heaven, Earth, and the Human, where the Human means ritualized culture bearing conventional meanings that can tie emotions to their appropriate objects. Xunzi's approach to ritual is extraordinarily complicated.

Of the many places where ritual is important, according to Xunzi, one is in the interactions among different social classes. To oversimplify his position, in a well-ordered society, rituals exist by virtue of which lower classes defer to higher classes and higher classes provide for the needs of lower classes. In a poorly ordered society, those rituals do not exist, with the consequences of class warfare and broken economy; everyone suffers, especially the poor. More important for Xunzi's Confucian sensibilities, in a poorly ordered society people cannot treat one another with humaneness because their classes are at odds with one another. In a true Confucian sense, deference is not only the attitude of lower classes toward higher classes, but the attitude of anyone regarding anyone else with humaneness. The higher classes in a well-ordered society defer to the lower classes and their needs, in appropriate ways that both recognize their humanity and provide for them. Xunzi sought for large-scale social rituals within which each social class could function in an harmonious dance with the others, paying deference to the others even when not sharing the values or interests of the others. The sharp point of Xunzi's conception of ritual is that the individuals and groups participating in the rituals do not need to share common interests and in fact can be in deep conflict, so long as they play the rituals together so as to keep an effective political economy going.

Nowadays, we strive to overcome economic class differences, not to accept them, and believe in social engineering in ways of which the ancients could not conceive. Very often we want rightly to break down rituals that perpetuate injustice. Nevertheless, many kinds of differences between people exist that prevent them from dancing with one another in appropriate humane ways. One contribution to overcoming the barriers to multiply-focused humaneness among people and groups is the development of rituals that allow them to interact with one another in "harmony" even while competing and disagreeing over fundamental values.

Put in a preliminary way, I advocate a Confucian project of social analysis that inquires into the existence of rituals that inhibit or prevent the expression of humaneness across social barriers, and that goes on to develop rituals for the interaction of contending groups that allows for all participants to treat one another humanely even while in conflict. These are two distinct steps.

The first is the development of a contemporary Confucian discipline for discerning ritual behavior and analyzing what it allows and what it prevents. This discipline should take advantage of all the social science methodologies for understanding ritual. But it should be guided by the Confucian theme of analyzing how specific rituals increase or inhibit humaneness, how they treat some people humanely and objectify others so as to dehumanize them. The Confucian sensibility about humaneness in diverse contexts is far subtler than that in late-modern and postmodern social sciences that try to be "value free."

The second step in a contemporary discipline of ritual analysis is the invention of new rituals that would replace dysfunctional ones or that would integrate people and social functions that ought to be integrated but are not. "Inventing rituals" is a strange idea, because we usually take rituals to emerge from below, as it were. But because all human interactions, including those of social entities, are mediated by rituals, to care for others means to care for the rituals needed for mediation. Therefore, creativity in enhancing human relations includes creativity in the invention of rituals that make them possible. Confucius thought the problem with his time was that there were insufficient rituals for civilized life. So he claimed to recover the rituals of the ancients and taught them to his pupils. But in fact by and large he was inventing the rituals that he taught. This proactive approach to ritual-making is fundamental to the argument of chapter 15.

HUMANENESS, RITUAL, AND OTHERNESS

Before we can say much about rituals that foster the expression of humaneness across barriers, however, a further word needs to be said about humaneness itself. Some Western philosophers recently have been concerned to understand human beings as "Others." This concern arises out of two longstanding problems in Western thought.

One is that in many contexts we conceive world history and our societies in the form of narratives, as we saw in the previous chapter. The vast complexities of nature and human society are simplified and given meaning through stories. A narrative gives meaning by connecting things in a comprehensible story line, but it also gives meaning by excluding from that narrative all the other things that happen that are not part of the narrative. A narrative is a license to not pay attention to those things, including people, who do not count for much in the story. In both the *Philosophy of Right* and the *Lesser Logic*, Hegel argued that the actual is the rational and the rational is the actual.[9] By "rational" he meant the unfolding of the narrative logic of nature and history. He admitted that there exist some groups of people who do not fit into that narrative but said they are not "actual": because they do not contribute to the story, it is as if they were only *possible*, not actual. In a narrative, some people inevitably are marginalized or ignored completely. But that is not humane: these neglected "Others" need to be recognized. Their experience, perspectives, and social locations need to count if they are to be treated humanely.

The other longstanding problem is the conviction that a human being is a subject who looks out onto a world of objects. For any given subject, according to this conviction, other people are not themselves subjects, but rather objects, reduced to what they might be in the mind of a subject to whom they appear. This point is associated in Western philosophy with Descartes, who famously identified the self with consciousness for whom "objects" are things within consciousness; he solidified the meaning of "objectivity" as reality-for-a-mind.[10] The focus on otherness is a correction that cultivates the experience of other people as themselves being subjects, not merely objects.

With regard to the problem of humanely treating individuals and groups that have been marginalized or entirely written out of the story of a given society, rituals that exclude them can be identified and deconstructed, and new rituals can be developed so that they are engaged and their perspectives are made to count in the social whole. Michel Foucault has inspired a strong strain of postmodern reflection on rituals of power that subtly marginalize various classes of people.[11]

On the political side, the development of rituals to include the marginalized and neglected is part of the project of democracy. The required rituals comprise not only explicit forms of voting and decision-making, but also the rituals of education and community formation that facilitate participation. On the economic side, rituals need to be developed that bring all people into the economy, making sure that basic needs are met for widows and orphans, ethnic minorities, the disabled, and others who are likely to be neglected or marginalized. On the personal side, rituals are required that educate all people in all social locations about the nature of those in other social locations, especially neglected or marginalized ones. Instead of thinking about world history or our societies in terms of narratives, we should learn to think of them in terms of vast, complicated dances of multiple, interacting rituals.

With regard to the problem of humanely treating individuals as subjects in their own right, and not only as functions of our own experience, we can appeal to the ancient Confucian discipline of learning to play interactive rituals with others in such a way as to defer to others as also being subjects playing within the rituals.

Humane deference is not achieved by a kind of universal acknowledgment that every other person is also a subject, even though that is true. Rather, one person's subjectivity is mediated through the particularities of body, family and friends, social structures, social location and historical position, ethnic identity, personal history, age, and a host of other elements. This first of all applies to the particularities of the life of the person who is deferring to another: I defer to another through the particularities of my own life. Until I have a grasp of what those particularities are, and the roles they give me in the many rituals in which I take part, I cannot defer to another particularity. But that deference is not actually achieved until I have some fairly profound feeling for how the other is a subject through the particularities of the other's own life. Just as my human deference to others is expressed through the particularities of my own life, the others cannot be identified as particular subjects until I grasp how they are subjects in their own particularities. Of course this requires both an elimination of bigotry that would blind me to the others and the achievement of the erudition needed to understand what the others' lives and circumstances are like.

Here is where love or humaneness "with distinctions" is so important. The fundamental meaning of family rituals, for instance, is that each person is allowed to be a particular subject while playing the various roles that define a complex family social location. Because of the intimacy of family culture, all the individuals within a family are alike in many respects, and they can learn to imagine what it is like to be someone else in the family (although I do not want to minimize the difficulty of maturation in this sense). But think how difficult it is to recognize the particular subjectivities of people vastly different from oneself, people of other families, other cultures, other social locations. The social barriers across which it is so hard to express humaneness are precisely those things that make it difficult to perceive or imagine how others inhabit their particular subjectivities.

Surely, an imperative deriving from humaneness is for all people to become educated about what it is like to be persons on the other side of social barriers. But education is not enough. We need the rituals so that people across social barriers can engage one another. But that also is not enough. We need to learn to play those rituals so that in the very engagement with those others we can come to recognize and defer to the others in their particular subjectivities. This includes recognizing conflicting interests and perhaps even deep hatred. To be humane to others does not depend upon them being humane to us.

Humaneness or love with distinctions gets its character from the specifics of ritual engagement across barriers. We should not think to love all people the way we should love our family members. Different social locations present different problems for achieving recognition and deference to other people's particular subjectivities, and in contemporary society those social locations are often in flux. Different forms of humaneness are appropriate for different kinds of social relations, especially those across barriers that make recognition of particular subjectivities of various "others" difficult. What an extraordinary moral task for the social sciences informed by Confucianism to investigate the ways rituals prevent the expression of humaneness across social barriers, and to invent better rituals that facilitate genuine humaneness with appropriate distinctions!

The preceding remarks have been given in a hortatory tone. This is a traditional Confucian posture. The argument has been that Confucianism has two important contributions to make to the contemporary problem of exercising humaneness across social barriers. One is its conviction that humaneness means different things in different situations and for different people, and that to treat everyone equally is not to be humane. The other is the Confucian sense of ritual as a conventional form of social interaction that allows people who are in deep conflict still to act together to make possible what their common ritual makes possible. These contributions are especially to be appreciated in contexts in which being humane requires recognizing the marginalized and objectified as subjects in their own right. Contemporary Confucians can enter the philosophical and spiritual conversation with these contributions.

What has not been said here is that Confucianism has often failed in these important tasks. For many people in traditionally Confucian societies, there is an history of treating people only as objectified in ritualized roles, eliminating their subjectivity. This has been true in assigning women demeaning roles and in establishing social hierarchies in which the people on top do not serve but take advantage of those lower down. Anger against Confucianism is justified in these respects. And yet these grave downsides of Confucian culture are perversions of the Confucian ideals precisely because they distort humaneness and use rituals to make impossible good things such as universal human flourishing. Precisely because Confucian rituals and practices of humaneness need to reach everyone in appropriate ways, the bad effects of historical Confucian rituals prove that they are bad rituals. The contemporary need is for new rituals that do not marginalize anyone in some social narrative and that do not objectify them. Contemporary Confucian spirituality should find this an exhilarating challenge.

Chapter Fifteen

Confucianism and the Feminist Revolution

Ritual Definition and the Social Construction of Gender Roles

INTRODUCTION

Confucianism has not fared well under the critical onslaught of the feminist revolution. But then none of the other ancient philosophical and religious cultures has escaped serious criticism also. As the ancient peoples around the globe emerged into historical modes, all were deeply formed by the evolutionary pressure to develop male dominance. Big, strong men are required for tribal warfare, hunting big game, and tilling the soil, while women are required for the bearing and the nurture of children for which they need big hips but not huge upper body strength. Of course there were many different social arrangements for the division of labor in a primitive group. Evidence exists that the degree to which women participate in public life is positively correlated with the degree to which fathers participate in the rearing of small children. But evolutionary biology favored big men who could make decisions in a hurry for the safety of the group, which also favored their dominant authority over women and children.[1]

The Axial Age philosophies, religions, and civilizations arose in part when social arrangements no longer required rigid stratification of social roles for survival and could impose cultural values that in some cases ran against the evolutionary pressures. So, for the first time it could be imagined that all human beings are "Under Heaven," as the Confucians put it, and therefore owe more loyalty and deference to anyone making a claim on being human than to members of one's tribe. Universal love and universal justice were ideals in all the Axial Age religions, however much those ideals were compromised by the adaptive pressures for survival.[2] In principle, social roles could have been adjusted to give women equality with men where the childbearing and nurturing were not at issue; sometimes those social roles were helpfully adjusted, as in the first and second generation of Christians but not the third and subsequent generations. The recognition of universal humanity was not translated very often into rearrangement of social roles that allowed women to flourish to the best of their ability. Partly, this was because of social inertia, lack of imagination for new social arrangements, and surely the reluctance of men to give up privilege. This was true for just about every culture during the Axial Age.

Let me tell an anecdote that illustrates this with regard to Confucianism in our time. In 1991 I attended the Second Confucian-Christian Dialogue. Two of the papers were presented by women, both East Asian. These women attacked Confucianism fiercely, assaulting it for the terrific demeaning of women in Confucian societies, citing among other things the authoritative rituals that subordinated women. Their arguments were so obvious and persuasive that all the males, Confucian and Christian, hid their faces. Then some of the male East Asian Confucians made the argument that primitive East Asian cultures were indeed patriarchal and that Confucianism in fact was a counterforce for the liberation of women. The patriarchal primitive under-layers of East Asian cultures proved to be too strong for the equalizing effects attributed to Confucianism, they said, and so Confucianism accommodated to primitive patriarchy when it could not do otherwise. This argument was not very persuasive, especially to the women in the room, because of Confucianism's actual history of institutionalizing the oppression of women, as we would now call it. Confucianism has been too deliberate for too long in its fostering of rituals and social structures that are very bad for women and thus are quite properly subject to attack from within the feminist revolution.

My purpose in this chapter is to revive and improve upon the argument made by the shamed men at this conference, namely, that patriarchy has an evolutionary base that needs to be brought under control by higher values, including those advocated by feminists (and defenders of sexual minorities). I will also argue that Confucianism can be developed in new directions that align it with feminist values, even if it has rarely if ever done so this far. For this argument, it is important that I am a contemporary Confucian philosopher willing to transform what Confucians have done thus far. As a male, I do not approach this topic as a woman demanding my rights, although I am nervously mindful of my mother, wife, two daughters, and three granddaughters looking over my shoulder. I argue rather as a Confucian seeking to improve Confucianism so that women and sexual minorities do get their rights and support for flourishing.

In most discussions from the standpoint of liberation movements, the oppressing institution, in this case various Confucian traditions, is viewed rather strictly in ways limited to its manifestations that are oppressive. Usually in these discussions, Confucianism is defined or characterized by its ways of oppressing women. This is true of all the fine essays in the powerfully illuminating 2003 collection *Women and Confucian Cultures in Premodern China, Korea, and Japan*, edited by Dorothy Ko, JaHyun Kim Haboush, and Joan R. Piggot. It is true also of the late nineteenth- and early twentieth-century Chinese feminist essays collected in 2013 in *The Birth of Chinese Feminism*, edited by Lydia H. Liu, Rebecca E. Karl, and Dorothy Ko. The obvious justification for this externalist approach to Confucianism is that these feminist authors are presenting perspectives obscured or demeaned in their social situation, and Confucianism is one of the main sources of this marginalization.

I want to take another approach, however, identifying Confucianism from the inside where it has resources for transforming itself so as to embrace and enable the flourishing of women and everyone else. The previous chapters of this book have built my case. The usual liberationist approach objectifies Confucianism in its modes of being oppressive, which ironically also objectifies women as the victims of oppression. I want to speak from the inside of ever-changing Confucianism to recommend more changes that transforms *us*, not some "other." Not in the slightest do I contest the historical accusations of the feminists that Confucianism has been oppressive of women and sometimes transformed a situation of relative equality into something much worse.[3] Parallel accusations are on target with most other civilizations. My concern rather is with liberative transformation.

NATURE, SOCIETY, AND PERSONS

One of the most important elements of Confucianism is the continuity it asserts and assumes from the broadest expanse of nature to human individuals, their social affiliations, and the achievement of high civilization. The special and remarkable character of this can be seen through a brief comparison. The West Asian cultures and religions, including Judaism, Christianity, and Islam, assume a rather sharp break between the human sphere and all the rest of nature. The common text for this is the first chapter of Genesis in which the creation of the Heavens and the Earth, and all the plants and animals of every kind, takes place before the creation of human beings. And then human beings are instructed to care for nature as a garden because all of nature is for the use of human beings. The first human, called Adam, cannot find companionship within nature and so one of his ribs is removed and turned into a woman, thus making Adam sexually male. Sexuality is interpreted as the search for the reunion of male and female, and the Genesis gloss on marriage says that the man shall leave his family and cleave to the woman and they shall become one flesh. No mention is made of children or reproduction and so their union is not within nature in that sense but wholly within the personal sphere. This view of marriage is rejected in most of the rest of the Hebrew Bible, in which it is said that the woman shall leave her family and cleave to the man for the sake of giving him children. Interestingly, when Jesus cited the basis for marriage, it was to the Genesis passage, saying it was a human union with no "natural" connection with children. For the West Asian religions, the background assumption is that the whole of creation is to be understood in terms of the affairs of human beings, however much that assumption is contested today.

In the South Asian religions associated with Buddhism and Hinduism, the important community comprises all sentient beings, not the human alone. The reincarnation culture supposes that souls move through many sentient life forms, and all must be revered as in continuity. In past lives you might have been an insect, then a cow, and now a human; if you are female, you have to wait for the next life to be born a man, but if you are a man now you might have a shot at enlightenment or liberation if you are smart, lucky, and have a good teacher nearby. Buddhists and Hindus have many, often contradictory, versions of this. Continuity with trees, mountains, and oceans is minimal on this view, a hard point for Buddhist and Hindu environmentalism.

In the East Asian religions, refined for us as Daoism and Confucianism, the continuity of the whole of nature, known and imagined, is affirmed. Everything is made of the powers of dynamic processes, from the stars and bounds of the Earth down to human bodies, souls, and activities. Social institutions constituting the specifically human realm within nature are themselves interpreted as parts of nature. On the material plane, everything is a mixture of yin-yang vibratory harmonies. On the Heavenly plane, all things have the shape they do because of the principles of harmony, which sometimes can connect things and sometimes cannot.

The distinction between Daoism and Confucianism, as it worked itself out through history, was something like this. The Daoists accept the continuity of nature and the human in principle, but are seriously skeptical about the capacities of the human to stay in touch with the Dao of universal nature. Daoists have been critical of the Confucian projects of guiding the human sphere to build the institutions of an artificial edifice of social organization and high civilization that is subject to corruption. Goodness knows, social institutions can be corrupt and we should promote Daoist critics. In addition, Daoism in some ways has retreated from the continuity of nature with high civilization in order to address the excesses of wild nature dangerous to humans. Daoists sometimes turn to potions and practices that respond to nature as dangerous and that seek release into some non-natural ontological realm where you can be a baby again or negotiate a heavenly bureaucracy.

The Confucians accept the whole of the continuity. One of the best illustrations of this is Wang Yang-ming's famous statement at the beginning of his *Inquiry on the Great Learning*, building on Mencius's "authoritative" well scene, in which universal human compassion was displayed. Speaking of the "small man," Wang said,

> Therefore when he sees a child about to fall into a well, he cannot help a feeling of alarm and commiseration. This shows that his humanity (*jen*) forms one body with the child. It may be objected that the child belongs to the same species. Again, when he observes the pitiful cries and frightened appearance of birds and animals about to be slaughtered, he cannot help feeling an "inability to bear" their suffering. This shows that his humanity forms one body with birds and animals. It may be objected that birds and animals are sentient beings as he is. But when he sees plants broken and destroyed, he cannot help a feeling of pity. This shows that his humanity forms one body with the plants. It may be said that plants are living things as he is. Yet even when he sees tiles and stones shattered and crushed, he cannot help a feeling of regret.[4]

Note that this asserts not only a metaphysical continuity among all things but also the human capacity to grasp this. The underlying cultural imagery for this continuity was the yin-yang cosmology that dated at least as far back as the *Yijing*. The Neo-Confucians further interpreted this in various versions of the interactions of principle (*li*) and material force (*qi*). While affirming this continuity across all of nature, the Confucians have focused attention on those domains subject to human influence and control, both concerning individuals for whom the ideals of the sage were developed and also institutions for whom the concerns of the scholar-official were developed. Confucius sought to recover a robust high civilization in a time of brutal social disharmony.

I bring up the continuity of nature with high civilization not to suggest that the male-female binary coded in traditional Confucian social rituals is natural, as has been suggested sometimes by apologists for male dominance. No, exactly the opposite. The yin-yang cosmology says, under many different interpretations, that anything in nature, from mountains to individuals, to the social institutions of high civilization, is a combination of yin and yang. Furthermore, anything in nature is a matter of changes in yin-yang balances, becoming more yin and less yang in some respects and more yang and less yin in others. The dynamic relations among things are themselves matters of more yin in some respects and more yang in others. There is considerable precedent for identifying yin with the female and yang with the male.

But this should not be heard with Western, Aristotelian, substantializing ears. Because all things are changing, the yin in something is always becoming greater or less, and so is the yang. So to apply the gender symbolism across nature, we should say that things are in constant change, with their many components feminizing and defeminizing, masculinizing and demasculinizing. But because these gendered descriptions are so far from the definition of real gender roles in human ritualized society, it seems to me hardly profitable at this point to use the gender labels outside the context of human relations.

One more point about the continuity of nature is in order, however. It has been tempting to many Westerners, and East Asians also, to hope that the yin-yang change model depicts a world in harmony. They hope that an increase in yin is accompanied by a decrease in the relevant yang, and vice versa. Thus reality is supposed to be a model of harmony. Nature is supposed to keep things in balance, and humans are supposed to go with the flow. The supposition here is that the cosmos, or the Earth, or our bodies, or society, is in dynamic homeostasis, and that changes are made internally to sustain that homeostasis. When bad food distorts that homeostasis, a change in diet can restore it.

But the yin-yang cosmology does not imply this. Yin can increase without a balancing decrease in yang; yang can extend itself without a timely retreat to yin. Stars go supernova in an unstoppable whoosh of yin, mountains erupt in fiery plumes of yang, jungles turn to deserts, human homelands flood, men become brutes, women collapse in passivity, economies destroy themselves, civilizations teeter on the cusp of collapse, and climate change threatens the entire human habitat. Nature in the wild is not scaled to the harmonious balances needed for the flourishing of human life: it treats people like straw dogs.[5] More profound than this, however, is that homeostasis is not the norm, change is. When the Earth falls into the sun, that's the Dao.

In the face of this, the human sphere within nature needs to take action to secure the harmonies necessary for human flourishing. If I might indulge a literary flourish, the Daoists, suspicious of big government, righteous norms, and ritual organization, seek out protected pockets where they can duck the forces of nature and drink cinnabar. The Confucians by contrast build dikes and establish granaries. The human efforts to modify nature to support human flourishing are not anti-nature. Rather they are the employment of the forces of nature to tame wilder nature so that the natural human habitat and social organization of high civilization can flourish. Otherwise the human habitat is threatened by the evolving patterns of change. But the conditions are always changing, and so both the habits of government and the habits of personal cultivation need always to be changing in response. Plato said this as well as Confucius.

I noted at the beginning that in prehistoric times humans evolved, on average, big bodies and aggressive hormones for men and nurturing bodies and hormones for women, at the same time that they developed seriously dimorphic social roles for the maintenance of their small groups. I say "on average" because both male and female biological characteristics fall under a range within a bell curve. Most men are big and aggressive, but some are super big and aggressive. Biologically, most men have XY chromosomes, but some significant few have XYY chromosomes that make them hyperaggressive and prone to violence. These XYY men have high status in a warrior culture but find it hard to hold jobs in industrial societies; today, a high percentage end up in prison. Other men are not so big and aggressive, perhaps meeker and smaller than most women. Most women are potentially nurturing and built for childbirth, but some are Amazonian on one side of the bell curve and on the other side are women so empathic and caring that they have trouble being tough enough to nurture in hard times. In prehistoric and ancient times, these bell curves are distorted into rather simple dimorphic roles, or so people believe. In our time, the social roles can be more flexible in adjusting to the spread of bell curves and the much more complicated set of issues for social flourishing—not all just reproduction and aggressive action.

Of course, these are not the only biocultural bell curves involved. There are sexual orientation bell curves for liking men and women, ranging from hetero- to homosexual. There are gender definition bell curves for female, male, and intersex genitalia, and gender identification bell curves for female, male, and transgender sensibilities. In prehistoric times perhaps the exigencies of survival pressured people to exclude consideration of people on the slopes of these bell curves because only the crude dimorphic social role classification of female and male was practicable. Now, however, more complicated social roles are possible and desirable in order to be sensitive to nature.

RITUAL

The feminist protest against Confucian influence on culture is aimed mainly at the rituals that demean women in various ways and at the formation of consciousness and authority structures cultivated by the rituals. These rituals involve both the actual roles to which women are consigned and the locus of authority within the ritual systems. Let me reiterate that I agree with these critiques. Whatever merit the Confucian rituals might have had in the conditions of Confucius's culture or in the situation of Zhu Xi, they plainly have great liabilities in contemporary cultures where families, jobs, affiliations, mobility, communications, education, and government are radically different from even a half century ago and are changing as we speak.

Let me reinforce the insider Confucian position, however, by mentioning again in this book what rituals are good for in the first place, indeed what they are necessary for. That we have socially maladaptive rituals now may not mean that we do not need rituals at all, only better ones. I will speak briefly again of Xunzi's classic theory of ritual that has been analyzed in earlier chapters.[6]

Xunzi observed, in his essay on Heaven, or Nature (*Tian*), that our biological heritage from Heaven and Earth gives us wonderful bodies with great flexibility. It also gives us capacities for emotional feelings across a wide range, plus intelligence to understand things and a capacity to govern and control ourselves. We can easily give modern scientific equivalents of this that take into account evolution. What nature does not give us, however, is the coordination of these things. We do not automatically fear the right things, love the right things, or think in intelligent ways. We can control our conduct, but to what end? There are many different ways we can walk and we need to learn a specific style of moving. We can make all kinds of sounds but have to learn a specific language so as to communicate. There are all sorts of ways we can greet one another, but need to develop specific ones that relate us to others.

According to Xunzi, the role of ritual learning, that is, learning conventions and embedding them as habits, is to make appropriate connections for individuals and social groups that pull together our natural endowments. When Xunzi speaks of the trinity of Heaven, Earth, and the Human, the contribution of the human is mainly ritual, that is to say, sign-shaped behaviors. Without the human contributions of ritual, or semiotically organized behavior, Heaven and Earth are insufficient to make people human. Humans become human by employing ritual conventions.

The positive and necessary role of ritual is to make human life possible in its many dimensions. Beginning with bodily habits such as walking, a style has to be learned, and the conventions of movement within East Asian societies are recognizably different from those from the West; we can even recognize different styles of movement within families, demonstrating the closely related but different conventions. We cannot greet one another without conventions of greeting, and if those are lacking, human encounters devolve toward fight or flight. To communicate we need some language, and the conventions of Chinese and those of English, though different, are roughly equal in utility. Some languages as learned are impoverished, however, and others can be learned so as to turn speaking into an art form. Without rituals of family life, at best there could be sexual intercourse with offspring. But then, human beings as they have evolved biologically would not have so evolved if there were no rituals that allowed for family protection and nurture in long gestation and childrearing. With hunting rituals, people can collaborate in the hunt. With political rituals, people can live in social groups for mutual support. With laboring rituals, economic systems are possible. With friendship rituals, friendship is possible. With aesthetic rituals, fine arts are possible. With court rituals, societies can be organized from micro-levels to macro-levels. With rituals of reading and writing, great literature is possible. The possibility of high civilization requires a ritual base of countless networks that must be kept in order, repaired when necessary, and invented when needed. Rituals are needed for a sufficiently efficient society so as to modify nature to protect and rebalance the human habitat.

Rituals are social habits connecting people as in a dance: rituals give the outline of the steps for interacting, but the rituals must be individuated in order to be played. A language makes speech possible but does not determine what to say, only what cannot find expression. Confucians have always understood that rituals are necessary to make the flourishing of human life possible. Confucians have also understood that rituals alone are not enough: individuals must learn to play them and to individuate themselves in that playing, as previous chapters here have explained.

Rituals are conditioned from many sides, beginning with elementary human capacities of the sort Xunzi noted; our capacities are changing. Rituals must also be conditioned by the situations in which they might be played, and these situations are also changing. Rituals are conditioned by the history and development of the various groups who play them: language rituals in a peasant household are different from those needed to function in an industrial society, and these are different again from those employed by people with university education, those involved with people from other cultures, and those employed by people who deliberately attend to the identification and rectification of bad rituals and the invention of new ones. These conditions are constantly changing.

The development, deployment, and eventual dissolution of rituals are temporal matters. The rituals for walking, greeting, speaking, and family life need to be learnable in about five years. Rituals for economies working the land or inventing new technologies take longer and last longer. The rituals for organizing a culture or high civilization need constant rebalancing, like riding a log down river rapids. From the standpoint of any moment, the rituals in play might seem to be natural in the biological sense, not learned, and they might seem to be static, just the way things are or should be. But in point of fact, everything is changing and the rituals are deep social constructions. Anthropologists might imagine a dynamic but unchanging culture. Confucians might imagine that there is an ideal system of rituals for any Confucian society. But those cultures and societies are constantly changing, even if unnoticed, to address new conditions. A ritual is good if it promotes and sustains human flourishing under the conditions arising, and it is bad if it inhibits this. Confucians stress, or should stress, the constant vigilance, the skills at discernment, and the political powers steadily to innovate opportunistically to keep the rituals fit for human flourishing for the conditions of each time and place.

GENDER ROLES AND RITUALS

Opportunities for women have been changing their ritual structures too. The social conditions for women in America underwent huge changes during World War II when so many men went into the military that women had to build ships, tanks, and bombs. In fact, women had to take over for men in just about all professions, and they did so. After the War was a time of great prosperity in America when a great many women as well as men went to college and then entered the work force. Given modern technology, such as levers controlled by computers, there was almost no kind of work that women could not do as well as men, from farm and factory labor to business and finance. Preschool programs and all-day grade schools have taken over much of the work of nurturing children. The rituals of family roles and gender relations including sex and marriage, and economic life, had to be modified to accommodate these changed conditions.

Of course the older habits of mind have not been easy to erase. In America we still struggle to ritualize the economy so that women get equal pay relative to men for equal work, and to allow women to rise to the topmost positions that in many areas are still reserved for men. The preservation of male privilege is rarely a matter of law anymore, but it is still powerful in ritual expectations. As women have come more and more to occupy positions previously reserved for men, they are breaking into the ritualized authority structures that previously let only men determine women's opportunities.

To be sure, there are subcultures in America where men and women are expected to be married, for the men to earn the money to support the family, and where women are supposed to raise the children and take care of the house. In some of those subcultures, ritualized thinking limits marriage to heterosexual couples. But there are no real conditions of marriage, economic or affectional, that cannot also be supportive of same-sex marriage, which is becoming legal in more and more places. The American system of economic and social opportunity is by no means universal across the world. But there is an inexorable pressure to change economic, social, and affectional rituals to accommodate the fact that women can do heavy lifting with levers and computers, with education, and with experience in public. The rituals now also allow men to participate in nurturing and domestic management if the needs and their cultivatable talents are fit.

The feminist critiques of Confucianism identify it with its traditional rituals that do not allow women to flourish in ways not limited by biology. These rituals usually have not let women function much in public so that they could compete with men and learn from and about public affairs, limiting them rather to the privacy of the home. The sorry claim that Confucian rituals promote yin-yang equality by putting women in charge in the house while men are in charge outside of the house fails to understand the oppression of being confined to domestic roles. The rituals have forced gender identities to conform to narrow categories, for both women and men, when in fact the bell curves of gender are very broad indeed. The rituals have often given to men the authority to determine what women are allowed to be and do, making women too much the creatures of men's intentionalities. Feminist critiques of Confucianism identified with these traditional rituals are far more nuanced, broader, and deeper than I have indicated here, but my main point is obvious.

OBSERVATIONS ON TRANSFORMATION

Permit me now to summarize my argument and make some observations about the transformation of society so as to be more just to women and sexual minorities:

First, Confucianism is superlative among world cultures at recognizing the continuity of nature from its farthest and least human-scaled aspects to the human sphere of institutions and high civilization. The human situation is conditioned by evolving human biology, by changing climate, and by other natural dynamics that might emerge. Therefore, the social constructionist view of gender roles is not the whole story.

Second, by the same token however, because of the Confucian recognition of the ubiquitous roles of rituals in the human sphere, there is no part of the human situation in which the social construction of roles is not present, and often very important.

Third, the rule for nature across all its stretch is change. The powers of yang and yin do not naturally harmonize, especially at the human scale. Homeostasis is not the rule, despite what many have thought and hoped for. Therefore, the conditions of human society are in constant change, however much we might miss or even deny those changes.

Fourth, the flourishing of human society requires strong efforts to cope with the effects of nature that are not scaled to support the human habitat. In the old days, the Confucians built dikes and granaries. Now the needs to defend the human habitat are extraordinarily more complex, including coping with vast populations that need food and education, transforming economies to deal with threatening climate change, and meliorating the effects of human competition and warfare based on defensive projects.

Fifth, the efforts to build a human habitat within the larger maelstrom of nature include the development of layers upon layers of matrices of rituals including family life and government, all the way up to our very vulnerable rituals of high civilization. Rituals defining gender relations are among these.

Sixth, while it is tempting to think of the human habitat as something static that has to be maintained by the constant addition of energy to support a social order in entropic decay, the fact is, Confucians should say, that the very nature of the human habitat should be understood as itself changing relative to external and internal conditions. Science fiction imagination needs cultivation in addition to reverence for history.

Seventh, while it is tempting with the feminists to see oppressive rituals as only negative, Confucians should see rituals as first the conditions for the possibility of semiotically structured human relations and institutions. If the rituals are oppressive regarding gender relations (or political relations, or economic class conditions, etc.), they should be transformed where possible into non-oppressive gender relations in which all participants can be respected humanely.

Eighth, while it is tempting to think that the rituals at hand are stable and homeostatic, Confucians should be the first to say that rituals need to be in constant, if opportunistic, revision and adaptation to changing conditions, and in point of fact have always been so as is apparent to taking a long view of history. Resisting the pull of nostalgia and defense of outdated privilege, Confucians should be alert to analyze the operative rituals at hand and devise better ones.

Ninth, better rituals are those that on the one hand are alert to the changing natural conditions, including social, institutional, and ritual conditions, in which they enable the human habitat and on the other hand are alert to the values embodied in or excluded from those rituals. Confucians have never limited the forces of nature to mere power but have always seen them as configurations that bring or preclude coherence and the harmonies that constitute good life and high civilization.

Tenth, our current situation is that rituals can be devised that define gender roles that respect the natural capacities of women as well as men, and those of sexual minorities, including individuals off to the edges of the bell curves. These ideal rituals will be different in different circumstances, and also should be readied for further change.

Eleventh, Confucianism sometimes has been its own worst enemy regarding ritual by acting as if nature did not change and that rituals conform to some image of static, harmonious, nature that also should not change. Confucians sometimes deserve the reputation of being social conservatives.

But twelfth, the real resources of Confucianism are its conviction that nature is in constant change, belying temporary stability, its human imperative to modify parts of nature so as to foster human flourishing, and its appreciation of ritual as the heart of what makes human life possible. New rituals are needed to make possible gender relations and their surrounding conditions that allow women as well as men and sexual minorities to flourish. New rituals are also needed to cope with global hostilities and uneven social development, economic competition, and struggles over cultural hegemonies. But new rituals for gender relations are at the forefront of progress. Progressive Confucianism should take this on as a central task. This would be a major contribution to world culture.

Epilogue

The underlying purpose in the essays collected in this book has been to contribute to the development of contemporary Confucianism so as to make it a wiser and more effective player in the global philosophical and religious conversation. As a non–East Asian Confucian, also identified as an American pragmatist, a Platonist as in chapter 1, a Christian, and a primarily Western-educated philosopher with a comparative commitment, my contribution to contemporary Confucianism comes from an odd angle, to say the least. I am especially grateful for the fact that there are so many other different kinds of Confucians contributing to this development, including a vigorous new generation of Chinese philosophers in China as well as the three friends to whom this book is dedicated.

A summary reflection on the themes named in this book's subtitle is in order: metaphysics, morals, rituals, institutions, and gender. The preface discussed three of them, metaphysics, morals as not exhausted in virtue-ethics, and personal identity as a function of ritual playing rather than a contrast between individualism and group identity. These three were set in the context of representing contemporary Confucianism as ready to address gender issues as raised by feminists and advocates for sexual minorities. Gender issues are a problem for Confucianism because of changing institutional structures in a global society of interacting cultures.

The problem for contemporary Confucian metaphysics is to find ways of expressing classical themes such as change and harmony in ways that relate to the global discussion. Much contemporary metaphysics, when it is not frightened of its own existence, still expresses a substantialist set of assumptions. Confucianism can challenge this, as in chapter 15 and elsewhere. Similarly, against the view that nominalistic accounts of things are necessary to be consistent with science, and the view that mathematics is the paradigm of relation, the Confucian theory of principle or coherence can be articulated so as to express layers and trajectories of coherence and incoherence amid changes, as in chapter 1 and elsewhere. Most importantly, Confucianism can bring fresh insight to the sense of value found in coherence, so that nature, social institutions, as well as human beings can be acknowledged as bearing value, as in chapters 1 and 3 and nearly every other one as well.

Realism with regard to value in all things potentially engaged is the metaphysical background for the sense of Confucian morals for which I have argued here. Whereas it is common for Confucians to emphasize the internal development of virtue, taken in the deep sense of humaneness (*ren*), this has led to a false sense of the importance of subjectivity and of kinship with Aristotelian virtue ethics, as interpreted by Alasdair MacIntyre. Without diminishing the importance of self-cultivation, Confucianism also needs to emphasize the vast problematic of discerning what to do, looking to see what is coherent and incoherent in the environment, and hence what is good and bad. This includes, of course, cultivating the individual self so that its biases do not get in the way. But it also includes, perhaps more importantly, the need for humane learning, for science, for artistic imagination to pick up on the subtle values of things, for abilities to track real changes that have significance. In our time, understanding the world often requires collaborative work, institutions of cooperation in inquiry and in correction of mistakes. The emphasis on learning is ancient in Confucianism and needs to be given contemporary expression as a crucial component of moral life, balancing the emphasis on self-cultivation. The centrality of learning for morals would not be of major concern if there were no real values in things and morality could limit itself to the cultivation of good individuals. This is the reason, from the perspective of morality, for the importance of the metaphysical reality of value in a cosmos of constant change with shifting forms of coherence. The neglect of metaphysics in so many compartments of current global thinking has disastrous, distorting results for moral thinking and action, as many of the chapters in this book testify.

Ritual is the theme at the center of this volume. Because ritual playing is so central to the development of the individual, the traditional Confucian themes of self-cultivation need to be expressed in terms of the developing virtuosity of ritual playing itself. This is not to say that playing rituals will make a person virtuous: it can make one merely boring. But one of the most important and pervasive venues for learning virtue and being virtuous is in ritual playing, from infancy onward. Furthermore, the playing of rituals intrinsically binds people with others, with institutions, and the natural environment; those things are internally related to an individual and yet remain external as elements in ritual play. For this reason, the typically Western division between individualism and self-identification with a social group can be replaced in the current conversation with a Confucian model of ritual participation, sometimes prioritizing an individual, sometimes a group, but always attending to the patterns of the ritual participation.

The other important point about ritual is that it is the primary medium through which individuals engage the world and touch upon what is really valuable. So, the Confucian sensibility is, or at least should be, critically aware of what values are achieved by the playing of a particular ritual and of how the ritual affects the values of the players and their environment, particularly their involvements in other rituals. On the other side, the Confucian sensibility ought to analyze how particular rituals have negative value, how they negatively affect the people, institutions, and environment in which they are played. Sexism and racism are ritualized behaviors, consisting of countless ritualized ways of behaving and thinking. Confucian analysis can say how this is so. Of course, the Confucian answer to most social problems is to change the rituals, as chapter 15 argued with regard to gender. Nearly all of the chapters here have dealt with ritual in this complex sense, especially chapters 10 and 11.

A Confucian understanding of institutions, exhibited throughout these chapters, emphasizes that they are complex, interlocked sets of rituals that need to be played in a society if certain social functions are to take place. Although institutions can be understood from the standpoint of those who play the rituals within them, as discussed earlier, they should also be understood from the standpoint of their objective social functions. It is in these objective social contexts that most of their moral worth can be exhibited, criticized, and amended. What the Confucian sensibility brings to the appreciation of institutions is a grasp of the possibilities they actualized that are not easily, if at all, broken down into the actualities of the people playing the rituals. A civilization has institutions of art, justice, government, economy, and the rest that achieve these values of high civilization and that depend on one another; when such social institutions are broken, the civilization is in trouble. Confucian moral concern should attend to this. So, it is important to keep in mind, as these chapters argue, that institutions themselves need to be cared for and supported in ritual ways. Rituals not only relate people to one another, and people to the natural environment. They also relate people to the institutions that make possible all this ritual play. For this reason, being a "scholar-official," ministering to institutions themselves, is not just one job among others, as chapter 5 argued. It is part of the virtue of being a humane human being.

Now as to the issues of gender, this book says very little that is new or creative. Rather, gender is situated as a set of issues for which

Confucians need a deep understanding of institutions, rituals, morals, and metaphysics. If Confucians (or anyone else) think of the evils of the oppression of women and sexual minorities only in terms of their social expressions, then the best that can be hoped for is an outcry against those social expressions and a general rejection of a society as wrong. The better path, blazed somewhat in these chapters, is to appreciate these and other social evils as malfunctions of rituals and institutions that themselves are the means for the appreciation, expression, and creation of valuable life. The malfunctions should be identified and corrected, within the limits of whatever is possibly coherent. The powers to cultivate the discernment of what is wrong and what would fix it are within the achievements of human civilization that Confucians can point out and cultivate.

Notes

PREFACE

1. See my *Boston Confucianism: Portable Tradition in the Late-Modern World.* Full bibliographical information for this and all other titles is given in the bibliography.

2. See also Anna Sun's *Confucianism as a World Religion: Contested Histories and Contemporary Realities*, an outstanding discussion of the history of Confucianism from a sociological perspective.

3. The term "situation ethics" was made popular by Joseph Fletcher in his *Situation Ethics: The New Morality*. The general approach was not as new as he thought.

CHAPTER ONE. THE GOOD IS ONE, ITS MANIFESTATIONS MANY

1. From Zhu Xi's *Reflections on Things at Hand*, 49:8b, 49:10b–11a, translated by Wing-tsit Chan in his *A Source Book in Chinese Philosophy*, 638.

2. Plato's *Republic*, book 6, 508b, 509b, translated by Paul Shorey, in *The Collected Dialogues of Plato Including the Letters*, edited by Edith Hamilton and Huntington Cairns, 743–744.

3. See Paul Weiss's *Modes of Being.*

4. I have developed this analysis of determinateness relative to the one and many in several places. See Robert Cummings Neville, *God the Creator*, part 1, and *Ultimates: Philosophical Theology Volume One*, part 3.

5. These five ultimates are discussed in greater detail, with nigh mind-numbing arguments, in my *Ultimates.*

6. This is the argument of Zhou's "Explanation of the Diagram of the Great Ultimate" in Chan's *A Source Book in Chinese Philosophy*, chapter 28.

7. For a fascinating discussion of relevant texts, see Philip J. Ivanhoe's *Readings from the Lu-Wang School of Neo-Confucianism*, 38–43.

8. A theory of temporality consistent with this is in my *Eternity and Time's Flow.*

9. This theory of value was first developed in my *The Cosmology of Freedom*, chapter 3, and more lately in my *Religion in Late Modernity*, chapter 9.

CHAPTER TWO. CONTEMPORARY CONFUCIAN COSMOPOLITANISM

1. See Hall and Ames's *The Democracy of the Dead: Dewey, Confucius, and the Hope for Democracy in China.*

2. See Dewey's *Democracy and Education* and his *Lectures in China: 1919–1920.*

3. See Jeffrey Stout, *Democracy and Tradition.*

4. *Mencius*, 2A:6. See Chan's *A Source Book in Chinese Philosophy*, 65.

5. *Xunzi*, book 23, "The Nature of Man Is Evil," and book 17, "On Nature (or Heaven)."

6. See Tu Wei-ming's *Humanity and Self-Cultivation: Essays in Confucian Thought.* For my analysis of Tu's thought on this point, see my *Boston Confucianism: Portable Tradition in the Late-Modern World*, chapter 5.

7. See my *Ritual and Deference.*

8. These five dimensions themselves are associated with, indeed are derived from, a metaphysical and cosmological theory of nature in its ultimate boundaries. For the arguments, see my *Existence: Philosophical Theology Volume Two*, part 1.

9. See Angle's *Sagehood*, especially chapter 2.

10. See ibid., chapters 7–9.

11. See Stout's *Democracy and Tradition*, chapter 10.

12. Ibid., chapters 10–11.

13. Ibid., chapter 5.

14. I have worked to extend this line in *The Cosmology of Freedom*, chapter 3; *Recovery of the Measure*, chapter 7; *Normative Cultures*, chapter 7; *Realism in Religion*, chapter 8; and *Religion: Philosophical Theology Volume Three*, chapter 9. Chapter 3 of the current volume lays out the theory in my terms.

15. This is the beginning of Zhang Zai's "Western Inscription," translated by Wing-tsit Chan in his *A Source Book of Chinese Philosophy*, 497.

16. See Wang's discussion in Chan, *A Source Book of Chinese Philosophy*, 659–667,

17. *Xunzi*, books 17 and 19.

18. See Tu's *Humanity and Self-Cultivation*, chapter 6.

19. See my analysis of poise in my *Religion in Late Modernity*, chapter 2.

20. An extensive discussion of value-identity is in my *Existence: Philosophical Theology Volume Two*, chapter 4.

21. Two splendid studies of this theme in Wang are Antonio Cua's *The Unity of Knowledge and Action: A Study of Wang Yang-ming's Moral Psychology*, and Warren G. Frisina's *The Unity of Knowledge and Action: Toward a Nonrepresentational Theory of Knowledge.*

22. See John H. Berthrong's *All under Heaven.*

CHAPTER THREE. SYSTEMATIC METAPHYSICS AND THE PROBLEM OF VALUE

1. Alfred North Whitehead, *Process and Reality: An Essay in Cosmology*, 3.

2. "Vagueness" is a logical term whose definition was developed by Charles S. Peirce.

3. See Chung-ying Cheng, *New Dimensions of Confucian and Neo-Confucian Philosophy*, part 3.

4. See, for instance, Antonio S. Cua's *The Unity of Knowledge and Action: A Study in Wang Yang-ming's Moral Psychology*, and Warren G. Frisina's *The Unity of Knowledge and Action: Toward a Nonrepresentational Theory of Knowledge.*

5. Terrence W. Deacon, *Incomplete Nature: How Mind Emerged from Matter*, chapter 1.

6. Stephen C. Angle, *Sagehood: The Contemporary Significance of Neo-Confucian Philosophy.*

7. See Hans-Georg Gadamer, *Truth and Method*, part 2, chapter 2.

8. Wing-tsit Chan, *A Source Book in Chinese Philosophy.*

9. See Angle's *Sagehood*, chapter 2, and Brook Ziporyn's *Ironies of Oneness and Difference: Coherence in Early Chinese Though; Prolegomena to the Study of Li.*

10. See Angle, *Sagehood*, chapter 4.

11. This theory of determinateness as harmony and as always bearing value is treated more expansively in my *Ultimates: Philosophical Theology Volume One*, especially part 3.

12. If this were to be elaborated, it would become apparent that there are five things that are "ultimate conditions" for the existence of any world of determinate things: form, components formed, existential relations to others with respect to which a thing is determinate, the value-identity achieved by a harmony, and the fundamental ontological context in which different things can exist together as mutually relevant. This is the "title thesis" of *Ultimates.*

13. "Contrast" and "definiteness" have their background in the technical discussions in Whitehead's *Process and Reality* and are discussed in my *Religion: Philosophical Theology Volume Three*, chapter 9.

CHAPTER FOUR. NEW PROJECTS FOR CHINESE PHILOSOPHY

1. This view is embodied in Wing-tsit Chan's *A Source Book in Chinese Philosophy*, a remarkable anthology of Chan's fine translations of basic texts that is still the standard over a half century after its publication.

2. The English-language embodiment of this movement to recover Chinese philosophy is perhaps best epitomized by the *Journal of Chinese Philosophy*, founded and edited by Professor Cheng Chung-ying of the University of Hawai'i, who also founded the International Society for the Study of Chinese Philosophy, similarly devoted to this recovery.

3. The great "father" of these Western students of Chinese philosophy was James Legge. He was a missionary, not a philosopher as such, and yet his critical commentary and translations brought Chinese philosophy into the Western philo-

sophical world. See the magisterial study of Legge, and of Max Mueller, by Norman J. Girardot, *The Victorian Translation of China: James Legge's Oriental Pilgrimage.*

4. These contributions of Xunzi are discussed in my *Ritual and Deference*, chapter 3, and in chapters 11 and 14 of the present book.

5. The "portability" of ancient Chinese philosophy was discussed at length in my *Boston Confucianism: Portable Tradition in the Late-Modern World.*

6. My own main contribution to cosmogony is in *God the Creator* and *Ultimates: Philosophical Theology Volume One*; my discussions of Chinese cosmogonies are in *The Tao and the Daimon*, chapter 7, and *Ritual and Deference*, chapter 4.

7. For instance, in conceptions of the Golden Egg, *Hiranyagarbha.*

8. This classification is elaborated in my *Realism in Religion: A Pragmatist's Perspective*, chapter 11.

9. The most thorough development of the mutually helpful connections between Chinese philosophy and Whiteheadian process philosophy has been made by Professor John H. Berthrong. See his *All under Heaven: Transforming Paradigms in Confucian-Christian Dialogue, Concerning Creativity: A Comparison of Chu Hsi, Whitehead, and Neville*, and *Expanding Process: Exploring Philosophical and Theological Transformations in China and the West.* He is anxious to be a process philosopher without the finite process God, which would ill-fit Chinese comparisons.

10. See Wing-tsit Chan, *A Source Book in Chinese Philosophy*, 463.

11. See my analysis in *Reconstruction of Thinking*, part 1.

12. The detailed cosmology is in *Process and Reality.* The point about value is more artfully made in *Science and the Modern World, Adventures in Ideas*, and *Modes of Thought.*

13. See Berry's *The Great Work: Our Way into the Future* and *Buddhism.*

14. See, for instance, Terrence W. Deacon's *The Symbolic Species: The Co-evolution of Language and the Brain* and *Incomplete Nature.* For an overview of the important moves in this regard, see Patrick McNamara, editor, *Where God and Science Meet: Evolution, Genes, and the Religious Brain.*

15. *The Tao and the Daimon*, 136–139.

CHAPTER FIVE. PHILOSOPHY'S FIGHT BETWEEN ENGAGEMENT AND DISTANCE: A CONFUCIAN RESOLUTION

1. For a magisterial study of the Axial Age, see Robert N. Bellah's *Religion in Human Evolution: From the Paleolithic to the Axial Age.*

2. See Eric A. Havelock's *Preface to Plato.*

3. If I may speak personally for a moment, I have participated in academic life by being the chair, dean, or director of every academic unit I have been in, from 1966 until 2009 when I turned seventy. I also have been active in the leadership of many professional and community organizations, including this society (The International Society for Chinese Philosophy). My sabbaticals have been too few, but always thoroughly enjoyed! At seventy, recognizing that I was not even close to Confucius's ideal of being able to trust the trained instincts of my heart without calculation, I nevertheless did resolve to begin a final withdrawal from my perhaps obsessive participation in academic life. I gave up all official administrative responsibilities and begged off committee work as much as possible,

taking on only those rare responsibilities where a younger person's career might be vulnerable and my own is not. I am free as a full-time teacher and love to participate in conferences such as this that are organized by others. It is time for me to make way for others and learn to be satisfied with only the honor of being a keynote speaker. Soon even that will not happen much. Instead of a family tablet in a closet in my grandchildren's house, I'm lucky to have books in libraries that might last longer; books last longer than digital publications, and I'm lucky also to be in the generation I am, after acid-free paper but before dependence on "the Cloud." Because I have worked on the rhythms of engagement and withdrawal, I am learning how to anticipate a world without me. This is one of the closing acts of a scholar-official.

CHAPTER SIX. WILLIAM ERNEST HOCKING: THE FIRST BOSTON CONFUCIAN

1. The title "Boston Confucianism" was first used at a conference on Confucian-Christian Dialogue in Berkeley, California, in 1991. It was used to describe four participants from Boston who subscribed to the traits described in the text here. I subsequently presented a paper to the American Academy of Arts and Sciences entitled "The Short Happy Life of Boston Confucianism," and the book, *Boston Confucianism.* Now, in addition to Confucians who accept the aforementioned description, there is a working group of Confucian scholars in Boston that accepts the title of Boston Confucians. The "Boston" part is still a joke—the school includes anyone who treats Confucianism as an important resource for philosophical problems of cultures outside the East Asian sphere, particularly modern Western urban cultures (such as Boston's); the joke is that many Bostonians regard themselves as living at the "Hub," the center of the world, the creed of the Boston *Brahmins.* For a discussion of the Boston Brahmins and of Hocking as one of the most distinguished of them, see C. T. K. Chari's "Human Personality in East-West Perspectives," in Leroy Rouner's edited *Philosophy, Religion, and Coming World Civilizations: Essays in Honor of William Ernest Hocking.*

2. Although most of Hocking's academic career was spent at Harvard, beginning in 1914, soon to be Royce's successor in the Alford Chair of Natural Religion, and surely part of the Harvard Boston Brahmin society, he was in fact bred and raised in the Midwest. Born in Cleveland, he was educated through high school in Joliet, Illinois, began college in Iowa, and finished at Harvard. His first academic teaching job (he had previously been a grade school principal) was in comparative religion at Andover Newton Theological School (1904–1906), then in philosophy at Berkeley (1906–1908), and at Yale (1908–1914) where he published his first major book, *The Meaning of God in Human Experience* (1912).

3. Hocking's work in *Re-Thinking Missions* was the report he edited, and mostly wrote, of a commission to study the effects of Christian missions in China, Japan, and India-Burma. It was intended not for ecclesiastical authorities but for laypeople in churches who had been supporting missions about which Hocking was dubious.

4. His most important book on religion was *The Meaning of God in Human Experience.* His most systematic treatise in political philosophy was *Man and the*

State. See also *The Spirit of World Politics.* In many respects, his *Human Nature and Its Remaking* combines both the religious and political interests, but does so by placing both in an evolutionary context with nature.

5. See Hocking's "Value of the Comparative Study of Philosophy." This was the conference volume from the 1939 Hawai'i conference that Hocking himself was not able to attend, though his article introduced the conference.

6. "Review of *Religious Trends in Modern China* by Wing-tsit Chan."

7. For a broader discussion of science, see Hocking's *Science and the Idea of God.*

8. "Value of the Comparative Study of Philosophy," 109.

9. In *Science and the Idea of God*, chapter 4, Hocking discussed science, especially physics and astronomy, as abstractions that leave out purpose and value.

10. *Science and the Idea of God*, 108.

11. Hocking used a 1922 translation (by J. Percy Bruce) of Zhu Xi's works. Hocking also knew Bruce's commentary (1923). A more up-to-date translation is available by Wing-tsit Chan, a friend of Hocking's, in his *Source Book* and elsewhere.

12. "Chu Hsi's Theory of Knowledge," 113.

13. Ibid.

14. Ibid., 111–112.

15. Ibid., 112.

16. Ibid., 110.

17. Ibid.

18. Ibid., 117.

19. The most outstanding contemporary proponent and expositor of the Confucian project of becoming a sage is Tu Wei-ming; see his *Humanity and Self-Cultivation* and *Confucian Thought.* Most remarkable in this regard is Hocking's own *Human Nature and Its Remaking*, a Confucian project of personal and species transformation if there ever was one, but employing only Christian metaphors, not Confucian ones. Hocking's discussions of Christian virtues are extraordinarily Confucian!

20. There were in fact many Buddhist schools that Zhu Xi would have known, including Hua-yen, T'ien-t'ai, and the Yogacara (Consciousness-Only) schools.

21. "Chu Hsi's Theory of Knowledge," 125.

22. Ibid., 127.

23. Ibid., 125.

24. On Peirce, see my *Eternity and Time's Flow*, chapter 1.

25. See Tu's *Humanity and Self-Cultivation*, chapter 8, and *Way, Learning, and Politics*, chapter 8.

CHAPTER SEVEN. CHENG CHUNG-YING AS A CONSTRUCTIVE PHILOSOPHER

1. As to journals, see, for instance, the *International Review of Chinese Religion and Philosophy* and *Dao: A Journal of Comparative Philosophy.* The *Journal*

of Chinese Philosophy has always been complemented by its older sister at the University of Hawai'i at Mānoa, *Philosophy East and West*, whose current editor, Roger T. Ames, is a giant in his own right in the comparative interpretation of Chinese and Western thought and the translations of classic Chinese texts.

2. See the *Journal of Chinese Philosophy* 30/3–4 (September/December 2003), thirtieth anniversary edition. See also the volumes that feature a new generation of scholars along philosopher Cheng's (and my) age, *The Examined Life: Chinese Perspectives—Essays on Chinese Ethical Traditions*, edited by Xinyan Jiang, and *Comparative Approaches to Chinese Philosophy*, edited by Bo Mou.

3. See John H. Berthrong, "From Xunzi to Boston Confucianism."

4. See Cheng Chung-ying, *Tai Chen's "Inquiry into Goodness": A Translation of the "Yuan Shan" with an Introductory Essay.*

5. *Peirce and Lewis's Theories of Induction.*

6. *Encyclopedia of Chinese Philosophy*, edited by Antonio S. Cua. This long list indicates significant trust in Cheng as an authority. Lest anyone think he is just a special friend of Cua, the editor, the governing editorial board includes, besides Cheng himself, Roger T. Ames, Chad Hansen, Shu-hsien Liu, David S. Nivison, Donald J. Munro, Vincent Shen, Kwong-loi Shun, David B. Wong, and Ying-Shih Yu, a veritable "Who's Who" of contemporary scholars representing many different and competing fields. The essay "Philosophy: Recent Trends Overseas" contains Cheng's interpretation of himself as one of those trends, a fascinating bit of intellectual autobiography set in relation to his peers. I have written a somewhat parallel interpretation of him in relation to his peers, with some different peers, in *Boston Confucianism: Portable Tradition in the Late-Modern World*, chapter 3.

7. One of his most recent expressions of this is "Inquiring into the Primary Model: *Yi Jing* and the Onto-hermeneutical Tradition." A variant of this essay is "Inquiring into the Primary Model: *Yi-Jing* and Chinese Ontological Hermeneutics," in Bo Mou's *Comparative Approaches to Chinese Philosophy*, 33–59.

8. For one of the most recent of Cheng's comparisons of Chinese and Western notions of ultimate reality, see his "Ultimate Origin, Ultimate Reality, and the Human Condition: Leibniz, Whitehead, and Zhu Xi."

9. His most formal interpretation of my work is "On Neville's Understanding of Chinese Philosophy: Ontology of *Wu*, Cosmology of *Yi*, and Normalogy of *Li*," in *Interpreting Neville*, edited by J. Harley Chapman and Nancy K. Frankenberry. My "Responding to My Critics" in the same volume (291–328) contains my dialectical appreciations. I wrote the foreword to his *New Dimensions of Confucian and Neo-Confucian Philosophy*. He read a draft of my *Normative Cultures* and wrote a wonderful interpretation of Confucian ritual propriety, in partial contrast to my interpretation, which I incorporated into the final text (164–165). My "Metaphysics in Contemporary Chinese Philosophy," which has become chapter 3in this volume, deals in part with his work.

10. For instance, Whitehead had recourse to Platonism to answer the question of how mathematics might apply to the world whose commonsense interpretation made mathematical relations impossible. Plato knew nothing of the modern mathematizing interpretation of nature. See Whitehead's *Science and the Modern World*.

11. For a technical discussion of how vague categories used systematically can surmount the postmodern criticism of theory as such, see my *The Highroad around Modernism*, chapter 6.

12. This theory of understanding history through core texts and motifs is explained and illustrated at greater length in my *Boston Confucianism*, chapters 6–9.

CHAPTER EIGHT. WU KUANG-MING AS ONE OF THREE STOOGES

1. See his *Chuang Tzu: World Philosopher at Play* and *The Butterfly as Companion: Meditations on the First Three Chapters of the "Chuang Tzu."*

2. See Wu's *History, Thinking, and Literature in Chinese Philosophy.*

3. See Northrop's *The Meeting of East and West.*

4. For a systematic elaboration of the points made here about my view, see *Recovery of the Measure.*

5. This theory of comparative inquiry is developed in my *Normative Cultures* and is illustrated at length in my three volumes of the Cross-Cultural Comparative Religious Ideas Project, *The Human Condition*, *Ultimate Realities*, and *Religious Truth.* See especially chapters 8 and 9 of *Ultimate Realities*, "On Comparing Religious Ideas" and "How Our Approach to Comparison Relates to Others," by Wesley J. Wildman and myself; I was first author on chapter 8 and he on chapter 9.

CHAPTER NINE. SPIRITUAL FOUNDATIONS OF CHINESE CULTURE

1. The distinction between conditional and essential components in a harmony is of general metaphysical application and I have developed it in great detail in *Ultimates*, chapter 10.

2. The beginning of Zhou's "An Explanation of the Diagram of the Great Ultimate," translated by Wing-tsit Chan in his *A Source Book in Chinese Philosophy*, 463.

3. *Analects*, 2.4, translated by Chan in his *Source Book*, 22.

CHAPTER TEN. SELFHOOD AND VALUE: PRAGMATISM, CONFUCIANISM, AND PHENOMENOLOGY

1. Pragmatism took its initial shape in the works of Charles Sanders Peirce, William James, and John Dewey. It had American antecedents in Jonathan Edwards and Ralph Waldo Emerson, and close neighbors in Josiah Royce, who called himself an "absolute pragmatist"; George Santayana, a fellow naturalist; and Alfred North Whitehead, who called his epistemology "pragmatic." Whitehead was the doctoral mentor of Charles Hartshorne and Paul Weiss, who edited Peirce's philosophical papers in six large volumes. Since the middle of the twentieth century pragmatism has seen a revival in several directions, including analytic pragmatism associated with Richard Rorty, Donald Davidson, and Robert Brandom, and

African American ethical-theological work associated with Cornel West, Victor Anderson, and Eddie Glaude. These and other branches of "neo-pragmatism" have been insightfully analyzed recently by Richard J. Bernstein in *The Pragmatic Turn*. But the pragmatism I work to extend is not these directions, although I learn from them. Rather my interest is in the metaphysical, cosmological, and religious dimensions of the early pragmatists. These dimensions, as well as my colleagues in this extension of the early pragmatists, are ignored by Bernstein. A better analysis of pragmatism, from the standpoint of my direction, is John E. Smith's older *Purpose and Thought: The Meaning of Pragmatism*. I sometimes call myself a "paleo-pragmatist" to distinguish myself from the "neo-pragmatists."

2. See Hall and Ames's *The Democracy of the Dead: Dewey, Confucius, and the Hope for Democracy in China* and Ames's more recent *Confucian Role Ethics: A Vocabulary*.

3. The word "interaction" was popularized by John Dewey, who also sometimes used the word "transaction." I often use the word "engagement" to stress the explicit or implicit intentionality in interpretive interactions. But as I shall argue here, much interpretive interaction is not conscious and so is not always deliberate engagement.

4. Peirce used this formulation in many places. See for instance his early (1868) papers "Questions concerning Certain Capacities Claimed for Man" and "Consequences of Four Incapacities," both in *The Essential Peirce: Selected Philosophical Writings: Volume 1 (1867–1893*. Those papers are frequently anthologized.

5. The valuational theme in Peirce is emphasized by John E. Smith in *Purpose and Thought*. I have developed it at great length in my trilogy, *Axiology of Thinking*, consisting of *Reconstruction of Thinking*, *Recovery of the Measure*, and *Normative Cultures*.

6. This essay was originally prepared as a paper for an Eastern Division American Philosophical Association panel with Cheng Chung-ying and Edward Casey, chaired by Linyu Gu. These informal musings are illustrative of the interpenetration of interpretations the text is citing.

7. See "Gibson's Affordances," by James G. Green.

8. See Barrett's "Skillful Engagement and the 'Effort after Value': An Axiological Theory of the Origins of Religion," in *The Evolution of Religion*, edited by Fraser Watts and Leon P. Turner.

9. For an expansion of this point, see my "Self-Reliance and the Portability of Pragmatism."

10. See Peirce's "Questions concerning Certain Capacities Claimed for Man," cited in note 4 in this chapter. On the basic background difference between the continental tradition's transcendental supposition and the naturalistic interactionist model in pragmatism, see my "Self-Reliance and the Portability of Pragmatism."

11. See Merleau-Ponty, *Phenomenology of Perception*.

12. See Heidegger's important essay, written shortly after *Being and Time*, "On the Essence of Truth."

13. Peirce described his categories in many places. See, for instance, *The Essential Peirce: Selected Philosophical Writings: Volume 2 (1893–1913)*, chapters 11 and 12.

14. The central text in Xunzi is his essay on *Tian*, translated Heaven or Nature, chapter 17, in volume 3 of the Knoblock translation. Edward J. Machle gives a particularly apt translation and careful analysis in his *Nature and Heaven in the Xunzi: A Study of the "Tien Lun."* A more recent set of studies of Xunzi on ritual is *Ritual and Religion in the Xunzi*, edited by T. C. Kline III and Justin Tiwald. Pragmatic Confucians might also want to look at my *Ritual and Deference: Extending Chinese Philosophy in a Comparative Context.*

15. I have elaborated in detail this pragmatic-Confucian theory of ritual, connecting pragmatic semiotics with ritual theory, in my *Normative Cultures*, which contains in its seventh chapter a long letter from Professor Cheng commenting on it.

16. This sense of the self as a continuum between the inner heart and the things of the world is based on the Doctrine of the Mean. I develop it at length in *Boston Confucianism.*

CHAPTER ELEVEN. INDIVIDUATION AND RITUAL

1. Various dimensions of ritual are discussed in several chapters of this book. Earlier and more extensive developments of my theory of ritual are found in *Normative Cultures*, chapter 7; *Boston Confucianism*, chapter 2; and *Ritual and Deference*, chapter 3.

2. See *Xunzi*, book 17, in volume 3 of the Knoblock translation; it is also in Chan's *Source Book*, chapter 7. Edward Machle's discussion of this chapter is very fine.

3. *Xunzi*, book 17; Knoblock translation in volume 3, 16.

4. See *Xunzi*, Knoblock translation, volume 3, 15.

5. See John Searle's *Speech Acts*, especially chapters 2–4.

6. The most famous text is Zhu Xi's *Family Rituals.*

7. This seems to be the critical focus of Seligman and his coauthors.

8. See Angle's *Sagehood*, chapters 6–11, for a beautiful analysis of the education of the sage in the depths of *li.*

9. See, for instance, Confucius's *Analects*, 13.18, in Chan's *Source Book*, 41.

10. See Emmanuel Levinas's *Totality and Infinity: An Essay on Exteriority* and Jean-Luc Marion's *Being Given: Toward a Phenomenology of Givenness.*

11. Confucians differ on the extent to which they emphasize continuity, although all accept it. Wang Yang-ming is a striking example. See Warren G. Frisina's *The Unity of Knowledge and Action: Toward a Nonrepresentational Theory of Knowledge.*

CHAPTER TWELVE. AUTHORITY IN SOCIAL INSTITUTIONS, ACCOUNTABILITY, AND CREDIBILITY

1. See his *Centrality and Commonality: An Essay on Confucian Religiousness*, especially chapter 3.

2. The democratic and divine representative models are familiar in the history of the Christian West. More obscure from our current vantage point but

very important is the continuation and expansion of the model of the Roman patriarch, especially as developed in Hellenistic and late Roman paganism and influential on Christianity. See the writings of Pierre Hadot, for instance, *Philosophy as a Way of Life* and *The Inner Citadel: The "Meditations" of Marcus Aurelius.*

3. The opening lines of the Doctrine of the Mean, translated by Wing-tsit Chan, in his *A Source Book in Chinese Philosophy*, 98.

4. See Tu Wei-ming's *Humanity and Self-Cultivation.*

5. See my *Boston Confucianism*, especially chapters 4 and 10.

6. See John Rawls, *A Theory of Justice*, especially chapter 2.

7. A quotation from the Great Learning illustrates this point and several of the points made earlier about Confucianism:

> The ancients who wished to manifest their clear character to the world would first bring order to their states. Those who wished to bring order to their states would first regulate their families. Those who wished to regulate their families would first cultivate their personal lives. Those who wished to cultivate their personal lives would first rectify their minds. Those who wished to rectify their minds would first make their wills sincere. Those who wished to make their wills sincere would first extend their knowledge. The extension of knowledge consists in the investigation of things. When things are investigated, knowledge is extended; when knowledge is extended, the will becomes sincere; when the will is sincere, the mind is rectified; when the mind is rectified, the personal life is cultivated; when the personal life is cultivated, the family will be regulated; when the family is regulated the state will be in order; and when the state is in order, there will be peace throughout the world. From the Son of Heaven down to the common people, all must regard cultivation of the personal life as the root or foundation. (Wing-tsit Chan translation, in his *Source Book*, 86–87)

8. *Mencius* 1B:8

9. Paul writes in Romans 13:1–7,

> Let every person be subject to the governing authorities; for there is no authority except from God, and those authorities that exist have been instituted by God. Therefore whoever resists authority resists what God has appointed, and those who resist will incur judgment. For rulers are not a terror to good conduct, but to bad. Do you wish to have no fear of the authority? Then do what is good, and you will receive its approval; for it is God's servant for your good. But if you do what is wrong, you should be afraid, for the authority does not bear the sword in vain! It is the servant of God to execute wrath on the wrongdoer. Therefore one must be subject, not only because of wrath but also because of conscience. For the same reason you also pay taxes, for the authorities are God's servants, busy with this

very thing. Pay to all what is due them—taxes to whom taxes are due, revenue to whom revenue is due, respect to whom respect is due, honor to whom honor is due. (New Revised Standard Version)

10. The seventh president, Jackson was in office from 1829 to 1837.

CHAPTER THIRTEEN. CONFUCIANISM AND TOLERATION

1. See Anna Sun's *Confucianism as a World Religion: Contested Histories and Contemporary Realities*.

2. As the author of *Boston Confucianism: Portable Tradition in the Late-Modernity*, I obviously believe that Confucians do not have to be culturally East Asian any more than Platonists have to be culturally Greek. That volume sorts through the issues of what needs to be carried over from one culture to another when a critical philosophy spreads.

3. For a reflection on Confucian themes filtered through a focus on political contexts of tolerance, see my "Culture, Religion, Nation-States, and Reason in the Politics of Tolerance."

4. To say that religious philosophies, or religions and their theologies, "take their bearing from what they consider to be ultimately important" is not an innocent observation. It is a surface expression of an extremely complex theory of religion and metaphysics of ultimacy articulated at length in my *Ultimates, Existence*, and *Religion. Ultimates* develops the metaphysics of ultimacy and the analytical tools of a theory of worldviews. Religion explores the relation between a situation and living according to a religious worldview.

5. See John H. Berthrong's *All under Heaven* for an explication of that phrase in a cross-cultural context.

6. See Peter L. Berger, *The Sacred Canopy: Elements of a Sociological Theory of Religion*.

7. See my *Ultimates*, chapter 4.

8. These are spelled out at length in *Ultimates*, chapter 4.

9. Tu Wei-ming goes so far as to say that Confucianism involves an existential decision to become a sage, which he likens to Kierkegaard's notion of existential decision as a leap of faith. See his *Humanity and Self-Cultivation: Essays in Confucian Thought*, 89. Not all self-proclaimed Confucians are this serious! See Stephen C. Angle's *Sagehood: The Contemporary Significance of Neo-Confucian Philosophy* for a careful analysis of the progressive depths of cultivated Confucian sagehood.

10. Samuel P. Huntington, *The Clash of Civilizations and the Remaking of World Order*.

11. From the Great Learning, translated by Wing-tsit Chan in his *A Source Book in Chinese Philosophy*, 86–87. A longer quote, containing these lines, is in a footnote in chapter 12 here.

12. See Wing-tsit Chan's editorial comments in his introduction to the Great Learning, *Source Book*, 84–85.

13. For a detailed development of this critique of narrative, see my *Ultimates*, chapter 8, and *Existence*, chapter 9.

14. The interpretation of principle as harmony or coherence has been beautifully elaborated by Stephen Angle in his *Sagehood*. The metaphysical thesis that things are harmonies of multiplicities and that harmonies are valuable in themselves is common to Plato and Abhinavagupta as well as to Confucians. I have given extensive defenses of it in my *Ultimates*, *Existence*, and *Religion*.

CHAPTER FOURTEEN. CONFUCIAN HUMANENESS ACROSS SOCIAL BARRIERS

1. Jaspers's seminal discussion was in *The Origin and Goal of History*. For more recent comparative historical discussions of the Axial Age, see Karen Armstrong's *The Great Transformation: The Beginning of Our Religious Traditions*, and Robert N. Bellah's *Religion in Human Evolution: From the Paleolithic to the Axial Age*.

2. *The Mo Tzu*, part 2 (chapter 15), translated by Wing-Tsit Chan in his *Source Book*, 213.

3. Ibid., part 2 (chapter 26), in Chan, *Source Book*, 218.

4. Confucius said, "Does Heaven (T'ien, nature) say anything? The four seasons run their course and all things are produced. Does Heaven say anything?" *Analects*, 17.19. Chan, Source Book, 47.

5. *Analects*, 13.18; Chan, *Source Book*, 41. Note the similarity of this argument to that of Socrates in Plato's *Euthyphro*.

6. See Samuel P. Huntington's *The Clash of Civilizations and the Remaking of World Order*.

7. For philosophical reflections on alienating social structure, focusing on the Chinese tradition, see *Harmony and Strife: Contemporary Perspectives, East and West*, edited by Shu-hsien Liu and Robert E. Allinson.

8. For this interpretation of the familial center of humaneness or love, see Tu Wei-ming's *Centrality and Commonality*. For my comments on Tu's view, see *Boston Confucianism*, 96–101.

9. See Hegel's *Philosophy of Right*, 10, and *The Logic of Hegel*, 10.

10. For an extraordinarily acute analysis of this point for Descartes and Western philosophy, see the essays by Anderson Weekes in Michel Weber and Anderson Weekes, editors, *Process Approaches to Consciousness in Psychology, Neuroscience, and Philosophy of Mind*.

11. See, for instance, Foucault's *The Order of Things* and *The Use of Pleasure*. One of his most influential followers is Judith Butler, author of *Gender Trouble: Feminism and the Subversion of Identity*.

CHAPTER FIFTEEN. CONFUCIANISM AND THE FEMINIST REVOLUTION: RITUAL DEFINITION AND THE SOCIAL CONSTRUCTION OF GENDER ROLES

1. See the survey of the biological and evolutionary conditions for male dominance in Wesley J. Wildman's *Science and Religious Anthropology: A Spiritually Evocative Naturalist Interpretation of Human Life*, chapter 7.

2. For a defense of this interpretation of the Axial Age revolution, see my *Religion: Philosophical Theology Volume Two*, chapter 2.

3. See, for instance, Hai-soon Lee's "Representation of Females in Twelfth-Century Korean Historiography," Jian Zang's "Women and the Transmission of Confucian Culture in Song China," and Noriko Sugano's "State Indoctrination of Filial Piety in Tokugawa Japan: Sons and Daughters in the Official Records of Filial Piety," all in Ko, Haboush, and Piggott, eds., *Women and Confucian Cultures in Premodern China, Korea, and Japan*.

4. Translated by Wing-tsit Chan in his edited *A Source Book in Chinese Philosophy*, 659–60.

5. See Franklin Perkins's *Heaven and Earth Are Not Humane: The Problem of Evil in Classical Chinese Philosophy*.

6. For a recent collection of studies of Xunzi on ritual, see T. C. Kline III and Justin Tiwald, eds., *Ritual and Religion in the Xunzi*. Edward J. Machle, who has an essay in that collection, has a full-length study of Xunzi's essay on "Tian," *Nature and Heaven in the Xunzi: A Study of the "Tien-Lun."* See Kurtis Hagen's *The Philosophy of Xunzi: A Reconstruction*, especially chapter 4; Hagen's preface has a helpful discussion of recent translations and commentaries on Xunzi. See also my *Ritual and Deference*, chapter 3.

Bibliography

Ames, Roger T. *Confucian Role Ethics: A Vocabulary*. Honolulu, HI: University of Hawai'i Press, 2011.

Armstrong, Karen. *The Great Transformation: The Beginnings of Our Religious Traditions*. New York, NY: Knopf, 2006.

Angle, Stephen C. *Sagehood: The Contemporary Significance of Neo-Confucian Philosophy*. Oxford, UK: Oxford University Press, 2009.

Barrett, Nathanial F. "Skillful Engagement and the 'Effort after Value': An Axiological Theory of the Origins of Religion." In *The Evolution of Religion*, ed. Fraser Watts and Leon P. Turner. Oxford, UK: Oxford University Press, 2012.

Bellah, Robert N. *Religion in Human Evolution: From the Paleolithic to the Axial Age*. Cambridge, MA: Harvard University Press, 2011.

Berger, Peter. *The Sacred Canopy: Elements of a Sociological Theory of Religion*. Garden City, NY: Doubleday, 1967.

Bernstein, Richard J. *The Pragmatic Turn*. Cambridge, UK: Polity Press, 2010.

Berry, Thomas. *Buddhism*. New York, NY: Hawthorne, 1967.

———. *The Great Work: Our Way into the Future*. New York, NY: Bell Tower/Crown, 1999.

Berthrong, John H. *All under Heaven: Transforming Paradigms in Confucian-Christian Dialogue*. Albany, NY: State University of New York Press, 1994.

———. *Concerning Creativity: A Comparison of Chu Hsi, Whitehead, and Neville*. Albany, NY: State University of New York Press, 1998.

———. "From Xunzi to Boston Confucianism." *Journal of Chinese Philosophy* 30/3&4 (September/December 2003), 433–450.

———. *Expanding Process: Exploring Philosophical and Theological Transformations in China and the West*. Albany, NY: State University of New York Press, 2009.

Bo Mou, ed. *Comparative Approaches to Chinese Philosophy*. Burlington, VT: Ashgate, 2003.

Bruce, J. Percy. *Chu Hsi and His Masters: An Introduction to Chu Hsi and the Sung School of Chinese Philosophy*. London: Probsthain, 1923.

Butler, Judith. *Gender Trouble: Feminism and the Subversion of Identity*. New York, NY: Routledge, 1999.

Chan, Wing-tsit, ed. *A Source Book in Chinese Philosophy*. Princeton, NJ: Princeton University Press, 1963.

———, ed. *Chu Hsi and Neo-Confucianism*. Honolulu, HI: University of Hawai'i Press, 1986.

———. *Chu Hsi: New Studies*. Honolulu, HI: University of Hawai'i Press, 1989.

Cheng, Chung-ying. *Peirce and Lewis's Theories of Induction*. Harvard University dissertation, 1964.

———. *Tai Chen's "Inquiry into Goodness": A Translation of the "Yuan Shan" with an Introductory Essay*. Honolulu, HI: East-West Center Press, 1971.

———. *New Dimensions of Confucian and Neo-Confucian Philosophy*. Albany, NY: State University of New York Press, 1991.

———. "On Neville's Understanding of Chinese Philosophy: Ontology of *Wu*, Cosmology of *Yi*, and Normalogy of *Li*." In *Interpreting Neville*, ed. J. Harley Chapman and Nancy K. Frankenberry. Albany, NY: State University of New York Press, 1999. 247–270.

———. "Ultimate Origin, Ultimate Reality, and the Human Condition: Leibniz, Whitehead, and Zhu Xi." *Journal of Chinese Philosophy* 29/1 (March 2002), 93–118.

———. "Inquiry into the Primary Model: *Yi Jing* and the Onto-hermeneutical Tradition." *Journal of Chinese Philosophy* 30/3&4 (September/December 2003), 289–312.

Cua, Antonio S. *The Unity of Knowledge and Action: A Study in Wang Yang-ming's Moral Psychology*. Honolulu, HI: University of Hawai'i Press, 1982.

———, ed. *Encyclopedia of Chinese Philosophy*. New York and London: Routledge, 2003.

———. "Early Confucian Virtue Ethics: The Virtues of *Junzi*." In Vincent Shen, ed., *Dao Companion to Classical Confucian Philosophy*.

Deacon, Terrence W. *The Symbolic Species: The Co-evolution of Language and the Brain*. New York, NY: Norton, 1997.

———. *Incomplete Nature: How Mind Emerged from Matter.* New York, NY: W. W. Norton, 2012.

Dewey, John. *Democracy and Education*. Ed. Jo Ann Boydston with Patricia R. Baysinger and Barbara Levine, with an introduction by Sidney Hook. Carbondale, IL: Southern Illinois University Press, 1980; original edition 1916.

———. *Lectures in China: 1919–1920*. Ed. and trans. from the Chinese by Robert W. Clopton and Tsuin-Chen Ou. Honolulu, HI: University of Hawai'i Press, 1973.

———. *Art as Experience*. New York, NY: Minton Balch, 1934.

Dilworth, David A. *Philosophy in World Perspective: A Comparative Hermeneutic of the Major Theories*. New Haven: Yale University Press, 1989.

Fingarette, Herbert. *Confucius: The Secular as Sacred*. New York, NY: Harper, 1972.

Fletcher, Joseph. *Situation Ethics: The New Morality*. Philadelphia: Westminster Press, 1966.

Foucault, Michel. *The Order of Things: An Archaeology of the Human Sciences*. New York, NY: Pantheon, 1970.

———. *The Use of Pleasure*. Trans. Robert Hurley. New York, NY: Random House, 1985.

Frisina, Warren G. *The Unity of Knowledge and Action: Toward a Nonrepresentational Theory of Knowledge*. Albany, NY: State University of New York Press, 2002.

Gadamer, Hans-Georg. *Truth and Method*. New York, NY: Seabury, 1975.

Girardot, Norman J. *The Victorian Translation of China: James Legge's Oriental Pilgrimage*. Berkeley, CA: University of California Press, 2002.

Green, James G. "Gibson's Affordances." *Psychological Review* 101/2 (1994), 336–342.

Hadot, Pierre. *Philosophy as a Way of Life*. Trans. Michael Chase and ed. with an introduction by Arnold I. Davidson. Oxford, UK: Blackwell, 1995.

———. *The Inner Citadel: The "Meditations" of Marcus Aurelius*. Trans. Michael Chase. Cambridge, MA: Harvard University Press, 1998.

Hagen, Kurtis. *The Philosophy of Xunzi: A Reconstruction*. Chicago and La Salle, IL: Open Court, 2007.

Hall, David L. *The Civilization of Experience*. New York, NY: Fordham University Press, 1973.

———. *The Uncertain Phoenix*. New York, NY: Fordham University Press, 1982.

———. *Eros and Irony: A Prelude to Philosophical Anarchism*. Albany, NY: State University of New York Press, 1982.

Hall, David L., and Roger T. Ames. *Thinking Through Confucius*. Albany, NY: State University of New York Press, 1987.

———. *Anticipating China*. Albany, NY: State University of New York Press, 1995.

———. *Thinking from the Han*. Albany, NY: State University of New York Press, 1998.

———. *The Democracy of the Dead: Dewey, Confucius, and the Hope for Democracy in China*. Chicago and LaSalle, IL: Open Court, 1999.

Havelock, Eric A. *Preface to Plato*. New York, NY: The Universal Library, 1967.

Hegel, G. W. F. *Philosophy of Right*. Trans. T. M. Knox. Oxford, UK: Oxford University Press, 1942; originally published 1896.

———. *The Logic of Hegel*. Trans. William Wallace. Second edition. Oxford, UK: Oxford University Press, 1963.

Heidegger, Martin. "On the Essence of Truth." Trans. R. F. C. Hull and Alan Crick. In *Existence and Being*, ed. Werner Brock. Chicago, IL: Henry Regnery, 1949. 317–351.

Hocking, W. E. *The Meaning of God in Human Experience*. New Haven, CT: Yale University Press, 1912.

———. *Human Nature and Its Remaking*. New Haven, CT: Yale University Press, 1918.

———. *Man and the State*. New Haven, CT: Yale University Press, 1926.

———. *The Spirit of World Politics: With Special Studies of the Near East*. New York, NY: Macmillan, 1932.

———. *Re-Thinking Missions: A Layman's Inquiry after One Hundred Years*. New York, NY: Harper and Brothers, 1932.

———. "Chu Hsi's Theory of Knowledge." *Journal of Asiatic* Studies 1/1 (1936), 109–127.

———. "Value of the Comparative Study of Philosophy." In *Philosophy—East and West*, ed. Charles A. Moore. Princeton, NJ: Princeton University Press, 1944. 1–11.

———. *Science and the Idea of God*. Chapel Hill, NC: North Carolina University Press, 1944.

———. "Review of *Religious Trends in Modern China* by Wing-tsit Chan." *Philosophy East and West* 4 (1954), 175–181.

———. *The Coming World Situation*. New York, NY: Harper and Bros., 1956.

Huntington, Samuel P. *The Clash of Civilizations and the Remaking of World Order.* New York, NY: Simon & Schuster, 1996.

Ivanhoe, Philip J., trans. with introductions. *Readings from the Lu-Wang School of Neo-Confucianism*. Indianapolis, IN: Hackett, 2009.

Jaspers, Karl. *The Origin and Goal of History*. Trans. Michael Bullock. New Haven, CT: Yale University Press, 1953. From the original *Vom Ursprung und Ziel der Geschichte*. Zurich: Artemis, 1949.

Jiang, Xinyan, ed. *The Examined Life: Chinese Perspectives—Essays on Chinese Ethical Traditions*. Binghamton, NY: Global Publications, 2002.

Ko, Dorothy, JaHyun Kim Haboush, and Joan R. Piggott, eds. *Women and Confucian Cultures in Premodern China, Korea, and Japan*. Berkeley, CA: University of California Press, 2003.

Kline, T. C., III, and Justin Tiwald, eds. *Ritual and Religion in the Xunzi*. Albany, NY: State University of New York Press, 2014.

Leder, Drew. *The Absent Body*. Chicago, IL: University of Chicago Press, 1990.

Lee, Hai-soon. "Representation of Females in Twelfth-Century Korean Historiography." In Ko, Haboush, and Piggott, eds., *Women and Confucian Cultures in Premodern China, Korea, and Japan*.

Levinas, Emmanuel. *Totality and Infinite: An Essay on Exteriority*. Trans. Alphonso Lingis. Pittsburgh, PA: Duquesne University Press, 1969.

Liu, Lydia H., Rebecca E. Karl, and Dorothy Ko, eds. *The Birth of Chinese Feminism: Essential Texts in Transnational Theory*. New York, NY: Columbia University Press, 2013.

Liu, Shu-hsien, and Robert E. Allinson, eds. *Harmony and Strife: Contemporary Perspectives, East and West*. Shatin, Hong Kong: Chinese University Press, 1988.

Machle, Edward J. *Nature and Heaven in the Xunzi*. Albany, NY: State University of New York Press, 1993.

MacIntyre, Alasdair. *After Virtue: A Study in Moral Theory*. Second edition. Notre Dame, IN: University of Notre Dame Press, 1984.

Marion, Jean-Luc. *Being Given: Toward a Phenomenology of Givenness*. Trans. Jeffrey L. Kosky. Stanford, CA: Stanford University Press, 2002.

McNamara, Patrick, ed. *Where God and Science Meet: Evolution, Genes, and the Religious Brain*. London, UK: Praeger, 2006.

Merleau-Ponty, Maurice. *Phenomenology of Perception*. Trans. Colin Smith. London, UK: Routledge & Kegan Paul, 1962.

Neville, Robert Cummings. *God the Creator*. Chicago, IL: University of Chicago Press, 1968; Second edition with a new introduction, Albany, NY: State University of New York Press, 1992.

———. *The Cosmology of Freedom*. New Haven, CT: Yale University Press, 1974; revised edition, Albany, NY: State University of New York Press, 1995.

———. *Reconstruction of Thinking*. Albany: State University of New York Press, 1981.

———. *The Tao and the Daimon: Segments of a Religious Inquiry*. Albany, NY: State University of New York Press, 1982.

———. *Recovery of the Measure*. Albany, NY: State University of New York Press, 1987.

———. *The Highroad around Modernism*. Albany, NY: State University of New York Press, 1992.

———. *Eternity and Time's Flow*. Albany, NY: State University of New York Press, 1993.

———. "Confucianism as a World Philosophy." *Journal of Chinese Philosophy* 24 (1994), 5–25.

———. *Normative Cultures*. Albany, NY: State University of New York Press, 1995.

———. *Boston Confucianism: Portable Tradition in the Late-Modern World*. Albany, NY: State University of New York Press, 2000.

———, ed. *The Human Condition*. Albany, NY: State University of New York Press, 2001.

———, ed. *Ultimate Realities*. Albany, NY: State University of New York Press, 2001.

———, ed. *Religious Truth*. Albany, NY: State University of New York Press, 2001.

———. *Religion in Late Modernity*. Albany, NY: State University of New York Press, 2002.

———. "Culture, Religion, Nation-States, and Reason in the Politics of Tolerance." In *Tolerance in the Twenty-First Century: Prospects and Challenges*, ed. Gerson Moreno-Riano. Lanham, MD: Rowman & Littlefield, 2006. 67–80.

———. *Ritual and Deference: Extending Chinese Philosophy in a Comparative Context*. Albany, NY: State University of New York Press, 2008.

———. *Realism in Religion: A Pragmatist's Perspective*. Albany, NY: State University of New York Press, 2009.

———. *Ultimates: Philosophical Theology Volume One*. Albany, NY: State University of New York Press, 2013.

———. "Self-Reliance and the Portability of Pragmatism." *American Journal of Theology and Philosophy* 35/2 (May 2014), 94–107.

———. *Existence: Philosophical Theology Volume Two*. Albany, NY: State University of New York Press, 2014.

———. *Religion: Philosophical Theology Volume Three*. Albany, NY: State University of New York, 2015.

Northrop, F. S. C. *The Meeting of East and West*. New York, NY: Macmillan, 1946.

Peirce, Charles Sanders. *The Essential Peirce: Selected Philosophical Writings: Volume 1 (1867–1893*. Ed. Nathan Houser and Christian Kloesel. Bloomington, IN: Indiana University Press, 1992. Volume 2 (1893–1913). Ed. The Peirce Edition Project. Bloomington, IN: Indiana University Press, 1998.

Perkins, Franklin. *Heaven and Earth Are Not Humane: The Problem of Evil in Classical Chinese Philosophy*. Bloomington, IN: Indiana University Press, 2014.

Plato. *The Collected Dialogues of Plato, Including the Letters*. Ed. Edith Hamilton and Huntington Cairns. New York, NY: Bollingen Foundation, 1961.

Rawls, John. *A Theory of Justice*. Cambridge, MA: Harvard University Press, 1971.

Rouner, Leroy S., ed. *Philosophy, Religion, and Coming World Civilization: Essays in Honor of William Ernest Hocking*. The Hague: Martinus Nijhoff, 1966.

———. *Within Human Experience: The Philosophy of William Ernest Hocking*. Cambridge, MA: Harvard University Press, 1969.

———. "The Surveyor as Hero: Reflections on Ernest Hocking's Philosophy of Nature." In *Contemporary Studies in Philosophical Idealism*, ed. John Howie and Thomas O. Bulford. Cape Cod, MA: Claude Stark & Co., 1975. 53–68.

Searle, John. *Speech Acts: An Essay in the Philosophy of Language*. Cambridge, UK: Cambridge University Press, 1969.

Seligman, Adam B., Robert P. Weller, Michael J. Puett, and Bennett Simon. *An Essay on the Limits of Sincerity*. New York, NY, and Oxford, UK: Oxford University Press, 2008.

Shen, Vincent, ed. *Dao Companion to Classical Confucian Philosophy*. Dordrecht: Springer, 2014.

Smith, John E. *Purpose and Thought: The Meaning of Pragmatism*. New Haven, CT: Yale University Press, 1978.

Stout, Jeffrey. *Democracy and Tradition*. Princeton, NJ: Princeton University Press, 2004.

Strong, David. *Crazy Mountains: Learning from Wilderness to Weigh Technology*. Albany, NY: State University of New York Press, 1995.

Sugano, Noriko. "State Indoctrination of Filial Piety in Tokugawa Japan: Sons and Daughters in the Official Records of Filial Piety." In Ko, Haboush, and Piggott, eds., *Women and Confucian Cultures in Premodern China, Korea, and Japan*. 170–189.

Sun, Anna. *Confucianism as a World Religion: Contested Histories and Contemporary Realities*. Princeton, NJ: Princeton University Press, 2013.

Tillman, Hoyt Cleveland. *Confucian Discourse and Chu Hsi's Ascendancy*. Honolulu, HI: University of Hawai'i Press, 1992.

Tu Wei-ming. *Humanity and Self-Cultivation: Essays in Confucian Thought*. Berkeley, CA: Asian Humanities Press, 1979. Reprint edition with a new preface and a foreword by Robert C. Neville; Boston, MA: Cheng & Tsui, 1998.

———. *Confucian Thought: Selfhood as Creative Transformation*. Albany, NY: State University of New York Press, 1985.

———. *Way, Learning, and Politics: Essays on the Confucian Intellectual*. Singapore: Institute of East Asian Philosophies, 1989.

———. *Centrality and Commonality: An Essay on Confucian Religiousness*. Revised and enlarged edition. Albany, NY: State University of New York Press, 1989.

Watson, Walter. 1985. *The Architectonics of Meaning: Foundations of the New Pluralism*. Albany, NY: State University of New York Press.

Weber, Michel, and Anderson Weeks, eds. *Process Approaches to Consciousness in Psychology, Neuroscience, and Philosophy of Mind*. Albany, NY: State University of New York Press, 2009.

Weiss, Paul. *Modes of Being*. Carbondale, IL: Southern Illinois University Press, 1958.

Weissman, David. *Truth's Debt to Value*. New Haven, CT: Yale University Press, 1993.

Whitehead, Alfred North. *Science and the Modern World*. New York, NY: Macmillan, 1926.

———. *Adventures of Ideas*. New York, NY: Macmillan, 1933.

———. *Modes of Thought*. New York, NY: Macmillan, 1938.

———. *Process and Reality: An Essay in Cosmology*. Revised edition by Donald Sherburne and David Ray Griffin. New York, NY: Free Press, 1978.

Wildman, Wesley J. *Science and Religious Anthropology: A Spiritually Evocative Naturalist Interpretation of Human Life*. Burlington, VT: Ashgate, 2009.

Wu, Kuang-ming. *Chuang Tzu: World Philosopher at Play*. With a foreword by Robert Neville. Chico, CA: Scholars Press, 1982.

———. *The Butterfly as Companion: Meditations on the First Three Chapters of the "Chuang Tzu."* With a foreword by Robert Cummings Neville. Albany, NY: State University of New York Press, 1990.

———. *History, Thinking, and Literature in Chinese Philosophy*. Taipei: Sun Yat-Sen Institute for Social Sciences and Philosophy, 1991.

———. *On Chinese Body Thinking: A Cultural Hermeneutic*. With a foreword by Robert Cummings Neville. Leiden: Brill, 1997.

———. *On the "Logic" of Togetherness: A Cultural Hermeneutic*. With a foreword by Robert Cummings Neville. Leiden: Brill, 1998.

Xunzi. *Xunzi: A Translation and Study of the Complete Works*. Three volumes. Trans. and ed. John Knoblock. Stanford, CA: Stanford University Press. Volume 1, Books 1–6 (1988). Volume 2, Books 7–16 (1990). Volume 3, Books 17–32 (1994). See also *Xunzi: The Complete Text*. Tran. with an introduction by Eric L. Hutton. Princeton, NJ: Princeton University Press, 2014.

Zang, Jian. "Women and the Transmission of Confucian Culture in Song China." In Ko, Haboush, and Piggott, eds., *Women and Confucian Cultures in Premodern China, Korea, and Japan*.

Zhu Xi. *The Philosophy of Human Nature by Chu Hsi*. Ed. and trans. J. Percy Bruce. London: Probsthain, 1922.

———. *Reflections on Things at Hand: The Neo-Confucian Anthology Compiled by Chu Hsi and Lu Tsu-Ch'ien*. Ed. and trans. Wing-tsit Chan. New York: Columbia University Press, 1969.

———. *Chu Hsi: Learning to Be a Sage*. Trans. with commentary by Daniel K. Gardner. Berkeley, CA: University of California Press, 1990.

———. *Chu Hsi's Family Rituals: A Twelfth-Century Chinese Manual for the Performance of Cappings, Weddings, Funerals, and Ancestral Rites*. Trans. with annotation and introduction, Patricia Buckley Ebrey. Princeton, NJ: Princeton University Press, 1991.

Ziporyn, Brook. *Ironies of Oneness and Difference: Coherence in Early Chinese Thought; Prolegomena to the Study of Li*. Albany, NY: State University of New York Press, 2012.

———. *Beyond Oneness and Difference: Li and Coherence in Chinese Buddhist Thought and Its Antecedents*. Albany, NY: State University of New York Press, 2013.

Index

Doctrine of the Mean, xiii, 9, 25, 178, 226–27